THE AMERICAN KENNEL CLUB

1884 ~ 1984

A SOURCE BOOK

THE AMERICAN KENNEL CLUB

1884 ~ 1984

A SOURCE BOOK

Edited by Charles A.T. O'Neill
and the Staff of The American Kennel Club

HOWELL
BOOK
HOUSE

Main entry under title:

The American Kennel Club, 1884-1984.

   Includes index.
   1. American Kennel Club—History. 2. Dog shows—
United States—History.   I. O'Neill,   Charles A. T.
II. American Kennel Club.
SF421.A44   1985   636.7'06073   85-24915
ISBN 0-87605-404-1

Table of Contents

Appendices

Acknowledgements

As the American Kennel Club approached its centennial year, the Board of Directors agreed that an effort should be made to compile a comprehensive history of the organization and of the sport of pure-bred dogs in America. I was assigned the task of coordinating the efforts in preparing this historical source book. The efforts of many people went into the finished product.

The first ten chapters of this book are substantially based upon material written by John T. Marvin. Mr. Marvin also supplied a large number of pictures from his personal collection; they appear in the book with his credit. The chapter on Obedience was written by James E. Dearinger, Director of Obedience, and Marion Lane of the AKC Staff. The Field Trial chapter was written by another member of the AKC staff, A. Hamilton Rowan, Director of Field Trials.

I would like to express my appreciation to a number of members of the AKC staff who contributed their time and energy in compiling the appendix material. These included, alphabetically, Pat Beresford, Roy H. Carlberg, James P. Crowley, Michael Liosis, John J. Mandeville, Robert G. Maxwell, Grace Schwartz, Fred Sheppard, William Secord, W. Terry Stacy, William F. Stifel, Roberta Vesley, and Hilde Weihermann.

Two members of the AKC staff who did extensive work in researching facts and proofreading the manuscript at various stages of its development were Roberta Vesley and Hilde Weihermann. Their work in ensuring the historical accuracy of the text was invaluable.

Finally, I would also like to acknowledge the efforts of Alice O'Connell and the members of her staff for the effort that was made to put the text into typeset form.

Charles A. T. O'Neill
August 1985

Preface

by Charles A. T. O'Neill

On a warm late-summer day, September 17, 1884, a group of twelve dedicated sportsmen, responding to a "meeting call" from Messrs. J. M. Taylor and Elliot Smith, met in the rooms of the Philadelphia Kennel Club, at the northeast corner of 13th and Market streets, Philadelphia, Pennsylvania. Each member of the group was a representative or "delegate" from a dog club. Each of those dog clubs had, in the recent past, held a benched dog show or had run field trials.

The delegates were deeply committed to the sport of pure-bred dogs. They shared a common desire to establish a "Club of Clubs." The new club would undertake to consider "all dog matters concerning bench shows and field trials." These basic subjects and many more will be dealt with in historical perspective in the text that follows.

In 1884 travel was not the pleasure that it can be today. Distances that we regard as "short drives" on the Interstate Highway system or on the turnpikes could, and very often did, require days of exhausting travel on the early steam-locomotive trains. The brave souls who responded to Messrs. Taylor and Smith's meeting call did so because they shared a common concern for the sport. The travel entailed was virtually an ordeal.

Air-conditioning was unknown. Ventilation consisted of "open windows." In a railroad car of that era, open windows meant cinders, soot, and smoke. On a warm day, travelers arrived at their destination looking like a group of coal miners after a hard day in the mine.

Because we at The American Kennel Club feel that a historic step was taken that day in Philadelphia, we would like to share with you a photo-reproduction of the hand-recorded minutes of that meeting, called to establish a "Club of Clubs." The club the group of sportsmen founded on September 17, 1884, was The American Kennel Club.

Philadelphia, Pa.
Sept. 17th 1884.

In pursuance of a call by Major J. M. Taylor & Mr. Elliot Smith for each & every club having held a bench show or formed for that purpose both in the United States and Canada to be represented by a delegate, a large number of men met at the rooms of the Philadelphia Kennel Club at the North East corner of 13th and Market Streets Philadelphia.
At 8:30 P.M. meeting called to order moved and 2nd that Mr. Elliot Smith act as chairman at the meeting pro. tem. also moved and 2nd that Mr. Samuel G. Dixon act as secretary pro. tem. Objects of meetings stated to be for the purpose of forming a club of clubs. to consider all dog matters concerning Bench Shows & Field Trials. Moved by J. M. Taylor that a com. of three be appointed by the Chair to examine

Philadelphia. Pa.
Sept. 17th 1884.

In pursuance of a call by Major
J. M. Taylor & Mr. Elliot Smith for
each & every club having held a bench
show or formed for that purpose both
in the United States & Canada to be
represented by a delegate, a large
number of men met at the rooms of
the Philadelphia Kennel Club at the
North East corner of 13th & Market
Sts Philadelphia.

At 8.30 P.M. meeting called to order.
Moved & 2nd that Mr. Elliot Smith
act as chairman of the meeting
pro. tem. Also moved & 2nd that
Mr. Samuel G. Dixon act as secretary
pro. tem. Objects of meeting stated
to be for the purpose of forming a
Club of Clubs. to consider all dog
matters concerning Bench Shows
& Field Trials. Moved by J. M.
Taylor that a com. of three be
appointed by the chair to examine

*report on the credentials of the delegates.
Chair appointed the following committee:
Samuel G. Dixon, Geo. N. Appold, & C. M.
Munhall. Moved by Maj. Taylor that a list of
clubs be made & the credentials produced.*

Illinois (Chicago)	*represented*	*by*	*J. M. Taylor*
Cincinnati	''	''	'' '' ''
Philadelphia	''	''	*Sam'l G. Dixon*
Westminster (N.Y.)	''	''	*Elliot Smith*
Montreal	''	''	*Jas Watson. proxy.*
New England (Boston)	''	''	*J. A. Nickerson*
New Haven	''	''	*G. E. Osborn*
Kentucky (Louisville)	''	''	*J. M. Taylor*
Baltimore	''	''	*G. N. Appold*
Cleveland	''	''	*C. M. Munhall*
New Brunswick (Canada)	''	''	*Elliot Smith*
London (Canada)	''	''	*Jas. Watson*
St. Louis	''	''	*J. W. Munson*
Knickerbocker	''	''	*R. T. Green*

*Moved & 2nd that a recess of ten minutes be
taken to allow com. to examine credentials.*

report on the credentials of the
delegates. Chair appointed the
following Committee: Sam'l G. Dixon
Geo. N. Appold. & C. M. Numhall.
Mond by Maj. Taylor that a list
of Club be read & the Credentials
produced.

Illinois. (Club) represented by J. M. Taylor
Cincinnati   "   "
Philadelphia."   "   Sam'l G. Dixon.
Westminster (NY)   "   Elliot Smith.
Montreal   "   "   Jas. Watson. proxy.
New England. (Boston)   "   L. A. Nickerson.
New Haven.   "   G. L. Osborn.
Kentucky (Louisville)   "   J. M. Taylor.
Baltimore "   "   G. N. Appold
Cleveland "   "   C. M. Numhall
New Brunswick (Canada)   "   Elliot Smith
London   (Canada)   "   Jas. Watson.
St. Louis   "   "   J. M. Hanson.
Knickerbocker.   "   R. G. Green

Mond & 2nd that a recess of ten
minutes be taken to allow the Com. to
examine Credentials.

Report of Com. on Credentials chairman Sam'l G. Dixon reported that ''The following named gentlemen having appeared before us and made their respective statements and produced their credentials according to which we have formed our decisions. Mr. Dorsey from Howard County Kennel Club having stated that his club was not formed for the purpose of holding Bench Shows - our decision is that he is not a proper representative to this meeting. The following men accepted

St. Louis	*J. W. Munson*
Philadelphia	*Samuel G. Dixon*
Westminster	*Elliot Smith*
Montreal	*Jas Watson proxy.*
New England	*J. A. Nickerson*
New Haven	*G. E. Osborn*
Kentucky	*J. M. Taylor*
Baltimore	*G. N. Appold*
Cleveland	*C. M. Munhall*
New Brunswick	*Elliot Smith. proxy*
London	*Jas. Watson. proxy*

Report of Com. on Credentials Chairman
Saml. G. Dixon reported that "The following
named gentlemen having appeared
before us and made their respective
statements and produced their Credentials
according to which we have formed
our decisions. Mr. Dorsey from Howard
County Kennel Club having stated that
his Club was not formed for the
purpose of holding Bench Shows – our
decision is that he is not a proper
representative to this meeting.
The following were accepted

St. Louis	J. W. Munson.
Philadelphia	Saml. G. Dixon.
Westminster	Elliot Smith
Montreal	Jas. Watson. Jersey.
New England	J. L. Dickerson.
New Hamp.	G. E. Osborn.
Kentucky	J. M. Taylor.
Baltimore	G. N. Appold
Cleveland	C. M. Munhall
New Brunswick	Elliot Smith. Jersey.
Dundee	Dr. Wim Temple Jas. Watson Jersey

Cincinnati   *J. M. Taylor*
Illinois   *J. M. Taylor*

Mr. R. T. Green of the Knickerbocker Kennel Club having produced a printed form of the by-laws & constitution of the Knickerbocker Kennel Club which did not mention Bench shows our decision is that he is not a proper representative to this meeting. Report of com. on credentials was accepted. Moved & 2nd & passed that Mr. Elliot Smith be elected permanent Chairman. Moved & 2nd that Chair appoint com. to draft a constitution & by-laws. Chair appointed.

Maj. J. M. Taylor
Mr. J. A. Nickerson
Mr. Sam'l G. Dixon

Mr. W. B. Shattuc & it was moved & 2nd that chairman be added to above com. Carried. Moved and seconded that the

Cincinnati   J. M. Taylor.
Illinois   J. M. Taylor.
Mr. R. J. Green of the Knickerbocker
Kennel Club having produced a
printed form of the by-laws &
Constitution of the Knickerbocker Kennel
Club which did not mention
Bench Shows our decision is that
he is not a proper representa-
tive to this meeting. Report of
Com. on credentials was accepted.
Mored & 2nd & passed that Mr.
Elliot Smith be elected permanent
Chairman.

Mored & 2nd that Chair appoint
Com to draft a constitution & by-
laws. Chair appointed.

My. J. M. Taylor.
Mr. J. A. Nickerson
Mr. Saml. G. Dixon
Mr. W. B. Shattuc. & it was
moved & 2nd that Chairman be
added to also Com. carried.
Mored & 3rd reminded that the

Meeting adjourn to meet at 8 o' clock pm on Oct 22nd 1884 in New York City 2nd & carried

> *Sam'l G. Dixon Sec'y P.T.*
> *per p.*

approved at N.Y.
Oct 22nd 84

meeting adjourn to meet at 8 oclock
P.m. on Oct 22nd 1884 in New York
City. 2nd & Carried

                    Saml. G. Dixon Secty.
                         per. X.

approvd at N.Y.
    Oct 22nd 84

It is literally impossible to encapsulate the dynamic growth of The American
Kennel Club through the ensuing century between the covers of this book. We have
tried to deal with the milestone events in the evolution of the sport of pure-bred
dogs as we have come to know it.

The Source Book brings you facts about the sport of "Pure-Bred Dogs"
before the founding of The American Kennel Club. It traces the growth of the sport
from the early years through the evolution of "Group Competition," the "Point
System," and "Obedience Trials" through the post-World War II period right up
to date.

We trust you will enjoy reading this Source Book as much as we at The
American Kennel Club have enjoyed preparing it. As the years go by you will find
yourself referring to its statistics, text, and photographs — and enjoying the wealth
of fascinating details. We hope the facts contained in this book contribute to your
enjoyment of the sport of pure-bred dogs.

1

Dogs, Dog Shows, and Dog Clubs–Beginnings

Man and dog have been inseparable companions for as long as records have been kept. Dogs are mentioned repeatedly in the early books of the Bible, and a representation of the dog may be found at the tomb of Amten in Egypt, which dates to the Fourth Dynasty, or 4000 to 3500 B.C. This supports the premise that the dog is one of the earliest domesticated animals.

Dog competitions of various kinds have been documented for centuries. While such events were informal, they did offer proving grounds for grading the hunting, coursing, and even fighting abilities of the several strains involved. Dogs are competitive by nature and will at the request of their masters enter adversary situations with both pleasure and abandon. This uninhibited compliance has generated reciprocal human attachment, which has been well documented through the years. Lord Byron wrote:

> But the poor dog, in life, the firmest friend,
> The first to welcome, foremost to defend,
> Whose honest heart is still his master's own,
> Who labours, fights, lives, breathes for him alone.

It is small wonder that the dog today is the most sought-after and trusted of animal species.

Dog shows, as we know them, are a relatively recent phenomenon. They follow by centuries man's use of dogs as hunting companions, coursing competitors, guard and dray animals, and companions. But unfortunately, dogs have also been sadly exploited by man in such macabre encounters as rat-killing contests, bull- and bear-baiting engagements, and dog fights. These brutal contests have often been referred to as "sports."

Man learned through these early uses of dogs, however distasteful some of them may have been, that selective breeding could produce offspring with predictable characteristics. Such characteristics include both the temperamental and phys-

Ad for an early pit fight, 1819. John T. Marvin Collection

A Grand Match at the Westminster Pit,
FOR 100 GUINEAS,
By 2 DOGS of 43-lb. weight each,
THE PROPERTY OF TWO SPORTING NOBLEMEN.
One, that famous
WHITE BITCH OF PADDINGTON,
Whose wonderful performances are so well known to the Fancy
to require no further comment—the other
A BRINDLE DOG OF CAMBRIDGE,
A remarkable and well known favorite, as his fame bears ex-
tensive proof—to fight from the scratch,
ON WEDNESDAY, 16th of JUNE, 1819,
at 6 o'clock in the evening precisely.—Doors open at half past 5.

ical, so that shape, size, temperament, and special abilities could be forecast. Thus, generations of the same strain were reasonably uniform with respect to these important attributes. ''Breeding in line'' became the rule, and although no accurate records exist, there is little doubt that knowledgeable dog men of yesteryear knew what to expect, within limits, from specific matings. This led to the consolidation of type, ability, and temperament.

English competitive activities prior to 1859 suggested a pattern for American efforts to follow. They were very informal affairs, staged without benefit of uniform rules. Strictly local in entry and attendance, these activities were most often held in neighborhood taverns. They were well received by townspeople, gaining steadily in popularity and frequency. One such exhibition is described in an article by Gerald Massey and is portrayed in an oil painting executed in 1855 by R. Marshall. The painting now hangs in the offices of The Kennel Club (London). It shows a group of fanciers together with their dogs around a ring formed by tables. Jemmy Shaw, owner of the tavern, is standing in the ring.

A match show at Jemmy Shaw's Queen's Head Tavern, 1855. From an oil painting by R. Marshall, 1855. John T. Marvin Collection

THE COUNTRY SQUIRE *taking a peep at* CHARLEY'S THEATRE WESTMINSTER, *where the performers are of the Old School.*

Local support for such efforts, generally referred to as "Pot House Shows," grew, while other, more gruesome competitions were often staged at the same locales. In fact, Jemmy Shaw advertised "Public Ratting Sports Every Tuesday Evening," followed on Wednesdays by "Canine Exhibitions." Shaw, like many proprietors of public houses, was involved deeply in a variety of dog-related contests and sports. In fact, he had catered to the "doggyset" at a tavern he previously owned, The Blue Anchor, which was the headquarters for the Toy Dog Club. One of these toy dogs was Shaw's own five-and-one-half-pound English Toy Terrier, Tiny the Wonder. Tiny held the record in a rat pit by killing 200 rats in fifty-four minutes, no small accomplishment. Early reports also list The Elephant and Castle, another tavern, as the site of various canine competitions, including a specialty show for Toy Spaniels in 1834. And the infamous Westminster Pit has gone down in history as the locale for such brutal encounters as bull- and bear-baiting by dogs, which continued to the death of one or more of the unlucky participants. Such public engagements disappeared gradually, although clandestine dog fights persist even today.

In addition to the public-house shows and the baiting and fighting encounters, dogs were also included in district-fair competitions for livestock, beginning in the late 1700s. Further, large landowners in the country who had substantial kennels of hounds put their bitches in whelp "out to walk" in the homes of tenants on their estates, where the puppies could be raised in a homelike atmosphere and where great personal care was given. The contact with people, including children, did

J. W. Walsh ("Stonehenge") judged the first organized dog shows in England, 1859.
John T. Marvin Collection

(Left) Bear baiting at Charley's Theatre Westminster—a drawing by H. Aiken, 1821. John T. Marvin Collection

much toward furthering the proper emotional development of the young stock. In time, local competition developed to the point that these youngsters met competitively and prizes were awarded for the best developed, most promising, and so on. Competition was keen and trophies were highly prized by the tenants, who became increasingly cognizant of the quality and condition of stock under their care. These local competitions, though relatively obscure and generally limited to the hound breeds, were important to the early development of dog shows; they alerted people in all walks of life to the importance of condition and uniformity of type, at the same time sharpening the competitive urge. Incidentally, the practice of putting bitches "out to walk" continued with variations well into the twentieth century.

By the late 1850s in England, informal matches and public-house shows were not enough. Forward-thinking fanciers began to seek other, better outlets for their interest. On June 28 and 29, 1859, the first organized dog show took place, staged out of the tavern atmosphere at Newcastle-on-Tyne. Though the entry was relatively small, the event was well organized. Pre-show entries were accepted, and a printed catalog was available. The show was advertised by *The Field* on May 28, 1859. The entry of sixty dogs was limited to Pointers and Setters, which suggests the major area of breed interest at the time. The judges for Pointers were J. Jobling, T. Robson and J.H. Walsh (Stonehenge), while the Setters were passed on by Robson, Walsh, and F. Foulgar. The Newcastle-on-Tyne show was followed the next year by one at Birmingham, which drew an entry of 267 dogs and included an all-breed classification. The all-breed classification was broken down between

Division 1 breeds (sporting) and Division 2 breeds (some workers, some nonsporting dogs, a few terriers, some toy dogs, and a class for foreign nonsporting dogs in which no prize was awarded as there were no entries). Division 2 at the 1860 Birmingham show was the forerunner of group divisions. In the years that followed, the number of established shows grew.

The first organized field trial was held on April 18, 1865, at Southill with Rev. Thomas Pearce (Idstone) and a Mr. Walder as judges. The trial was called a success, although this opinion occasioned considerable controversy in sporting papers. Only sixteen entries competed, including Pointers (large and small) and Setters (English, Irish, and Gordon). Subsequent trials, with improved turnouts, were staged at Stafford, Bala, Shrewsbury, and several other locations. These subsequent trials are reported in detail in the first volume of *The Kennel Club Stud Book,* which covers the years 1859-1874.

The first show staged under the aegis of The Kennel Club (England) was the Crystal Palace event of June 17-20, 1873, with an entry of 975 dogs. After this event, attention was turned to the production of a printed stud record for all registered dogs. After much discussion concerning an editor capable of producing such a book, Frank C. S. Pearce, the son of Rev. Thomas Pearce mentioned above, was selected. Pearce proved to be an excellent choice. The first volume of *The Kennel Club Stud Book, A Record of Dog Shows and Field Trials* appeared in 1874. The book is quite formidable, including over 600 pages with breeding particulars for 4027 dogs together with show and field trial results dating to 1859. The honor of being Number 1 in this record belonged to G. T. Rushton's Bloodhound bitch, Abeille, who was whelped in 1865. Pearce continued as editor of *The Stud Book,* and the second volume was issued in July 1875.

The Kennel Club (England) experienced many of the problems that plague infant organizations in an active field. Mature thinking and careful planning, however, prevailed. Some opposition to policies became apparent in 1875, but it was quickly resolved. Since then, The Kennel Club and its activities have progressed with minimal difficulty. For those who wish to learn more about the early development of this institution, E. W. Jaquet's book, *The Kennel Club, A History and Record of Its Worth* (London, 1905), is a fully annotated volume that offers historical background, biographical sketches of many important club members, a record of actions by the several committees, and much more. Jaquet was secretary of The Kennel Club at the time.

These early dog shows and events in England, which led to the birth of The Kennel Club (England), preceded American actions in this direction by several years. The English experience presages many of the problems that inevitably confronted Americans in their desire to become part of this new and exciting sport.

2

The Early American Scene

The early American pattern of development included dog fighting and baiting, though hunting and general field activities existed as well. Matches and field competitions involving Pointers, Setters, and hounds, while generally local in entry, were numerous and widespread. New-World dog fanciers were both active and knowledgeable, and many wealthy landowners maintained private packs of hounds for hunting. In so doing they kept detailed kennel records that demonstrated knowledgeable breeding practices designed to improve their stock.

Indeed, George Washington had a strong kennel of Foxhounds at Mount Vernon and maintained written records of individual dogs dating to 1758. He was very particular as to their bloodlines and kept detailed accounts of each of his dogs, including all new litters. During the Revolution his interest and affection for dogs led him to return a stray hound to General Howe, the British commander. The hound was identified by Howe's name on a collar. This return was made by special courier, under flag of truce. The courier also delivered this note:

> General Washington's compliments to General Howe,—does himself the plea-
> sure to return to him a dog, which accidentally fell into his hands, and by the
> inscription on the collar, appears to belong to General Howe.

In his reply, General Howe recognized that dogs have always provided a common meeting ground for all persons under all and sundry circumstances.

Washington's love of dogs continued long after the Revolution, and his kennel was enlarged by a gift of seven French hounds from General Lafayette in 1785. Washington hunted these dogs, and his diary contains a number of interesting observations upon their performance.

Washington's hound pack is only one of many that were documented during the eighteenth and early nineteenth centuries. This was to be expected, as most American sportsmen closely followed English activity in this area. Such sporting papers as John S. Skinner's *American Turf Register,* first published in 1829, includes both English and American field-sport information. Another early periodical, *The United States Sporting Magazine,* begun in 1835 and edited by C. R. Colden, has sections offering considerable information on hunting, dog training, dog care, and other related topics.

But the most important written effort in this area was Arnold Burges's book, *The American Kennel and Sporting Field.* This book was published in 1876, and it includes the first organized stud record to be published in America. The honor of being number 1 in this record went to a black, tan, and white English Setter, Adonis, owned by George Delano of New Bedford, Massachusetts. Adonis is listed as being sired by Leicester out of Doll, who was imported in whelp. Burges includes breeding particulars for a total of three hundred twenty-seven dogs: fifty-five English Setters, fifty Gordon Setters, seventy-one Irish Setters, sixty-four native Setters (basically, English Setters), forty-four cross-bred Setters (any com-

The title page of the first American stud book.
John T. Marvin Collection.

Arnold Burges,
"Father of the Stud Book."
John T. Marvin Collection.

THE

AMERICAN KENNEL

AND

SPORTING FIELD.

BY

ARNOLD BURGES,

(LATE EDITOR, "AMERICAN SPORTSMAN.")

NEW YORK:
J. B. FORD & COMPANY,
1876.

bination of English, Irish, and Gordon), thirty-four Pointers, and nine Spaniels of various breeds (Clumbers, Cockers, and Irish Water Spaniels).

Burges's book offers another important dividend: an annotated chronological listing of the first dog competitions held in America. It begins with the Illinois State Sportsmen's Association of Chicago event held on June 2, 1874. Since only a general commendation and no awards were given, this affair cannot be considered a true dog show. Problems plagued the second attempt, which was staged under the auspices of the New York State Sportsmen's Association at Oswego, New York, on June 22, 1874. Only two dogs and one bitch were entered, and under the circumstances, no awards were given.

On October 7, 1874, a show held at Mineola, New York, under the rules of The Kennel Club (England), had entries in Pointers, Irish Setters, Gordon Setters, and "Setters of any breed." There was a satisfactory entry, and this event is considered to be the first American Dog Show. The very next day, October 8, 1874, the Tennessee Sportsmen's Association held a combined dog show and field trial at Memphis, Tennessee. This was the first such combined event and the first organized field trial in America. Again the dog-show portion of the meeting was conducted under the rules of The Kennel Club (England). This event was followed on January 14 - 21, 1875, by a competition in Detroit that was open to "dogs besides those devoted to field sports" and was probably the first truly all-breed event in America. Unfortunately, the report in Burges's book on the Detroit show carries results limited to sporting breeds, which brings up the question of whether any other breeds were involved. Of interest, however, is the fact that classes for the Pointers were divided into Pointers over fifty-five pounds and Pointers not exceeding fifty-five pounds.

Other events held in 1875 included the Rod and Gun Club of Springfield, Massachusetts, show of April 28 - 29; the Watertown, New York, show of May 3; the Paris, Kentucky, show of June 3; the Mineola, New York, show of June 23 - 24 (its second event); and the New England Association Fair at Manchester, Vermont, of September 18.

The second annual event of the Tennessee Sportsmen's Association was staged on October 27 in Memphis. It was an unusual affair for this early date, with sweepstakes and puppy stakes together with classes for braces (the first in America) and a "free-for-all" stake open to Setters and Pointers, regardless of age, for the "Championship of America." Five entries competed for the cup, valued at $150, together with the considerable prize money of $250 for first place, $150 for second, and $100 for third. The entry fee was $25 per dog, which shows that high entry fees existed even then. The Memphis show had several other stakes, making it truly an event that departed from the simple format used for the early events.

Burges's 1876 book was basically a stud record that also reported the results of some early dog shows and some isolated field activities. Burges did not attempt to include reports of such exhibitions as fairs and farm events, where dogs, together with many other animals, were on exhibit. He had contemplated future editions of his stud record, but they did not come to pass. In 1882, a revised edition of *The*

American Kennel and Sporting Field was published; in his preface to this edition, Burges gave the following reasons for not continuing the effort:

> When six years since I wrote *The American Kennel and Sporting Field* and gave therein the first list of canine pedigrees ever issued in this country, I stated in the Preface my intention to revise that list from time to time so as to keep pace with the importations and breeding of sporting dogs. This intention was, however, frustrated by the organization of the National American Kennel Club, in 1876, having for its object, among others, the issue of an official stud book, and as I recognized the fact that a National Club could give to such a work a character no private individual could, I withdrew *The American Kennel and Sporting Field* from the competition. The book has consequently remained unrevised until now. . . . In a country where field sports have but recently come into general recognition, and where but a few years since canine breeding and selling was confined to a disreputable class, a short time naturally produces great alterations, and the writer who honestly tries to keep up with the developments of the day, will find himself compelled to retract assertions, made upon the authority of different circumstances.

Burges's perception was correct, as there had been substantial activity in several areas since the publication of the first edition of his work in 1876. The number of shows and entrants therein had burgeoned, and new breeds had appeared, as had a rival stud record, *The National American Kennel Club Stud Book*. But Arnold Burges was the first to publish a stud record in America, and in so doing emphasized the singular importance of such a record upon the growth of interest in pure-bred dogs. Burges died on March 10, 1888, long before he could see the consequences of his effort to establish a reliable record for posterity.

The National American Kennel Club rapidly became important in its field. It was founded at the Chicago show on January 26, 1876, with permanent headquarters in St. Louis. The officers and committee members elected at the Chicago meeting were Dr. N. Rowe, President; J. H. Whitman, First Vice President; E. C. Sterling, Second Vice President; C. H. Turner, Secretary; and Luther Adams, Treasurer. The executive committee consisted of L. H. Smith, P. H. Bryson, C. H. Raymond, L. V. Lemoyne, W. Jarvis, Arnold Burges, S. H. Turrill, E. O. Greenwood, and C. F. Demuth.

The majority of the new club's members were field-trial oriented and not active in dog shows. Preparation and publication of the stud book were made the responsibility of President Rowe, who had excellent credentials for the task. Rowe, editor of *The American Field,* a leading sporting paper of the time, was a well-known writer as well as an active dog breeder and exhibitor. Unfortunately, work on the registry was slow, and it was not until 1879 that the initial volume was published. This volume includes particulars for 1416 dogs registered through 1878. The registrants are broken down into seven major divisions: English, Irish, Gordon, and cross-bred Setters, Pointers, Spaniels, and Chesapeake Dogs and Retrievers. The Spaniel division embraces a number of variants, including Irish Water, Clumber, Cocker, Sussex, Retrieving, and Water Spaniels.

THE AMERICAN FIELD

THE SPORTSMAN'S JOURNAL.

Published by the American Field Publishing Co.

Four dollars a year; two dollars for six months; one dollar for three months; strictly in advance.
Money should be sent by Postal Order, Draft on Chicago, or by Registered Letter.
THE AMERICAN FIELD and NEW YORK SPORTSMAN $6 a year.
The Trade supplied by the American and Western News Companies.
Manuscript intended for publication should be written on one side of the paper only.
Communications must be accompanied by the writer's name and address, not necessarily for publication, but as a private guarantee of good faith, and all communications, upon any subject, or for any department, must be addressed

N. ROWE,
Editor and Manager American Field,
155 & 157 Dearborn St., Chicago, Ill.

GREAT BRITAIN OFFICE AND AGENCY:—The American Exchange in Europe (limited); Henry F. Gillig, General Manager, 449 Strand, W.C., London, Eng.

WESTERN OFFICE:--155 & 157 Dearborn Street, Chicago, Ill.
EASTERN OFFICE:--Office "New York Sportsman," Tribune Building, New York.
Address all communications to Western Office.

NEW YORK AND CHICAGO, SATURDAY, JULY 2, 1881.

THE AMERICAN FIELD.

In our last issue we announced that the CHICAGO FIELD Publishing Company having consummated arrangements with the incorporators of the AMERICAN FIELD Publishing Company for the sale of the CHICAGO FIELD, its good will, patronage, and everything appertaining thereto, this issue of the paper would be under the title of the AMERICAN FIELD.

The "AMERICAN FIELD," we think, will be generally recognized as a more appropriate name than the CHICAGO FIELD, since the paper has never been local nor sectional, but national, always maintaining that the sportsmen of America were a brotherhood, whose interests are identical, and consequently the interests of one section of as much import to the paper as those of another. The word "Chicago," therefore, to the casual observer, and one unacquainted with the true characteristics of the paper, localized it, which was extremely objectionable to the best interests of the paper, which is happily obviated by the substitution of the word "American."

Dr. Nicholas Rowe, c. 1880. John T. Marvin Collection. *Dr. Rowe's editorial comment (July 2, 1881) when the paper's name was changed from* The Chicago Field *to* The American Field, *its present name.* John T. Marvin Collection

The cross-bred Setter classification is interesting since it was not unusual at the time to mix blood in order to gain improved performance; cross-bred Setters were rather popular, which is evidenced by the 258 stud-book entries that include double and triple crosses of the Setter breeds. A note at the beginning of the cross-bred section suggests that the records were not always well kept. "Owing to the indefinite character of some of the pedigrees," the note reads, "it was impossible to decide to what breed certain dogs belonged. They are therefore included in the present class to save disregarding them altogether.'' This is indeed a frank and interesting statement!

Typical entry information in *The National American Stud Book* is offered here for the English Setter dog Adonis, Number 1: ''George E. Delano, New Bedford, Massachusetts, breeder, owner; whelped 1875; black, white, and tan; by Leicester by Llewellin's Dan, out of his Lill II.'' Adonis is the same dog recorded as Number 1 in Burges's earlier stud record, though there he is recorded as being sired by Leicester out of a bitch named Doll. The discrepancy illustrates that early records were not without error.

The first volume of this stud book also includes the constitution and bylaws of The National American Kennel Club, its bench-show and field-trial rules, breeding particulars for the 1416 dogs registered, and results for nine bench shows held from 1876 to 1878. The book also includes the results of five field trials: Memphis (1874, 1875, and 1876), Iowa (1877), and Nashville (1877).

Among the bench shows reported is The Westminster Kennel Club's first show, held on May 8 - 10, 1877. What is not mentioned is that the event was extended through May 11 as a result of the crowd's desire to view the 1201 dogs entered. This event is second only to the Kentucky Derby in terms of longevity among

The cover of the first Westminster catalogue cover, 1877. John T. Marvin Collection

First Annual N. Y.

Bench Show.

CATALOGUE

1877.

NEW YORK:
ROGERS & SHERWOOD, PRINTERS, 21 BARCLAY STREET.
1877.

consecutively held sporting events in America. A complete review of the history of the Westminster show appears in The Westminster Kennel Club's one-hundredth anniversary book, published in 1976.

Dr. Rowe continued to produce *The National American Kennel Club Stud Book,* publishing the second volume in 1885. This edition is marked as being "printed by N. Rowe for The National American Kennel Club" even though the club had changed its name in 1884 to The National Field Trial Club and had dropped all interest in bench shows. The American Kennel Club had been organized in 1884, and had assumed full jurisdiction over bench shows. In 1886, Dr. Rowe assembled and published the third volume of the stud record, which was issued in quarterly installments and entitled *The American Kennel Stud Book.* Dr. Rowe, who had full title to the stud record, subsequently offered the three initial volumes gratis to the infant AKC, which accepted them. Without Rowe's effort and generosity, the initiation of a stud book would have been delayed for many years and would not be as extensive as it is with respect to the early entries.

Dr. Rowe's effort to improve the lot of pure-bred dogs, particularly field dogs, never wavered and he worked tirelessly from about 1874 toward the completion of *The Field Dog Stud Book.* This effort was approaching fruition at the time of his death in 1896 at the age of fifty-four. Fortunately, Mrs. Rowe, who had always assisted her husband, carried on both *The American Field* magazine and the final preparation of *The Field Dog Stud Book. The Field Dog Stud Book* was published in 1901, and has been continued from that date, enjoying reciprocity with *The American Kennel Club Stud Book.*

A third national stud record, *The American Kennel Register,* backed by the Forest and Stream Publishing Company, appeared in 1881 as a monthly publication. It included a stud record (stud book with registration number assigned to each dog), show results, reports on important happenings, and probably the best editorial effort carried out by any of its contemporary periodicals. It ceased publication after the January/February 1889 issue. The newly founded American Kennel Club had offered to take over this stud book to insure continuity, but the offer was refused by the Forest and Stream Publishing Company, and *The American Kennel Register* disappeared from view.

The emergence of several organizations and several published stud records during these years pointed to the need for a cooperative effort to bring stability to the national interest in pure-bred dogs. With the consolidation of the stud records into *The American Kennel Club Stud Book* and with the formation of the AKC itself, the American stage was set for the future growth and development of the sport of pure-bred dogs.

3

The Birth of the
American Kennel Club

When the National American Kennel Club changed its name in 1884 to the National Field Trial Club and altered its direction to embrace field dogs only, dog shows suffered for want of a central governing body. However, many established bench shows continued because the public's interest in this activity grew steadily, and serious efforts to form a national kennel club came from several sources.

Major Taylor, an experienced dog judge and breeder, and Elliot Smith of the Westminster Kennel Club both put forth such an effort, but both attempts failed. However, a group of twenty-five dedicated fanciers petitioned Taylor and Smith to renew their efforts. This petition was in the form of a ''Call for a Kennel Club'' that appeared in the August 1884 issue of *The American Kennel Register*. It reads:

> *Editor American Kennel Register:*
> In view of the conflicting actions of the Westminster Kennel Club and of Major Taylor relative to the inception of a National Kennel Club, and the danger of the proposal falling through thereby, we respectfully ask you to issue a call for a meeting of exhibitors and clubs to form such a Kennel Club, and that you prepare a plan of organization, work, etc., for such a club, to be considered at this meeting. It seems very desirable that the co-operation of so respected and experienced a judge as Major Taylor, and so old and influential an organization as the Westminster Kennel Club, should both be secured to this object.

The ''call'' evoked substantial response from fanciers and clubs across the United States and Canada. Taylor and Smith both backed the effort and aided its progress in every possible way. A meeting was scheduled for September 17-18, 1884, in Philadelphia during the Philadelphia Dog Show. Delegates from clubs across the United States and Canada attended. These clubs included Illinois, Cincinnati, Philadelphia, Westminster (New York), Montreal, New England (Bos-

Major James M. Taylor. John T. Marvin Collection

ton), New Haven, Kentucky, Baltimore, Cleveland, New Brunswick (Canada), London (Canada), and Saint Louis—thirteen clubs in all. Several other groups had representatives who were not admitted to the meeting because their bylaws did not mention bench shows, a point of substantial importance at the time.

The major order of business at this meeting was twofold: first, to select a suitable name for the organization; second, to appoint a committee to draft a constitution and bylaws. The name proposed was the National Bench Show Association. It was also proposed that membership should consist of clubs only, and not individuals. A committee of delegates was formed to draft a constitution and bylaws. This committee was to make a report in New York during the week of the New York Non-Sporting Dog Show, October 21-22, 1884. The committee consisted of Elliot Smith, Chairman; J. A. Nickerson; General Shattuc; Major Taylor; and S. G. Dixon.

On October 22, 1884, the newly drafted constitution and bylaws were approved at the New York meeting and officers were elected for the ensuing year. The documents were approved after some changes and additions, including a change in name from the National Bench Show Association to The American Kennel Club. The officers elected were Major J. M. Taylor, President (Lexington, Kentucky); Elliot Smith, first Vice President (New York, New York); Samuel Coulson, second

Vice President (Montreal, Canada); Edward S. Porter, Secretary (New Haven, Connecticut); G. N. Appold, Treasurer (Baltimore, Maryland).

Thus, the October 22, 1884, meeting in New York marked the true beginning of The American Kennel Club as a structured organization—a club with a name, constitution, and bylaws, and a full complement of officers.

The second annual meeting of The American Kennel Club was held in Philadelphia on May 19, 1885. A hotly contested election of officers at that meeting bore the following results: Major Taylor, President (by a close six to five vote); Elliot Smith, first Vice President; A. W. Pope, second Vice President; G. E. Osborn, Secretary; and E. Comfort, Treasurer. That some friction existed in the new club is evidenced by the close margin of Taylor's election and that the "annual" meeting was convened only about seven months after the first meeting. In any event, the committee that had been previously appointed to revise the constitution and bylaws submitted a more concise version of these important documents, which was accepted.

At the same meeting, twenty-eight committees were appointed to consider the several breed standards to be adopted and used at shows held under the rules of the AKC. Some of the committees were confined to one breed, while others were to concern themselves with the standards for a number of breeds.

The friction within the club's hierarchy only increased after the May 19, 1885, meeting in Philadelphia. It was obvious that changes would be necessary if the young club was to progress. After a stormy seven-month period, Major Taylor submitted his resignation in December, 1885, and it was accepted by Elliot Smith, the first Vice President, who was then elected president. At a June 10, 1886, meeting the offices of Secretary and Treasurer were combined and Vredenburgh was elected as his successor. At a June 10, 1886, meeting, the offices of Secretary and Treasurer were combined and Vredenburgh became the guardian of the new office, a position he held until December 16, 1919.

During this period, it became apparent that the club had to have a reliable stud book. As mentioned earlier, The American Kennel Club agreed to take over *The American Kennel Stud Book* from Dr. Rowe in 1887, and to be fully responsible for its future publication. The introduction to the fourth volume of *The American Kennel Club Stud Book* (1887) acknowledges Rowe's gift of the initial three volumes. The quarterly frequency introduced by Rowe continued through 1888, but reverted to annual frequency with the fifth volume, issued in 1889.

Other important things occurred in the 1880s. At this time there was a restive atmosphere surrounding the Canadian-based clubs. Since the formation of The American Kennel Club, Canadian clubs had depended upon it for registrations, shows and trials, and the like. Early attempts to form a kennel club in Canada included the creation of the Dominion of Canada Kennel Club. According to the June 1883 issue of *The American Kennel Register,* the club held an annual meeting and elected officers, but no further report appeared, indicating that the club had failed. Activity in Canada continued, however, and in 1886 three Canadian clubs resigned from the AKC, reflecting growing schism that eventually led to the founding of the Canadian Kennel Club in 1888. An effort in this direction began at a meeting held in London, Ontario, in September 1887, followed by another meeting in London the next year, at which the Canadian Kennel Club was founded. Interestingly, Samuel Coulson, who had been elected a vice president of the AKC in 1884, was elected a vice president of the newly formed Canadian Kennel Club. A complete history of this club in this early years may be found in ''The Canadian Kennel Club Story,'' an article appearing in the seventy-fifth anniversary issue of *Dogs in Canada* (February 1963).

Another development that took place during this segment of the history of the AKC was the late entry of still another national kennel club into a field that was already strewn with memories of previously unsuccessful groups. This club was organized as the National Kennel Club of America on April 3, 1888. Its President was Dr. J. Frank Perry, who wrote extensively on dogs under the pseudonym of Ashmont. Perry had previously been active in attempts to form a national club, and he was a signer of the 1884 ''call'' for a national kennel club. The new group was the first to offer ''bargain rates'' to early joiners. At the July 5, 1888, meeting of the club, the following officers were elected: Dr. Frank Perry, President; Anna Whitney, Vice President; W. S. Jackson, Vice President; E. S. Porter, Vice President; Dr. C. E. Nichols, Vice President; and H. W. Huntington, Secretary/Treasurer. In addition, there was a fifteen-member executive committee elected in staggered terms of one, two, and three years.

The National Kennel Club of America is noteworthy for the election of Anna Whitney as Vice President, perhaps the first woman to become a national dog club officer in America. The National Kennel Club of America did not prosper, and gradually it faded from view as the AKC continued to gain.

4

Early Growth and the American Kennel Gazette

The last ten to twelve years of the nineteenth century were an exciting period for both pure-bred dogs and the infant American Kennel Club. Interest in the breeding of pure-bred dogs grew tremendously, and dog shows gained in popularity in all sections of the country. Much of this progress may be attributed to the marked reduction of friction between individuals and the several competing clubs as the AKC gained strength and support. Further, *The American Kennel Club Stud Book* was now the sole responsibility of the AKC, as the only competing stud book, *The American Kennel Register,* had passed into oblivion.

The American Kennel Club was strengthened further by the long-term incumbency of August Belmont, Jr., as President, a post that he held continuously from 1888 until 1915. Prior to this the club has had three presidents: Major Taylor (1884), replaced by Elliot Smith, who served two terms, and William Child, who assumed the office in 1887. Belmont replaced Child in 1888. The frequent changes in this office did little to instill confidence in the organization. Belmont's election and long incumbency, along with that of Alfred P. Vredenburgh as Secretary and later as Secretary/Treasurer, marked a change in direction and attitude, offering a stability that had heretofore been lacking.

In 1888, August Belmont proposed that the AKC publish a magazine, *The American Kennel Gazette,* which, he believed, would aid the club's growth while informing interested people of current matters pertaining to pure-bred dogs and dog shows. His idea met with some opposition; several members of the board were afraid that the cost of such a periodical would be prohibitive. Belmont countered with an offer to personally underwrite the effort by covering any deficit that might arise, up to five thousand dollars per year. The first issue of the *Gazette* appeared in January 1889 and carried the following statement:

> The American Kennel Club having adopted the plan of publishing a
> Gazette, in pursuance of your wishes in the matter, the officers have begun this,

its first publication, with the new year, 1889, and they will endeavor, as much as lies in their power, to meet what they feel the Kennel World requires in the shape of an official organ; taking as their guide the expressions of opinion on the subject from breeders and exhibitors, both in the past and since the adoption of the plan of publishing this *Gazette*.

It is proposed to afford the Kennel Club and its individual members an official medium for the publication of all proceedings and announcements bearing upon any subject embraced by the interests of the Kennel World, and to keep and publish a complete and official record of all that transpires during the year, either in connection with shows, field trials or matters affecting the breeding, kennel or field management of any known breed of dogs.

Alfred P. Vredenburgh, the third Secretary/Treasurer of the American Kennel Club, and AKC Secretary from 1886 until 1920.

Title page of a 1915 American Kennel Gazette. John T. Marvin Collection

The new magazine had a physical size approximating today's *Gazette,* but did not carry the editorial material that has since become an important feature of the publication. In fact, there was no editor or illustrations, and the first issue had a total of only twenty pages. Thereafter, the *Gazette* slowly expanded. James Watson, an established writer, judge, and a knowledgeable dog fancier, was appointed the *Gazette's* first editor. Watson gave the magazine a new look and began to include news items and informative articles concerning dogs as well as a record of the AKC's affairs. After Watson left the position in 1900, the *Gazette* was guided by an editorial board for 24 years, after which period the need for a full-time editor again became apparent. Since its inception, the magazine has grown steadily in size, circulation, and quality. A list of its editors includes James Watson, 1898-1900; editorial board only, 1900-1924; Louis de Casanova, 1924-1942; Arthur Frederick Jones, 1942-1968; Henry Bernacki, 1968-1978; Robert Sheretta, 1979-1980; and Pat Beresford, 1980-present.

The *Gazette* has always had approximately the same format and size, except from April 1942 through July 1952, when it was reduced in size to six by nine inches as a wartime conservation measure. Color plates and cover designs were introduced in the 1920s.

As the sport of pure-bred dogs continued to gain in popularity, the AKC prospered. New clubs came into the AKC's sphere of influence, and many of the older clubs gained in size and prestige. This growth necessitated many changes, and one of these concerned office space. In 1884, the infant group had no permanent office and held its meetings at various locations. As steady growth brought in new clubs, additional shows, more registrations, and an ever-expanding volume of records, the need for space grew. In 1887, the first official office was opened at 44 Broadway in New York City. It was a small room, but large enough to contain the sparse early records and to offer a site for delegates' meetings (delegates numbered fewer than twenty at the time). The first delegates' meeting of 1887 was held at this location on March 23, 1887, but as there was no quorum, the meeting was immediately adjourned. At the next meeting, the treasurer reported a balance on hand of $55.73.

By 1895, the sport had grown to the point at which the AKC required larger quarters, and a move was made to 55 Liberty Street, New York City, on May 9. This space was adequate for a few years, when it became necessary to obtain additional floor space. More suitable offices were rented at the same address, and they included separate rooms for the stud book and *Gazette* activities. At this time the office force had expanded to nine employees. The first telephone was installed in 1902. Its prospective installation caused considerable discussion before the heavy financial outlay of $75.00 per year for such service was approved.

In 1909, the 55 Liberty Street location had to be vacated, as the building was to be razed. The AKC moved its headquarters to the German-American Insurance Building at Liberty Street and Maiden Lane, New York City. There was space for a library and a meeting room together with additional rooms for several departments. These offices remained the club's headquarters until 1919, when new quarters were obtained at 221 Fourth Avenue. The club's offices remained at the Fourth Avenue address until 1964 when they were moved to the present location at 51 Madison Avenue.

Working agreements with foreign kennel clubs, including the Canadian Kennel Club, began in 1889. Also in 1889, the matter of incorporation was first introduced, though it was not to be resolved for a number of years.

In 1891, a technical problem arose when the American Bull Terrier Club applied for membership, at the same time requesting recognition of the breed. The matter was tabled while an investigation was held to determine whether there was such a breed. Initially, with the request for breed recognition, the alternative name of Boston Terrier had been submitted; the breed was finally recognized under the title of Boston Terrier in 1893.

The associate membership category, consisting of individuals rather than clubs, also caused problems during this period. The associate members were thorns in the side of the organization, and continually made suggestions and requests, often of a strictly local nature. In the 1890s a suggestion for a clubhouse was broached by the group but rejected. One of the most unusual proposals concerned the possibility of erecting dog kennels in New York City's Central Park. In 1923 associate membership in the AKC was finally eliminated.

Outside an early American dog show, c. 1890s. John T. Marvin Collection

Several interesting practices surfaced during this period. For example, the secretary had the power to approve or disapprove shows and the rules under which they were held. He had sweeping powers and he had the authority to decide whether or not a breed would be able to offer Winners Classes (Open Classes). In addition, it was not unusual for a breed with a small number of registrations to be relegated to the miscellaneous class. During this same general period, many of the smaller events were termed "ribbon shows," which closely approached today's sanctioned affairs. Fanciers complained, but it was some time before the secretary's powers were curtailed.

In 1895, a critical situation arose on the West Coast, where clubs were becoming restive concerning their position within the sport. The distance between the West Coast and the New York City headquarters made communications very difficult. In an attempt to alleviate such problems before they got out of hand, Secretary/Treasurer Vredenburgh went to the West Coast in 1895 to discuss problems with representatives of the clubs in that area. The trip was quite productive and resulted in the formation in 1896 of the Pacific Advisory Committee (PAC). This committee was to act as an intermediary between the AKC and the groups in the Far West. This move was effective for a time, but problems continued to surface, culminating in the formation of a short lived rival kennel club, the Pacific Coast Kennel Club. This organization quickly recruited some ten clubs, suggesting that the situation had become sufficiently critical to send Vredenburgh on another trip. It was finally decided to permit West Coast clubs to elect their own advisory committee rather than have it appointed in New York, as had been the practice. This helped, but it did not eliminate all of the problems; in 1911, for example, Oakland held a show under antagonistic rules on the same day that an AKC event was to be held by the Golden Gate Kennel Club in San Francisco. This action resulted in the suspension of the Oakland club and its officers, though they were subsequently reinstated.

Still, by 1913 the problems had grown more numerous as the PAC continually requested deviations from the rules in order to reduce the cost of events on the West Coast. The AKC consistently refused to grant such rule deviations. With no solution in view, members of the PAC resigned in 1913, effectively eliminating that committee. In its stead, the AKC appointed a trial board together with a West Coast agent. This action was met with mixed feelings, but accepted by the majority of clubs and fanciers.

The situation on the West Coast reached a climax in 1914 when the San Jose Kennel Club was disqualified for holding a show under the rules of a new group, the National Dog Breeders Association (which association failed shortly after inception). However, problems on the West Coast did eventually subside as travel arrangements and telephone service improved.

Other matters of national importance also required attention. One of the most urgent involved the proper approach to championship requirements. Then, as now, the making of a champion was of substantial importance and the establishment of procedures required much study and time. Early American shows followed precedents set in England with respect to the championship title and required three first place wins in the Open Class, which was generally divided by sex. Several changes were made by 1900, and the following point schedule emerged, based upon the total number of dogs at the show:

All-Breed Shows with under 250 dogs:	1 point
All-Breed Shows with 250 and under 500 dogs:	2 points
All-Breed Shows with 500 and under 750 dogs:	3 points
All-Breed Shows with 750 and under 1000 dogs:	4 points
All-Breed Shows with 1000 dogs and over:	5 points

The number of dogs in the breed was not considered, since the schedule applied to all breeds. All member club specialty shows were rated at four points, while nonmember club specialties were given a two point rating regardless of the size of the entry. The system had obvious inequities. For example, at an all-breed show with over 1000 dogs, a dog in a breed that had few dogs entered gained five points because of the size of the overall entry. The same dog could defeat a relatively large breed entry at a small event—under the 250-dog total— and gain only one point. In all instances, regardless of show or entry, an accumulation of ten points was required for the title of champion.

Beginning in 1904, other suggestions emerged when an attempt was made to rate shows in accordance with the prize money offered, as follows:

Shows offering at least $2000 in regular classes:	1 point
Shows offering at least $2500 in regular classes:	2 points
Shows offering at least $3000 in regular classes:	3 points
Shows offering at least $4000 in regular classes:	4 points
Shows offering at least $5000 in regular classes:	5 points

All specialty shows were automatically rated at four points, and shows held on the Pacific Coast were rated at one-half the monies in the above schedule. This proposal, while never placed into effect, raises some interesting points. First, the prize monies were obviously of greater importance than they were later; second, West Coast affairs were generally smaller in entry, probably because of the distances involved.

On May 26, 1908, the AKC was granted articles of incorporation under a special charter from the State of New York. The new constitution and bylaws were published in the June and December 1908 issues of the *Gazette* and were finally approved in January 1909, culminating work begun in 1889. About the same time, a prerequisite for a title was modified so that fifteen points had to be won, with some of the points awarded by three different judges. The year 1909 also marked the addition of trial boards to the club's hierarchy. Until then, the Board of Directors heard all controversies, settled all disputes, and levied all fines and penalties for infractions of the rules. Trial boards were established to hear complaints and controversies and to decide them, to levy fines, and to take care of other such business. Concurrent with this acton, rules governing superintendents were first placed in the rule book. Until this time, anyone could assume the role—a judge, a handler, a dealer—in fact, anyone who was in good standing with the AKC. The rule decreed that anyone acting as superintendent, show secretary, or veterinarian was prohibited from exhibiting or judging at any show that that officer or veterinarian supervised. While the problem was not widespread, conflicts of interest had occurred in the past.

Many of the rules governing dog shows also came under scrutiny. One concerned specialty shows, wherein the requirement was added that nonmember specialty clubs had to obtain permission from the parent breed club before staging any show. The second concerned dog show classes. At this time, the relatively new Graduate Class was eliminated and an American-bred Class was substituted. This new classification was for dogs bred and whelped in the United States, as is the case today. It became effective on January 1, 1910.

Though Pacific Coast shows were originally given a lower point-rating than eastern events because of the generally smaller entry, this changed in 1910. The new policy provided that all shows west of the eastern borders of Montana, Wyoming, Colorado, and New Mexico under the jurisdiction of the Pacific Advisory Council would be rated as follows:

Under 100 dogs:	1 point
Under 200 dogs:	2 points
Under 300 dogs:	3 points
Under 400 dogs:	4 points
400 dogs and over:	5 points

All member club specialty shows were rated at four points and all nonmember club specialty shows at two points. The new ratings for all-breed events were extremely helpful in building interest in the West, where the fancy had long been hampered by rules formed basically for East Coast shows. Nonmember specialty clubs could not have a rating over two points in spite of their overall entry, whereas member specialty clubs had a four-point rating. Why this latter restriction was applied is unclear, but it surely placed an unfair restriction on nonmember groups.

In 1911 a rule went into effect that concerned territorial protection. In large cities there was a trend toward developing several clubs, often formed by dissident groups. The first club established had no protection if other clubs endeavored to hold a show on a date that might be in conflict with the first club's show. The new rule gave sole privilege to the member club that had held the first show in a given area. No other event could gain show approval in the same area without first obtaining permission from the existing member club. But if the existing member club had failed to hold a show within a period of eighteen months, a show could be approved for another club without permission from the resident member club. Also, if the resident member club failed to hold a show within twelve months of said licensed show, an application for active membership in the AKC from the club formed later would be accepted without the consent of the existing member club. This rule prevented inactive member clubs from selfishly holding a territory, and gave an opportunity for other clubs to develop.

In 1911, definite rules for classified and unclassified special prizes were established. A classified special prize was one offered in a single breed, somewhat similar to an award for best of breed (although such a triumph was not recorded by the AKC). An unclassified special was a prize offered in classes involving multiple-breed competition similar to the present groups and best in show. This prize was competed for by representatives of several breeds in a single class. This, too, was an unofficial prize at the time and for several years after.

Judging procedures have undergone an amazing metamorphosis over the years. In the beginning, most shows did not offer a best-in-show award, and in any case there was no official award. Actually, there was no such competition unless a trophy was offered for the placement, which made the judging necessary. The first best-in-show award was claimed by an imported White Bull Terrier named Count at an 1885 Connecticut event, according to unofficial records. Thereafter, it was not unusual for awards to be offered for both best dog in show and best bitch in show. Further, the award could go to a dog that was not in breed-class competition but rather entered in the unclassified specials class. This grouping included dogs of several breeds that were not entered in the classes, and often entries reached seventy or eighty at some large events. This class was not even noted in many early catalogs. The number of judges for the class varied with time. For example, at Westminster in 1921, two judges and a referee were listed. The referee was to be

George Thomas and James Mortimer looking over the Wire-haired Fox Terriers at an early dog show. (Note Spratt's benching with straw bedding.) John T. Marvin Collection

used to break a tie between the two judges if this became necessary. This early period can be a confusing one to modern fanciers and exhibitors, who take for granted today's orderly sequence of elimination, which leads to the ultimate winner of best in show.

In its first thirty years The American Kennel Club established itself as the predominant national American club with regard to pure-bred dogs and dog shows. As the AKC approached the 1920s, it found itself to be an organization with a firm foundation and the proven ability to weather adversities and to administer a body of rules that served its membership and the interests of pure-bred dogs in this country.

5

The 1920s Changing Times and Changing Rules

The pattern of dog shows in America changed greatly during the 1920s. Previously, shows had been conducted with little guidance from The American Kennel Club, and there was little standardization in the procedures followed in holding shows. It was not until well into the 1920s that standardized procedures for dog shows began to emerge. It became apparent that uniform rules, applied equally to all dog clubs, were necessary if the sport was to continue to prosper. The situation of rather loose national control by more than one dog club was inadequate, as travel conditions improved and fanciers began to attend shows outside their immediate geographical area.

The AKC was aware of the problem, and in 1923, after a great deal of substantial study and discussion, it initiated a nationwide remedial program. A committee of directors was appointed to study the rules and to recommend changes. The existing rules, many of which had been held over from prewar days, did not enable the AKC to cope with the problems that surfaced as show activity increased. At one time, for example, a dog defeated in the breed classes could, under certain circumstances, be eligible to enter the competition for best dog in show, surely an undesirable situation.

The committee offered a number of recommendations, particularly with respect to show rules and judging procedures. One of the most important of these concerned the overall structure of dog shows. This entailed separating the several breeds into five groups and judging each breed in each group to a single winner: best of breed. These best-of-breed winners in each group were next judged to a best dog in that group, and finally, the five group winners met to decide the best dog in the show. The dog so designated had, in effect, defeated all other entrants. This was the beginning of the presently used group alignment system. The five group divisions decided upon were:

Group 1: Sporting Dogs. This division included all Pointing Breeds, Retrievers, and Spaniels as well as all Hounds.
Group 2: Working Dogs. This included all the Working and Herding Breeds.
Group 3: Terriers.
Group 4: Toy Breeds.
Group 5: Non-Sporting Breeds.

In 1920, sanctioned matches were begun. These matches provided useful training exercises for more formal events and they made dog owners more aware of correct show procedures.

By 1924, the new group alignment was in general use across the country. Exhibitors liked the new format, as it offered standardized competition among the entrants that made major awards meaningful. This could not be said about many high placements gained under the previous system. The Westminster Kennel Club was the first to include judging for best in show under the new format, and Ch. Barberryhill Bootlegger, a Sealyham Terrier owned by Bayard Warren, captured the award. A full review of the new show procedure was offered in depth in a detailed article by John F. Collins, "What the New Rules Mean," that appeared in the January 1924 issue of *The American Kennel Gazette*. The new rules had many virtues, the most important being that the dog judged best in show had, through the process of elimination, defeated all other competitors, as is the case today.

The new procedures also provided that a veterinarian had to be present at every show and that every dog entered had to be examined before being admitted to the show. This was an important rule, as it helped control the spread of distemper, a dreaded disease of the time.

It should be pointed out that the new judging arrangement was not mandatory, and any club could elect to forgo any placements subsequent to best of breed, providing this was advertised in advance. This policy still exists, and today the Saw Mill River Kennel Club, for example, elects to conduct its all-breed show under a format in which all judging is concluded after best of breed and/or best of variety.

The new rules seemed to encourage many more individuals to begin judging. Possibly this was at least in part due to the new uniformity in procedure. In any event, the May 1925 issue of *The American Kennel Gazette* carried a license committee notice concerning the requirements for being awarded a judging license. The requirements set forth in the notice were decided upon as the result of several years of study concerning the proper procedures for screening applicants for judging, and considerably reduced the number of new multi-breed and all-breed licenses gained in preceding years, when there had been few restrictions. Additional guidance was offered by this committee when it suggested that "in the variety classes [groups], each group must be judged by a judge or judges, judging the greatest number of breeds in that group at the regular show." Additional guidance was offered for arbiters of best in show: "The judges must be selected from judges of the variety classes." These suggestions, however, have long since been dropped.

The evolution of judging procedures makes one realize that today's smooth-running show format is not happenstance, but the result of many years of trial and error, constant evaluation, and the dedication of knowledgeable individuals pursuing the best interests of pure-bred dogs.

In 1926, the AKC felt that the dog fancy should participate in the national celebration of the nation's sesquicentennial (1776—1926), which was centered in the city of Philadelphia. To this end, the AKC sponsored its own show for the first time. The 1926 show, known as the Sesquicentennial Show, or Sesqui Show, was held in Philadelphia on September 30 through October 2, 1926. It was a huge success and had a lasting effect on the public.

Held under the new rules, there were five groups and a panel of thirty-one judges. The prizes were numerous and included a specially designed gold medal offered by the Sesquicentennial International Exposition to every best-of-breed or best-of-variety winner. The American Kennel Club itself offered solid gold medals to every Winners Dog and Winners Bitch and sterling silver medals to every Reserve Winner. In addition to these unusual prizes, monies were offered in all breeds and varieties as follows: $20 for first, $10 for second, and $5 for third in all the regular classes (Puppy, Novice, American-bred, Limit, and Open). Variety groups were even better provided for, with cash prizes of $50, $30, and $20 for the first three placements in each of the five groups, while best-in-show trophies of sterling silver were offered by The Kennel Club (England) and by Spratts Patent Limited. The generous trophy list undoubtedly had a bearing upon the entry of 2899 contestants.

The judging panel for the event included thirty-one of the most respected arbiters in the country. A number of the nation's top dog men were included on the panel, and today many are legends. A complete and informative biographical article on these judges appeared in the August 1926 issue of *The American Kennel Gazette*.

The benched all-breed dog show given by the AKC was held in the Auditorium, Sesqui Centennial International Exposition, Philadelphia. The hall was the largest ever to house a canine exhibition.

Mayor W. Freeland Kendrick, of the City of Philadelphia, presenting Best-in-Show Trophy to the Best-in-Show Sealyham, Ch. Pinegrade Perfection, handled by Percy Roberts, at the AKC Sesqui Centennial Show, Philadelphia, 1926. The drawing was made by B. Laurence Megargee, brother of the famous artist Edwin Megargee. From the Collection of William L. Kendrick

Ch. Pinegrade Perfection

Best in show at the Sesquicentennial extravaganza was captured by the Sealyham Terrier, Ch. Pinegrade Perfection, an imported bitch owned by Frederick C. Brown and handled by Percy Roberts. Interestingly, Mr. Roberts had two dogs eligible for the Terrier Group competition and opted to handle the other one, while sending in the Sealyham Terrier with Eland Hadfield. The judges saw it differently, however, and placed the Sealyham Number 1 in group. Roberts, of course, handled the bitch in the finals.

Five groups were judged, with all Sporting Dogs and all Hounds being grouped together. The remaining four groups were Working Dogs (Group 2), Terriers (Group 3), Toys (Group 4), and Non-Sporting Breeds (Group 5) . The top entry was in Wire Fox Terriers with 164 dogs (there were also 48 Smooths). Wires were followed by Shepherd Dogs with 139, Boston Terriers with 117, Pekingese with 89, Bulldogs with 82, Cocker Spaniels and Pointers with 75, English Setters with 71, and Airedales with 68. This entry sample gives an idea of contemporary breed popularity in the show ring.

(In the foregoing, the name ''German'' had been deleted from the ''German Shepherd Dog'' designation during World War I and was restored at a later date.)

Even though the Sesquicentennial Show was a success and gave pure-bred dogs tremendous publicity, using three judges in each group and five judges for best in show was an expense that few events could carry. In addition, the several restrictions placed upon judges limited those who wished to apply and expand their licenses. For these reasons, the format was changed after this show, and in a meeting of the license committee, held just two months after the Sesqui Show had scored its stunning success, its rules were revised and a notice appeared in the December 1926 *Gazette*. This notice set forth amended rules to become effective July 1, 1927, which relaxed the requirements for a judging license and allowed anyone in good standing with the AKC to judge. The edict also barred persons who were commercially connected with dog-related products. The new regulation effectively opened the way for a host of persons to judge, providing the superintendent submitted the name to the license committee six weeks before the show and followed certain other requirements.

A number of other matters came under consideration during the late 1920s. The most important of these was the board's decision to expand the number of groups from five to six with the new division of Sporting Dogs (Hounds), Group 2. This included all the hound breeds that had previously been classified in Group 1 with other sporting breeds. The new Group 1 continued to embrace Setters, Pointers, Spaniels, and Retrievers. The remaining four group divisions were renumbered but otherwise remained the same: Working Dogs (Group 3), Terriers (Group 4), Toys (Group 5), and Non-Sporting Dogs (Group 6). The name Sporting Dogs (Hounds) was changed subsequently to Hounds.

Other items of interest that occurred during the 1920s included a survey ending in August 1927 comparing entries at some of the country's top events over a five-year span. This table showed that only three events in the United States exceeded an entry of 1000 dogs; these were Westminster, the Eastern Dog Club, and a single Hollywood show. This is interesting when one considers that today most all-breed events annually exceed the entry figure of 1000.

A long-standing problem that was resolved during this period concerned the form for catalogs used at shows. Early catalogs listed the several breeds by physical size, beginning with the large breeds, then listing the medium-size breeds, and closing with the small dogs. The arrangement offered little uniformity from one show to the next, since one club would start with Mastiffs while another, for example, would begin with Great Danes. Later, the arrangement of breeds was modified so that all breeds were alphabetically arranged. This was satisfactory until the group system came into being. In the late 1920s, the problem was finally settled when all breeds were classified by group and arranged alphabetically within each group, which is the same procedure followed today.

In May 1927, the AKC tried to direct more attention to American-bred dogs by offering special incentives. The AKC announced that it would offer a fifty dollar cash award for best in show, if American-bred, at all member club events. The competition was limited to one year and did much toward improving interest in American-bred dogs.

Another change that transpired during the 1920s concerned the availability of AKC silver championship medals. These handsome mementos could be purchased by the owner of each new champion, but they were discontinued in the 1920s because of their high cost. The recurring complaint against ear-cropping was also raised during this period. England had outlawed the practice, and at the time, the English press had been full of pro and con arguments. The American Kennel Club Rules Committee aired the matter at a delegates' meeting, and after a lengthy discussion it was moved, seconded, and carried that no further action would be taken on the question of ear-cropping.

A highlight of the 1920s was the appearance of the first edition of The American Kennel Club book of standards, *Pure Bred Dogs,* in 1929. This effort, in the form of a hardbound book, has been maintained in an up-to-date format as far as new breeds and revised standards are concerned. In 1938, the book was renamed *The Complete Dog Book*. It has gone through numerous editions, as changes in standards occurred and new breeds were added to the Stud Book.

The 1920s were a critical period in the development of The American Kennel Club. The tremendous success of the Sesquicentennial Show brought dogs and dog shows sharply to America's attention. Even more importantly, the 1920s saw a marked development of standard rules and judging procedures instituted on a nationwide basis. The stabilization of these procedures began a process that has resulted in the uniform arrangement that governs the dog shows of today.

6

The 1930s
Innovation and
Consolidation

The 1930s was a time for both change and consolidation. While not so turbulent as the previous decade, there did take place during this period a host of innovative moves involving the sport of pure-bred dogs. While the country suffered through the Great Depression, registration figures and interest in dogs and dog shows grew. The number of recognized breeds increased from 83 in 1930 to 105 in 1940; the first AKC obedience trials were held; and AKC field trials grew in popularity and numbers. A milestone in the history of the club was reached in 1935 when the one-millionth dog was registered in the records of the AKC *Stud Book*. The dog was a Shetland Sheepdog named Sheltieland Alice Grey Gown, owned by Miss Catherine Edwards Coleman of Newport, New Hampshire. The certificate was personally presented to Miss Edwards by Russell H. Johnson, president of the club.

An action initiated in the late 1920s that bore fruit in the following decade concerned professional handlers. This group was composed of persons who exhibited dogs for pay (private) or for a fee (public). The AKC decided to require licenses of all persons who charged for these services. (Handlers' licenses were eliminated in 1978, and now anyone who is in good standing with the AKC may charge for this service.) In the 1930s, the licensing requirement led to the formation of an organization that could support the general interests of handlers as well as set up standards of conduct. This group was formed in 1931 and Leonard Brumby, Sr., was elected president. The Professional Handlers Association (PHA) grew and prospered. It held a number of conventions around the country, the first being at Cleveland in 1936. Years later, a second association, the Dog Handlers Guild, was formed, and it also became an organization with a substantial national membership.

Prior to 1932, the AKC had no complete book of rules specifically covering registration and dog shows. The initial issue of the rules was presented to the fancy in the November 1932 issue of the *Gazette*. This was followed by a separate book of

Russell H. Johnson, then president of the American Kennel Club, with the one millionth dog registered. John T. Marvin Collection

these rules. These rules were approved by the delegates at the December 1932 meeting. The general format was quite similar to that of the rules appearing in the modern AKC booklet, *Rules Applying to Registration and Dog Shows*. It is surprising to think that the club was able to function until as late in its history as 1932 without published rules. Since that time, however, the rules have been made readily available so that the ever-growing number of participants may have access to complete, up-to-date information concerning registration procedures, dog shows, field trials and obedience trials.

Another important activity that was begun in the 1930s was Children's Handling Classes, first held at the Westbury Kennel Association Show in 1932. This effort was initiated by the PHA and proved highly popular. The class designation was changed to Junior Showmanship Competition in 1950. Today, these classes are a popular adjunct to many shows.

Winners of the American-bred Group Awards for1938: Left to right: *Ed Sayres, Jr., handling the Kerry Blue Terrier, Ch. Bumble Bee of Delwin; Mrs. M. Hartley Dodge with her German Shepherd Dog, Ch. Giralda's Geisha; Mrs. Sherman R. Hoyt, with her Standard Poodle, Ch. Blakeen Jung Frau; H. E. Mellenthin with his Cocker Spaniel, Ch. My Own Brucie; John Royce with his Pekingese, Ch. Kai Lo of Dah-Lyn and Hans Sacher (handler) with the Smooth Dachshund, Ch. Herman Rinkton, owned by Mrs. Annis A. Jones.* John T. Marvin Collection

A far-reaching amendment to the rules was adopted at the December 12, 1933, delegates' meeting. This new rule dealt with the registration of litters, and it read in part:

> All litters of dogs eligible for registration and whelped in the United States of America on or before January 1, 1932, must be registered by their breeders or by the owners or lessees of the dams at the date of whelping and no single dog from any such litter will be otherwise eligible for registration. A single dog of a registered litter can be registered only by the breeder, owner of sire, owner or lessee of dam at date of whelping. . . . No dog of such registered litter shall be eligible for exhibition until it has been registered or listed in the usual manner.

This amendment was significant in that it required a statement of the number and sex of the puppies in a litter, and subsequent individual registration of the "get" was limited in number and sex to those noted on the litter registration. The registration required the signatures of the owners of both the sire and the dam. This rule is still in effect today. The rule did much to eliminate dishonest practices while greatly improving the validity of the Stud Book.

A very important addition to the AKC was made in 1934 when the club decided to establish a library. An early statement on this subject may be found in the November 1934 issue of the *Gazette,* and a definitive article, "How Our Library Could Function," by Anne Fitzgerald, appeared in the January 1935 issue. At its April 1934 meeting the board of directors decided to appoint a library committee to supervise the operation, and Hubert Brown was made chairman. Brown was assisted by William Cary Duncan (a club director), Louis de Casanova (editor of the *Gazette),* Edwin Megargee (a widely known fancier and artist), and James W. Spring (counsel for the AKC). The library continued under the supervi-

sion of this committee until 1958. In September 1937, a full-time librarian, Mrs. Peterson, was appointed. She held the post until her retirement on February 28, 1975. She accomplished much during her term, and the library grew tremendously. The library continued under the supervision of several well-schooled assistants until September 1979, when Mrs. Roberta Vesley was named library director.

The library now includes more than 15,000 volumes and has a full-time staff of four. It is considered to be one of the best and most complete libraries on dogs and related subjects in the world. A bibliography of books in the library appears in the *Gazette* issues from September 1977 through July 1978; the March 1977 issue includes a description of today's library and its operation.

In 1935, the club decided to stage a nationwide competition to emphasize the importance of American-bred dogs. The effort carried over into 1939, and each year a representative of each group was selected based upon the total group triumphs during the year of competition.

In 1938, The American Kennel Club published its first and last strictly commercial book, *The American Kennel Club Blue Book*. This book carried advertising from a host of the country's top kennels, including many of those whose dogs had captured the 1937 American-bred awards. In the foreword of this publication, Russell Johnson, president of the AKC, states, "the time was ripe for publication of a book clearly showing the present status of not less than ninety breeds by placing before the public pictures of standard specimens, so that one may at least see the state of perfection these breeds have reached by the year 1938."

The Blue Book included references to all phases of canine activity then under the AKC. In addition, *The Blue Book* offered a chapter on Greyhound racing, with emphasis upon AKC-registered dogs, together with field-trial and obedience sections that included such information as the listings of 1937 winners. The publication, however, omitted illustrations and descriptions of many worthy dogs, since inclusion was generally dependent on the purchase of an advertisement.

As previously mentioned, the American-bred competition continued through 1939. The effort to determine these winners generated tremendous competition among wealthy exhibitors who journeyed to all sections of the country, often on chartered airplane flights. This situation all but eliminated from competition dogs owned by people of more modest means. The publicity generated by the American-bred competition was generally unfavorable, and 1939 was the last year of competition.

During the 1930s a change in rules went into effect concerning breeds with varieties, such as Fox Terriers. The rule stated that variety winners should be judged to best of breed. This move reduced the number of group representatives for the breeds involved and caused considerable controversy among exhibitors for several years. The matter was not, in fact, resolved until about 1953, at which time all variety winners were again permitted into the group and the best of breed award was eliminated in the breeds with varieties at all-breed shows only. The long-term result of this action was to increase the number of varieties so that a given breed would gain additional representatives in the group competition. For example, in Cocker Spaniels, there was only one representative in the group in 1937, but by 1943 there were three: solid color, parti-color, and English type. Of course, since then, the English Cocker has gained breed autonomy and the solid color variety has expanded into two segments: black, and any solid color other than black, including black and tan. This was one of the many interesting and far-reaching maneuvers that with attendant controversy, required changes in the rule book. In fact, this rule change caused several breeds to install varieties where the possibility existed, thereby increasing the number of dogs eligible to compete in a given group.

An important milestone in the history of dogs and dog shows took place in 1939, when the Morris and Essex Kennel Club of Madison, New Jersey, enjoyed an all-time record entry at its May 27 show. There were a total of 3862 dogs on the benches and all were judged in one day.

Morris and Essex was a unique affair in that it was organized and conducted by Mrs. M. Hartley Dodge on her estate in Madison. The show was first held in 1927 and there were 504 dogs benched. The show grew steadily before reaching the peak noted above. Best in show at the 1939 landmark event went to the Cocker Spaniel, Ch. My Own Brucie, owned by H. E. Mellenthin. Morris and Essex was suspended during the war years of 1942—1945, but resumed in 1946 with an agenda limited to thirty-two breeds. Breeds were added until seventy-eight (with 2548 entries) were represented at the last show in 1957.

With the close of the 1930s, the nation was facing World War Two and The American Kennel Club was facing a tremendous challenge inherent in the strains that the war years placed upon the nation.

(Above) Aerial photograph showing the extent of the Morris and Essex Show held at Madison, New Jersey. The large ring in the foreground was used only for Group and Best-in-Show judging. Fifty or more rings were generally used. John T. Marvin Collection. *(Right) Morris and Essex Show—May 24, 1956.* From left to right: *Mrs. Dodge, Mrs. Edward P. Renner (judge), Mrs. S. K. Allman, Jr. (owner) and Charles Meyer (handler). The Best in Show is the Dalmatian, Ch. Roadcoach Roadster.* John T. Marvin Collection

7

The 1940s
Difficult but Interesting

The sport of pure-bred dogs in America was to a large extent shaped by the Second World War. The hostilities that began in Europe in 1939 had their first effect on the sport in America through a progressive reduction in the number of imported dogs. However, after the United States became actively involved, dogs did their part in the war effort. They distinguished themselves through the Dogs for Defense program with many heroic deeds in all arenas of action.

The war continued until 1945. Throughout the war years, American dog shows, field trials, and breeding activities struggled, but they did continue on a reduced scale. Dog shows offered a source of relief and relaxation to many in a nation at war. These activities helped many to continue their lives in a relatively normal manner in spite of the problems and sorrows that resulted from the conflict, which affected everyone to one degree or another. The continuation of dog shows, obedience trials, and field trials was a triumph of American ingenuity and was aided greatly by The American Kennel Club's flexible reaction to the difficulties that arose. The American Kennel Club permitted deviations from and even disregard of existing rules to permit dog clubs to continue to function.

The American Kennel Club's show canons were strict, and full compliance was impossible under wartime conditions and government-imposed restrictions. The AKC reacted quickly to this situation, and it was not long before long-standing rules and regulations were interpreted more loosely and, in many instances, disregarded altogether. A number of shows were approved to be held in the same building on consecutive days, using the same equipment (benching, ring barriers, and so on). This was necessary to overcome the hardship that resulted from gasoline-and-tire-rationing. Further, the number of unbenched shows increased, and geographic restrictions were relaxed. Other adjustments enabled exhibitors to conserve gasoline by relaxing the strict rules governing time schedules for arriving at and leaving events. This permitted exhibitors to cooperate with one another so that two or more, together with their dogs, could use the same vehicle. It was not

Members and guests at the Professional Handlers Association Convention of 1940 held on the estate of Mr. and Mrs. Harry Hartnett, Harrison, New York. From left to right, front row: *Harry Hartnett, Leonard Brumby, Nate Levine, John Goudie, Billy Lang, William Ackland;* second row: *Clinton Callahan, Tom Gately, John Murphy, Ernest Loeb, John McOwan, William Mattinson, Wallace Larson, Bob Craighead, Leslie Romine;* third row: *Mrs. Hartnett, Mrs. Levine, Mrs. Romine, Mrs. Harold Correll, Mr. Correll, Mrs. Craighead, Mrs. C. V. Blagden, Gordon Forsyth, Mrs. Emmett Warburton;* back row: *Mrs. Mattinson, Miss Joyce Mattinson, Stuart Richardson, and Mrs. Winifred Little.* John T. Marvin Collection

Best in Show, Morris and Essex, 1941: Mrs. Dodge with Enno Meyer, judge, awarding trophy to James M. Austin with the great Smooth Fox Terrier, Ch. Nornay Saddler. John T. Marvin Collection

Shieling's Signature with the James Mortimer Memorial Trophy for Best American-bred Dog in Show at Westminster in 1945; he was Best in Show all breeds, too.

Dwight D. Eisenhower and Mrs. Eisenhower at the Potomac Boxer Club's Specialty Show in 1948. John P. Wagner is the judge; Walter Foster has the lead on Merry Monarch and Nate Levine on El Wendy. John T. Marvin Collection

long before all those who wished to exhibit were able to do so. At the same time individual exhibitors gained information about the other fellow and his dog. This was a true learning experience. Actually, the adversity of the war years was a blessing in disguise, as it demonstrated that many of the past, highly restrictive rules were unnecessary and even undesirable.

The war, of course, had some negative effects on the world of the American pure-bred dog. The procedures mentioned above tended to obscure the identity of the several clubs involved. Exhibitors had difficulty in identifying the show-giving club in cluster situations without referring to a catalogue. But one must recognize that even in the 1980s the practice of clustering shows resulted in more entries and many more shows, more show-giving clubs, and more entries at the average event than ever before. During this period, The American Kennel Club sought to increase sanctioned match activity, and in 1947 even distributed a separate booklet of regulations for these events. This initiated many such informal affairs, which were in turn responsible for a host of new fanciers entering the sport.

In a move to comply with national wartime attempts to conserve paper products, *The American Kennel Gazette* was reduced in overall size to a format of 9$^{1}/_{2}$ by 6$^{1}/_{2}$ inches. This was attended by a reduction in type size that made reading difficult. But these changes accomplished their main purpose, which was conser-

An early meeting of the Professional Dog Judges Association with Henry D. Bixby, Executive Vice President of the AKC, in November 1945. Standing, left to right: *Joseph Burrell, Louis Murr, Dr. Charles McAnulty, and Leon J. Iriberry.* Sitting: *Alva Rosenberg, Anton Rost, Mr. Bixby, William Kendrick, and William F. Meyer. Several other members were not present.* John T. Marvin Collection

vation. The reduced size continued through the July 1952 issue, when a size approximating the original size was resumed.

In the middle 1940s, professional judges formed the Professional Dog Judges Association, which included many of the top all-breed judges of the time. The intent was to gain greater input on rule changes and other matters that affected them as a group. The association held several meetings, and in 1945 they met in New York City with Mr. Bixby, executive vice president of the AKC. The outcome of this and other meetings was an experiment offered at the Maryland Kennel Club show held on February 2 and 3, 1946. At this show, the judges commented upon the dogs as they judged. The result was not very well received, as few exhibitors appreciated having their dogs faulted before other judges and exhibitors. The panel for this show included Anton Rost (president of the judges' association), L.J. Murr, E. L. Pickhardt, W. L. Kendrick, Alva Rosenberg, and E. D. McQuown. Best in show was captured by a Standard Schnauzer, Ch. Winalesby Vaaben.

In the late 1940s, for the first time some benched affairs of two-day duration split their entry and benched and judged three groups each day. This reduced the amount of benching required as well as the minimum size of adequate show sites. It also lessened the hours that exhibitors were away from home. Many other changes were adopted during this period for the convenience of the exhibitor. Before the war, for example, dogs usually were required to be on their benches from 10 A.M. until 10 P.M., a rule that was strictly enforced. During the war, a 6 P.M. excusal time went into effect at most shows, so that exhibitors could leave at an earlier hour. Unbenched shows were even more useful, permitting exhibitors to come and go at will. Without the situation created by the war, two-day benched shows with hours from 10 A.M. to 10 P.M. might have remained the rule rather than the exception.

One important postwar move was the January 1946 appointment of Leonard Brumby, Sr., to the post of full-time field representative. Henry D. Bixby, prior to becoming executive vice president in 1942, had attended some shows in this capacity as early as 1936, but Brumby was the first full-time field representative. The field representative was to attend shows and trials and observe the actions of exhibitors and judges. The effort was an attempt to improve the overall quality and operation of each event attended. Brumby's early work in this area was well received by all, and it was most regrettable that Brumby died in office the year following his appointment.

Judging was another area that received attention in the 1940s. Judges and rules relating to them had always been difficult to administer. On October 1, 1947, a judges' directory, entitled "Licensed Judges," was issued. For the first time, there was made available a list of judges who held permanent licenses, giving their names, addresses, and the breeds involved. Prior to this, such information was carried only periodically by the *Gazette*. The directory also included judges who had been approved on a temporary basis, providing they had judged at a show held after January 1, 1944, or had held a temporary license granted since that date. This publication was followed in January 1949 with a new and revised list, titled "Dog Show Judges," which contained the names and addresses of all judges who were approved at the time.

Subsequently, another new rule allowed prospective judges to gain experience through an apprentice system. This involved being present in the ring and observing the procedures and placements of a licensed judge and possibly examining and discussing selected dogs with the judge, if time permitted. The apprentice judge was then required to report to the AKC the several shows at which he had observed. After several such assignments, the apprentice was generally approved to judge the selected breeds for which he had applied. Thereafter, apprenticing was not required for added breeds. The system was in effect for a number of years, but was dropped in 1970. It is doubtful if there will ever be a system satisfactory to all for gaining and training new judges, but the subject receives continued attention from the AKC because of its importance.

During the same general time frame, circa 1950, the Bred by Exhibitor Class came into being as the earlier Limit Class was dropped. This action confined the entry of imported dogs to the Open Class (previously, imports could be entered in the Limit Class).

Many procedures and rules were formed or reinterpreted during the 1940s. The stress that World War II placed on the people of the nation brought about changes and ultimately a body of rules that served the sport of pure-bred dogs well. Many of the new rules and the attitude changes set forth in the 1940s were developed further in the 1950s.

8

The 1950s
Problems and Solutions

War-related problems that had threatened the sport were no longer a factor as the 1950s began, but the times still made it necessary for AKC to exercise flexibility in the application of new rules and the interpretation and modification of old rules. Many changes became necessary because of the tremendous surge of national interest in pure-bred dogs and dog-related activities, whether it was conformation, obedience, or field. This expansion of activity brought about many new rules as well as a considerable amendment of many existing canons.

Two areas that enjoyed especially tremendous growth were obedience trials and field trials. As a result, the field-trial rules underwent some drastic changes during the early part of the decade. In addition, many new exhibitors entered the scene through obedience trials, where the activity was supplemented by an influx of ex-servicemen who had been connected with the war-dog effort.

Another important change enacted about 1950 involved the long-standing registration of a kennel name, or prefix, giving sole use of the name to the owner, with no time limitations. The change limited the exclusive use of a kennel name to a five-year term, with renewal available upon application and with payment of a fee.

With one-day shows becoming more numerous and with daylight hours for outdoor events being reduced during the early spring and late fall, a rule went into effect in January 1951 that restricted judges to twenty dogs per hour. This was subsequently modified to twenty-five dogs per hour, with the total number of dogs per day not to exceed two hundred. Also in the early 1950s, rules were instituted to require show-giving clubs that had limited entries to indicate the limitations on their premium lists.

One of the most controversial issues to be addressed surfaced at the December 1950 delegates' meeting, when an attempt to seat women delegates was made; the motion failed for want of a second. Until that time all delegates had been men. In March 1951, the matter was again brought up but was tabled until June 1951, when

Superintendents Conference at the American Kennel Club, 1952. John T. Marvin
Collection

a vote upon the proposal was scheduled for the March 1952 meeting of delegates.
At that time the motion failed.

In 1950, further amendments were made to the rules that substantially
changed the entire format of dog shows. It was determined that no show could
extend for more than two days unless specific permission from the AKC was
obtained. This restriction caused few hardships, and two-day shows decreased
steadily as the number of one-day events increased. Also in 1950, a recording fee
was imposed on each entry fee. The charge was a nominal twenty-five cents per
dog, but it did bring in considerable revenue in view of the burgeoning number of
shows and entrants. However, the collection of the recording fee was discontinued
by June 1954, despite that increase in revenue.

The 1950s was a period of transition, experimentation, and growth. Many innovations begun during the war years were held over with good effect. Of these, two of the most significant were one-day shows and the elimination of benching at many shows. Two-day shows steadily declined in number while those that continued initiated a split-group format with three groups being judged and benched each day and with best in show being judged the final day. This meant that only the previous day's group winners had to be held over. Benched, multiday events carried out in a leisurely fashion, which had been the backbone of the sport, became merely a memory. These events had been shows at which fanciers could learn about dogs through personal contact with others with greater experience, and have the opportunity and the time to discuss various points of interest. These learning experiences and opportunities as once known were lost.

In retrospect, the decade of the 1950s was one of consolidation. The American public was exposed to more and bigger dog shows held throughout the country.

These events generated substantial interest and led many to become involved with pure-bred dogs. These new fanciers began to breed and to exhibit their dogs, which swelled the number of entries at shows. Of course, many dropped out of the competition if they discovered their new purchase was not of show quality, but a substantial number gained enough pleasure and gratification to continue to breed and exhibit dogs. This group offered an ever-widening base for dog clubs and dog shows.

A glance at overall registration figures over the years of American Kennel Club stewardship tells better than words the story of growth in interest. Although it took fifty-one years for AKC to register its first million dogs, it required only twenty-one additional years for the AKC to reach the five-million dog plateau.

The 1950s was a period of steady, healthy growth. This period is important as it foreshadowed the pace with which the registration and interest in pure-bred dogs was to grow following the war years.

Dog Writers' Association Dinner, February 9, 1958, honoring George F. Foley; William L. Kendrick is the toastmaster. William Brown photo

The final lineup for Judge William Brainard, at Westminster, 1958. Left to right: *Bob Gorman with the Standard Poodle, Ch. Puttencove Promise; Ruth Williams with the Irish Setter, Ch. Kinvarra Kimson, Phil Marsh with the Boxer, Ch. Marjack's Windjammer; Jimmy Butler with the Wire-haired Fox Terrier, Emprise Sensational; and Harry Murphey with the Whippet, Ch. Laguna Lucky Lad. Tom Gately is gaiting the Pug, Ch. Pugholm's Pumpkin Eater. The Poodle placed Best in Show over an entry of 2,569 dogs.* John T. Marvin Collection

9

The 1960s Rule Changes and Growth

The sport of pure-bred dogs in America continued to grow at a rapid pace through the decade of the 1960s. As a reflection of this, by early 1964 The American Kennel Club had outgrown its quarters at 221 Park Avenue South. It became necessary for AKC to find larger accommodations, which led the club to a location at 51 Madison Avenue. It is interesting to note that the new quarters were on the site of the old Gilmore's Garden, where the first Westminster Kennel Club Show was held on May 8-10, 1877. Gilmore's Garden had been razed many years previously to make room for modern offices.

One of the first rules to be reconsidered in the 1960s concerned judging loads. Because of the prevalent one-day show format, there was no question that some restrictions were required if shows were to be concluded on time. At the earlier multiple-day benched events, a strict schedule was not so crucial since there was time to adjust to problems as they arose. At unbenched, one-day shows with a 10 A.M. to 6 P.M. format, it was necessary that judging proceed on a fixed schedule. Many clubs assigned their judges too many dogs. This caused considerable difficulty, particularly when the event was out-of-doors and available daylight hours were a factor. At the time, many events were concluded under less than satisfactory lighting conditions. For these reasons, fixed judging schedules were suggested, calling for a daily 175-dog maximum scheduled at 20 dogs per hour. The possibility of having a 200-dog load at 20 dogs per hour was also explored. Finally, it was concluded that the 175-per-day, 25-per-hour schedule was the most acceptable.

In 1962, the rule concerning apprentice judges was relaxed. The original canon, instituted in 1949, was changed so that a person who had apprenticed in one breed could apply to judge other breeds without having to apprentice. Also in 1962, stricter rules were enacted for benched shows that required dogs to be on their benches during the show hours except when being groomed or exercised or when their classes were being judged. Further, it became the club's responsibility to notify exhibitors in the premium list as to whether the show was to be unbenched or benched.

Throughout the 1960s, obedience and field-trial rules continued to undergo periodic examination and change that resulted in a host of new and amended rules designed to improve these activities. This brought many new entrants into these events.

In 1967, the long-used best-of-winners class was eliminated. In its place a system of judging best of winners during the judging for best of breed or best of variety of breed was established. If either winner went best of breed or best of variety of breed, it was automatically designated best of winners. This hastened the judging through the elimination of the time required to assemble an additional class.

Other important and interesting rule changes evolved during the same period

Westminster, 1960. The international press gives full coverage to Best-in-Show Pekingese Ch. Chik T'Sun of Caversham. Clara Alford, with her back to the camera, is the handler. John T. Marvin Collection

Hall of Fame presentations, 1968. Left to right: John Cross, Show Chairman; Ned Irish, President of Madison Square Garden; William Rockefeller, Westminster President; Percy Roberts, and Mrs. Anne Rogers Clark. Dr. Milbank, another electee, was not present. John T. Marvin Collection

and require mention. One was concerned with the development of shows that were limited to champions only and/or dogs having a certain number of championship points. This type of show was relatively rare and did not gain much support; it steadily lost its appeal. The same was true of other types of restricted shows. This lack of support may also be attributed to the ever-increasing number of handlers who could ill afford to attend such limited events when they could attend an unrestricted show and handle many more dogs.

In 1967, the condensed premium list was first approved. Prior to this, premium lists carried a great amount of information concerning trophies, their donors, and the like. The new rule provided that only certain limited information had to be included in the premium list, and the detailed trophy lists could be printed separately. With rising postage rates and printing costs, this was a welcome relief to most clubs. In the following year, 1968, new obedience regulations were proposed. These new regulations were a great improvement over the earlier canons and helped streamline the entire effort by making the rules more concise. The new regulations went into effect on January 1, 1969. They had been carried in full in the July 1968 issue of the *Gazette*.

An important new approach to approving conformation and obedience judges came upon the scene in November 1969 when the provisional judging system appeared. This was but one of the many continuing efforts through the years to improve judging by establishing more demanding requirements. New applicants with adequate breeding and exhibiting experience were permitted to officiate at three shows, after which the Board of Directors reviewed their performances. Thereafter the provisional judge was either certified or required to gain further training and experience. Unfortunately, the approval process for new judges will never be easy nor will the search for a better system ever end. People have different opinions, and to obtain an objective critique on something as subjective as judging is not easy.

The 1960s saw the continuation of the pace that had been set in the 1950s. The thrust in this decade was increasingly toward refinement in the areas of judging procedures and in the conduct and certification of judges.

Percy Roberts, one of the most prominent professional handlers, and later an AKC all-breed judge, pictured in the late 1960s. John T. Marvin Collection

10

The 1970s and 1980s
A New Approach

There was a tremendous and continuous growth in the sport of pure-bred dogs throughout the first century of The American Kennel Club's existence. As the end of the club's first hundred years approached, it was apparent that dogs had increasingly become greater factors in people's lives. George Crabbe's verse, however, describes better than statistics the nature of dogs and their relationship to human beings:

> With eye upraised his master's looks to scan,
> The joy, the solace, and the aid of man;
> The rich man's guardian and the poor man's friend,
> The only creature faithful to the end.

We can be proud of the AKC for recognizing and furthering this precious, age-old relationship.

Among the important accomplishments of the club during the 1970s was the extension of The American Kennel Club voting rights to women. Since its formation in 1884, only men had been permitted to serve as delegates to The American Kennel Club. No women were allowed to hold this office or to vote upon the many rules that affected all member and nonmember clubs. This situation was decried for many years, but previous attempts to rectify the situation had always met with failure. In 1973 and 1974, a new effort was launched to correct this inequity, and finally, on March 12, 1974, a motion to allow women to serve as delegates was seconded and carried by a vote of 180 to 7.

At the June 1974 meeting of the AKC, the first women delegates were elected: Mrs. Carol D. Duffy to represent the Mid-Hudson Kennel Club, Mrs. Gertrude Freedman to represent the Bulldog Club of New England, and Mrs. Julia Gasow to represent the English Springer Spaniel Club of Michigan. These three women attended their first delegates' meeting in September 1974, and since then there has been a steady rise in the number of female delegates. By December 1983 there were some 140 in office.

A rule change that became effective in September 1974 concerned premium lists, entry forms, and catalogs. Until then, all official documents had to follow a 6 by 9 inch format. As most commercial printers had adapted to a $5^1/_2$ by $8^1/_2$ inch format, it became obvious that the 6 by 9 inch format had become obsolete. The new rule provided that the pages in question could be anywhere between $5^1/_2$ by $8^1/_2$ inches and 6 by 9 inches.

A number of modifications to show procedures came into effect beginning in late 1973 when there was a serious fuel shortage. This situation resulted in policy changes with respect to territorial limits and show dates. During this period it was not unusual for several clubs to hold their shows at the same location on consecutive days. This minimized travel while offering additional shows with greater convenience for the exhibitors. These arrangements required a more flexible approach by the AKC, and the situation at large was reminiscent of the war years. At the same time, the maximum number of specialty shows permitted to participate in a combined event at the same location was raised from ten to twenty. The initial event approved under this new rule was the combined Specialty Clubs of Dallas in 1974.

The approval of multiple events at the same site on consecutive days for all-breed efforts (called cluster shows) was a step forward, as it allowed for the most efficient use of a facility, and in many instances enabled a number of clubs in the same general area to use the best possible facility in that area. The new approach gained impetus, and by 1982, 30 percent of the all-breed shows were being held as part of cluster arrangements.

In 1977 a fuel shortage again became a factor, and an increase in the number of requests for cluster shows resulted, particularly in the less populous regions. Clusters of shows in such areas offered an educational experience to the local population while assuring financial stability for the show-giving clubs. The practice also helped popularize dogs and dog shows in many regions where little interest had been apparent before these events were held.

The strongest argument against cluster shows was the possible loss of identity of the several show-giving clubs. Few people, including exhibitors and handlers, associated a town or city with a dog show that was held outside its geographic area. But on the other side of the coin, many smaller clubs that became involved in cluster activities had experienced difficulty in holding unsupported shows in their own areas because of expenses and the absence of suitable facilities. Without this approach these clubs would probably have had great difficulty holding independent events.

Another item of interest that occurred during the 1970s was an attempt at the delegates' March 1977 meeting to reinstate the recording fee that had been in effect during the 1950s. This fee (twenty-five cents per dog entered) was originally levied to help the AKC with show-related expenses. AKC had ceased collecting this fee in

1954. The proposal to reinstate the fee included a suggestion that the rule be amended to provide that the fee not exceed one dollar. There was considerable opposition, and at the June 1977 delegates' meeting the proposal was withdrawn.

An important change in rules occurred on January 1, 1978, when AKC ceased to license professional handlers. The licensing of handlers had been in effect since 1929. This change placed all handlers in the same category as other exhibitors, and anyone could then handle a dog for a fee. This removed a substantial load from the shoulders of the AKC office and field staff, permitting them to pursue other matters.

In January 1981 *The American Kennel Gazette* altered its long-standing format. Until this time, the *Gazette* had carried all club business, including the Secretary's Page, reports of delegates' meetings, listings of new champions, obedience title holders, and field-trial champions, new judges, listings of applicants for judging licenses, and so on. It also included a complete listing of show, obedience-trial, and field-trial awards. As shows and trials proliferated, this material became increasingly voluminous, creating problems in cost and in mailing. It was finally decided that *The American Kennel Gazette* would be offered as a separate entity from the awards section. The awards section would be mailed only to those who subscribed to it. This substantially reduced the printing and mailing costs of both sections.

The subject of a recording fee came up again in December 1977. The expenses related to administering shows and trials had risen dramatically over the years, with the entire burden for covering these expenses being placed on registration income. Among the services that had been added over the years was the enlargement of the field staff. The twenty-five-cent recording fee provided for in the rules was again put into effect on April 1, 1978. The fee was increased to fifty cents effective May 2, 1983. This was viewed as a way to gain income from the show-going segment of the fancy without having to further increase registration rates.

In 1983 a landmark change took place. It was decided to increase the number of groups from six to seven, the first change in the number of groups since the 1920s. This was accomplished by splitting the unwieldy Working Group into two segments: Working Dogs (Group 3) and Herding Dogs (Group 7). This change in format became effective following action by the delegates in March 1982.

In retrospect, in spite of fuel shortages and other problems, the period of the 1970s and 1980s was one of success for pure-bred dogs. This statement is supported by the registration figures. Registrations exceeded one million dogs in twelve of the fourteen years from 1970 through 1983. These statistics demonstrate that interest in the pure-bred dog has risen dramatically in the last hundred years, and through the guidance of The American Kennel Club this interest has grown in a way that the pure-bred dog, regardless of breed, has continued to improve in conformity and ability throughout the years.

11

Obedience

by James E. Dearinger

Obedience, as we know it today in America, owes its very being to Mrs. Helene Whitehouse Walker. In 1933 she had been breeding Standard Poodles for two years, and the dogs of her Carillon Kennels were fast gaining recognition as dogs of outstanding quality and character. But it nettled her that friends often badgered her by calling her Poodles "sissy dogs." She decided that the best way to convince everyone that Poodles, despite their fancy haircut, were as intelligent as any other breed was to have them perform in a series of obedience exercises.

What she had in mind was tests patterned after those held in England under sponsorship of the Associated Sheep, Police, Army Dog Society. This English society had recently modified the requirements of its field trials, making it possible to hold competitive tests at both indoor and outdoor shows, and—for the first time—opening the tests in England to all breeds.

Mrs. Walker approached dog clubs and private kennel owners with her idea of holding competitive tests in connection with dog shows here, and received a small but "most enthusiastic" response. Accordingly, the first obedience test in the United States for all breeds of dogs was held in October 1933 on the estate of Mrs. Walker's father at Mount Kisco, New York. There were eight entries: two Labradors, three Poodles, two Springer Spaniels, and a German Shepherd Dog.

The dogs were required to walk at their handler's side without leash; to retrieve a dumbbell, both on the flat and over an obstacle; to remain in the sitting and lying-down positions with their handlers out of sight; to come when called; and to leap a long jump on command. The judge was Robert Carr, a field-trial enthusi-

A heavy debt of gratitude is owed to Elsworth S. Howell of the Howell Book House, Inc., for kind permission to borrow liberally from *The Story of Dog Obedience,* by Blanche Saunders (New York, 1974). Much of the early historical material in this chapter is taken from Ms. Saunders' text, and in particular from chapters two through four.

Mrs. Helene Whitehouse Walker and Ch. Nymphaea Jason of Carillon—June 1931.

ast, and the winner a Labrador owned by William F. Hutchinson of Far Hills, New Jersey. This competition was cheered on by a gallery of over 150 people.

Dog training was already well known in the United States in the 1920s and early 1930s. There were a number of professional trainers who would board a dog and train him for the owner, or who would give private lessons to overcome special problems in the dog's behavior. A few of these trainers were Josef Weber (author of *The Dog in Training*, 1939); Carl Spitz (of Hollywood fame—"Buck" in *Call of the Wild* and Cairn Terrier, "Toto," in *The Wizard of Oz*); Hans Tossutti *(Companion Dog Training*, 1946).

Long before 1933, owners trained in groups, gave obedience exhibitions, and competed in trials. But these get-togethers were confined to the working breeds such as the German Shepherd Dog or the Doberman Pinscher.

The first all-breed obedience test in Mount Kisco in October 1933 gave dog owners the realization that no matter the breed, no matter that the owners were amateurs, here was the opportunity to show what one could do in the training field. "Train your own dog!" became a popular slogan, and dog owners from all parts of the country were quick to respond. The widening enthusiasm spurred Mrs. Walker to greater goals, and she began aiming toward the introduction of obedience at the next all-breed event—the North Westchester Kennel Club show. The show date was June 9, 1934, and that left little time. Mrs. Walker sent a letter to *Pure-Bred Dogs/American Kennel Gazette:*

> Test classes could become popular—not only to prove the value of developing a dog's brain, but in interesting the average visiting public at a show. The judging of dogs in the breed classes is a mystery to many, but a series of tests displaying the dog's brain is something they can actually see.

Obedience at this historic first test at an all-breed show was to consist of one class. The exercises were (1) heeling on leash (walking in a natural manner with dog as close as possible to handler's left knee, while judge directed a pattern of turns and a figure eight)—10 points; (2) heeling free (same as No. 1, except off lead)—30 points; (3) sitting two minutes (handler out of sight)—20 points; (4) recall to handler (including a drop, a sit in front, and going to heel on command)—25 points; (5) retrieving 2-lb. dumbbell on flat (moving at fast trot or gallop, no mouthing or playing with dumbbell, delivering to hand when ordered)—20 points; (6) retrieving 8- to 10-oz. dumbbell over 3'6'' obstacle (retrieving as in No. 5 but climbing obstacle both going and returning)—50 points; (7) long jump (6 feet)—30 points; and (8) lying down five minutes (handlers out of sight, all dogs in the ring together)—65 points.

In 1934, Mrs. Walker persuaded the Somerset Hills Kennel Club to join with the North Westchester Kennel Club in holding obedience tests. Their event, at Far Hills, New Jersey, took place on September 22, 1934. Somerset Hills thus became the second club to hold obedience tests in conjunction with an all-breed show.

Mrs. Walker then staged a second private event, held in Mount Kisco on October 21, 1935. For the first time, tracking tests were also included. There were eight entries in obedience and six in tracking. About five hundred spectators watched the tracking on the side of the hill and crowded about a large ring for the obedience test.

Obedience rules in 1933—1934 were far more lenient than they are today. Commands and hand motions automatically went together. The dog's name was used with signals as well as with commands, and—if the dog didn't obey the first time — there was always a second chance, though with a penalty. If an owner wished to take part in an obedience test, it was mostly a matter of obtaining a list of the exercises and then using whatever method he could to get the dog to obey. Performances in the ring varied, but there was little emphasis on handling.

From the sport's point of view, it is fortunate that the early rules were less demanding. Ease of training encouraged the amateur. Simplicity of the test retained the enthusiasm which today has brought obedience to such a degree of quality of performance, reflecting accuracy and precision as well as encouraging happiness and willingness on the part of the dog.

The four obedience tests held during 1933 and 1934 aroused great interest among spectators, kennel owners, pet owners, and dog clubs. More and more, people wanted to know where they could get information on training, what the dogs were required to do, and how one went about arranging for similar tests. Mrs. Walker got in touch with Charles T. Inglee, executive vice president of The American Kennel Club, and showed him the many newspaper clippings and the vast amount of correspondence from all over the country that gave evidence of the interest in training, and stressed that obedience was not a passing fad, but was destined to become an integral part of future dog activity. Mr. Inglee was interested.

Six obedience tests were held in 1935 in conjunction with all-breed dog shows. The sponsoring clubs were the North Westchester Kennel Club, the Lenox Kennel Club, the North Shore Kennel Club, the Westchester Kennel Club, the Somerset Hills Kennel Club, and the Kennel Club of Philadelphia.

Meanwhile, dog journalists were giving column space to the growing enthusiasm for dog training that was spreading across the country. In May 1935, the *Chicago Tribune* carried a column about the Amateur Training Club of Chicago, "one of the few schools in the country where the owner of a working dog can go to school and learn how to train his own canine." Six months later, the *New York Times* gave a full-page banner headline to a story recounting the intelligence and skill displayed by a champion Miniature Schnauzer in performing the Novice exercises in connection with the Kennel Club of Philadelphia's annual exhibition in Convention Hall.

Two other events of 1935 were to have a strong influence in the development of obedience in this country. First was the visit to America of Mrs. Grace L. Boyd, who brought along and demonstrated three of her obedience-trained Standard Poodles who were winning against all breeds in England. She later wrote a training leaflet for beginners that was widely distributed to the American public. Second, Mrs. Walker wrote a booklet called "Obedience Tests: Procedures for Judge, Handler, and Show Giving Club"; this was the first attempt to standardize the sport for this country. In addition to setting out procedures, the pamphlet addressed the important issues of professionalism and irresponsible judging. Mrs. Walker felt strongly that obedience must appeal to the amateur, one-dog owner who would bring his own dog to a show and handle it in the ring. She recommended that professional handlers and trainers be barred from the Novice class so that the amateurs would not become discouraged and drop out.

Mrs. Walker submitted this pamphlet of procedures to The American Kennel Club on December 7, 1935. On March 10, 1936, the Board of Directors of the AKC approved the procedures in principle, and one month later published in the *Gazette* the first official "Regulations and Standard for Obedience Test Field Trials." The regulations were eight pages long and adhered quite closely to Mrs. Walker's "procedures." One exception was that a third class, the Utility, was added to the rules, and this class alone was open to professional handlers as well as to amateurs. A dog was expected to "qualify" twice in each class in order to earn a title—that is, earn 80 percent of the available points in Novice and Open, and 70 percent in Utility. The Utility degree at this time also required that a dog pass a tracking test, and over half of the points in the class were designated to tracking. From the very beginning, a passing score in a class would count toward a title only if there was competition in the class: six dogs had to participate in Novice, four in Open, and three in Utility.

The first regulations contained the following exercises:

Novice

1. Heeling on leash	20
2. Heeling free	25
3. Coming when called	20
4. Sitting one minute	15
5. Lying down three minutes	20
	100

Open

1. Heeling on leash	40
2. Heeling free	50
3. Coming when called (including a "drop" on command)	25
4. Retrieving dumbbell on the flat (dumbbell to vary in proportion to size of dog)	25
5. Speaking on command	20
6. Long jump	30
7. Sitting three minutes (handler out of sight)	25
8. Lying down five minutes (handler out of sight)	35
	250

Utility

1. Tracking (¹/₄-mile track aged ¹/₂-hour)	225
2. Exercising scent discrimination (3 articles, one to be metal)	75
3. Seeking back (inconspicuous article dropped by handler)	60
4. Retrieving dumbbell over an obstacle (dog to climb jump going and returning; height to vary in proportion to size of dog, not to exceed 3'6'')	40
	400

The first licensed test held in accordance with these regulations took place on June 13, 1936, and appropriately enough, was held with the North Westchester Kennel Club all-breed show at Mount Kisco, New York. The test consisted only of a Novice class, and all dogs, regardless of whether they had competed in Open classes before, had to enter in Novice until they twice won more than 80 of the possible 100 points. There were twelve entries, and eight of the twelve qualified. The next day the Orange Kennel Club held an obedience test with its show, and eight qualified of the sixteen entered. Over this weekend the first six Companion Dog titles were earned: five went to Standard Poodles and one to a Miniature Schnauzer.

After a six-month trial period, The American Kennel Club issued a revised edition of "Regulations and Standards for Obedience Test Trials," as approved November 10, 1936.

The rules had been expanded. Probably the greatest change was that Novice and Open classes were now divided into "A" and "B" divisions— "A" being for amateurs only, and "B" being for professionals and amateurs. There were other slight changes. Speaking on Command was transferred from the Open to the Utility class. A Stand for Examination exercise was added to Utility. The Retrieve over the Hurdle, which had been in the Utility class, was transferred to Open, making the C.D.X. (Companion Dog Excellent) requirements the same as at present, although with differences in scoring.

The next amendment to the rules by AKC was in June, 1938, when sample judging charts were added. These broke the exercises down into parts, and showed the number of points to be awarded for each part. Also, beginning in 1938, dogs were required to "clear" rather than "climb" the jumps, and exceptions began to be made in the jump height requirements for certain breeds. The sample judging charts proved too complicated, and were dropped in the next revision, May, 1939. Also in 1939, the word "Test" was eliminated for the first time, and the new title became "Regulations and Standards for Obedience Trials." "Trials" it has been ever since.

Eighteen tests were held in 1936—the first year of AKC recognition. A total of thirty-three C.D.'s were awarded to dogs in nine different breeds: thirteen Standard Poodles, seven German Shepherd Dogs, six Doberman Pinschers, two Wire Fox Terriers, and one each to Great Danes, Newfoundlands, Irish Terriers,

Miniature Schnauzers, and Keeshonden. Three Standard Poodles earned the C.D.X. that first year.

In response to a suggestion made by Mrs. Walker, the AKC *Gazette* began in its October 1937 issue to list all obedience winners, along with their scores, the numbers competing, and the names of the judges. Until that time, only the dogs' names were published, and the extra detail helped to develop interest in the sport.

In 1937, eighty-two dogs won C.D. (Companion Dog) degrees, twenty earned the C.D.X., and four won U.D. (Utility Dog) titles. In this second year, a number of new breeds joined the ranks of title holders, so that by the end of 1937, twenty-five different breeds had at least one C.D. and eight breeds had made it to the C.D.X. level. The first four Utility Dogs (including the tracking requirement) were finished in 1937—two German Shepherd Dogs and two Standard Poodles. One of these Poodles was Carillon Epreuve. It passed its tracking test on the same day as one of the Shepherds, but since it had completed the U.D. work a month earlier than the Shepherd, this dog was credited as being the first dog of any breed to earn all obedience degrees. Carillon Epreuve was owned by Mrs. Helene White-house Walker!

Early in 1938, Henry R. Ilsley wrote in the *New York Times*, "The growth experienced by Obedience Tests during the last two years in the United States has been unprecedented in dog show history."

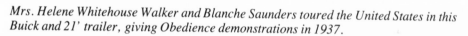

Mrs. Helene Whitehouse Walker and Blanche Saunders toured the United States in this Buick and 21' trailer, giving Obedience demonstrations in 1937.

With obedience growing by leaps and bounds and interest in exhibiting increasing with each event, the Obedience Test Club of New York was founded. This club was actually an outgrowth of the Bedford Hills Training Class, which had been formed by Mrs. Walker in December 1935. Since the intention was to set up a national all-breed obedience organization, the members chose the name "The Obedience Test Club of America." However, The American Kennel Club advised that it could not approve the words "of America" because this covered too much territory. Thus, the name was changed to the Obedience Test Club of New York. This club unquestionably was *the* dominant influence in the sport during the first four years of AKC jurisdiction, yet it was never recognized as a "parent club" by the AKC because its activities involved all breeds.

In addition to holding an annual obedience test, the O.T.C. conducted all-breed training classes and widely disseminated information on training and handling. It also established a list of approved judges, which started with five in 1936: Josef Weber, E. D. Knight, Mrs. Wheeler H. Page, W. C. Green, and Mrs. Whitehouse Walker. By 1938 the list had expanded to fifteen, including Major Bryant Godsol, the first "all-rounder" licensed for obedience. The club supplemented the roster of approved judges with a list of recommended judges, people

Blanche Saunders and Ch. Carillon Courage, CDX, 1938.

who were anxious to learn obedience and then be approved for judging. Some of the names on this list were Charles LeBoutillier, Jr., still active in 1984, Mrs. Henry Sabetti, Benno Stein, and Mrs. Charles Baiter. Maintaining these lists of approved and recommended judges was important to the development of the sport because, in the early days, there was more opportunity for discrepancy in judging than there is today. The judge interpreted the rules as he believed they should be interpreted, and if he felt like evaluating a dog's work on the basis of personal likes or dislikes, there was nothing in the rules that said he couldn't do it.

The Obedience Test Club of New York helped to standardize judging by establishing classes for judges. The idea was picked up first by other Eastern training classes and then by classes in other parts of the country. Through discussion groups, judging problems were worked out so that judges generally were approaching their assignments in the same way.

The O.T.C. was dissolved May 3, 1940. In spite of its prominent role in developing obedience, it had never become a member of the AKC; its members voted to operate independently. At the time of its dissolution, O.T.C. had fifteen affiliated clubs with a combined total of more than five hundred members.

In June 1941, the New England Dog Training Club, Inc., became the first

Doberman Pinscher "Fritz,"— Retrieve.

obedience club to become a member club of the AKC. This club was formally established on October 15, 1936. It held its first obedience trial specialty on February 21—22, 1937, in conjunction with the Eastern Dog Club show in Boston, Massachusetts, with twenty-four dogs competing in the five regular classes. The NEDTC is still in existence today and continues to hold its obedience trials in conjunction with the Eastern Dog Club's shows.

Very little change was seen in obedience trials during the next few years. Obedience was growing and the AKC kept vigilant watch on its progress. In 1941, a Hurdle and Bar Jump exercise was added to the Utility class. Initially this exercise was performed with the dog holding the dumbbell in the heel position, and jumping when commanded. In 1947 the regulations were changed so that the exercise was performed in the same way as the Broad Jump. The handler placed the dumbbell in the dog's mouth, left it in a sit-stay in front of the jump, and took up a position midway between the jumps. The dog then jumped on command and delivered the dumbbell as in the retrieving exercises. In 1950 the Hurdle and Bar Jump exercise was replaced by Directed Jumping.

An Obedience Advisory Committee was convened by the AKC in 1946 (the first such committee met in 1939) to consider changes to the regulations. This committee helped to standardize judging. The 1947 edition of the obedience regulations for the first time contained a section called ''Standard for Obedience Trial Judging''; heretofore this section had been called '' 'Suggestions' for Obedience Trial Judges.'' The standards for judging led to uniformity in judging in all parts of the United States. The principal part of each exercise was clearly defined in this new section, and the rules spelled out what constituted minor or substantial deductions.

In 1947, credit toward a title required that the dog earn more than 50 percent of each exercise as well as a minimum score of 170 points, with a required number of dogs competing. The total number of points for a perfect score was set at 200 for all three classes. Tracking was dropped as a requirement for the Utility title that year, and became a separate ''class'' although a dog was required to have a C.D. in order to enter a tracking test.

From almost the beginning of the sport until 1947, to Speak on Command was a part of the Utility class. The dog was required to bark continuously on command from sitting, down, and standing positions, and likewise, to stop on command. The rationale for this exercise was reported by Josef Weber in his book, *The Dog in Training:*

> In Europe this feat is of use in guide dogs for the blind, especially in dense and excited traffic in which the blind man may not be noticed. . . . In police work, speaking on command is used first to make the dog bark to attract the officer's attention when the dog has found his quarry or something of a suspicious nature.*

---

*Josef Weber, *The Dog in Training,* New York: Whittlesey House, Division McGraw-Hill Book Co., Inc., 1939, p. 160.

Nevertheless, many exhibitors did not like this exercise and owners of sporting dogs objected to it on the grounds that a dog giving voice was undesirable in the field. Further, many exhibitors did not want to teach their dogs to bark because of urban pressures, and many did not enter the Utility classes because of this exercise. The 1946 Advisory Committee recommended to eliminate the Speak on Command, and it was replaced in the 1947 regulations with the Signal exercise.

Until 1947, the handler in Utility had to bring only three articles of his choosing to the trial for the Scent Discrimination exercise, of which one had to be metal and none could be a handkerchief. The remaining "several articles" were provided by the judge. Numerous attempts were made by the Obedience Advisory Committee to standardize the Scent Discrimination exercise, so that all articles would be similar and all handlers had the same kinds of articles. Some felt that dissimilar articles permitted a dog to pick out his handler's by sight rather than by scent. When the committee recommended that the handler bring all fifteen articles to the trial, five each of wood, metal, and leather, warm debate followed. Many exhibitors did not like the idea that they had to provide fifteen articles, arguing that either the judge or the club should provide any required beyond the three that exhibitors had been bringing all along. One suggestion was that if there had to be a change, then the show-giving club could send three articles to each handler a few days before the show, or have each handler purchase three standard articles on the day of the test, with the club providing the balance of twelve.

In the end the Obedience Advisory Committee prevailed, and the AKC did approve that the handler should provide three groups of five "absolutely identical" articles, consisting of metal, wood, and leather objects. With the exception of deleting the wooden article by recommendation of a subsequent advisory committee, the requirements remain the same today.

Another Obedience Advisory Committee met in 1949, and primarily recommended changes for the Utility class. Directed Jumping was proposed to replace the Hurdle and Bar Jump. Instead of the handler leaving the dog, as he had in Hurdle and Bar, the dog was now to leave the handler, on command, and go forward (with no dumbbell) "at a smart pace" to the other end of the ring, sit on command, and finally jump as directed. The exercise was then repeated for the other jump.

Many felt that this would be too difficult to train. John Brownell, a member of the committee and later on the executive staff of AKC with responsibility for Obedience, wrote to AKC in support of this exercise:

> I discussed that part of the proposed exercise which involves sending the dog away in a straight line and making it sit at a distance, with our training director and our head trainer. They worked out a training method and tried it out on two or three of our advanced dogs. . . they were able to get the better dogs to do it in a reasonably short time, and while they think it will be quite difficult for some dogs, they both feel, as I believe all of your committee felt, that we need something more difficult in Utility.

The end of a successful track. Left to right: *Judge Wally Kodis; Richard Doyon and Sunshine Amber Princess CDX, TDX; Judge Tom Knott.*

Some trainers as well as clubs wrote the AKC objecting to this exercise. They felt people sought obedience training to teach their dogs to come when called, and could see no practical reason to teach a dog to go away from its master. This argument notwithstanding, the Directed Jumping exercise was instituted in 1950.

More was at issue here than changing an exercise. A conscious decision had been made that the Utility class in particular should present a significant challenge to both handler and dog. When faced with the prospect that the new exercise might put the Utility title beyond the reach of some, the committee did not compromise.

Nineteen-fifty also saw the new stipulation ''there shall be no penalty of less than $1/2$ point or multiple of $1/2$ point.'' Until then judges had sometimes scored in fifths or even tenths of points. The new rule brought more uniformity to judging. In 1964 the title of the rule book was shortened from ''Regulations and Standards for Obedience Trials'' to its present form, ''Obedience Regulations.''

As mentioned earlier, tracking originally was part of the Utility class, and a dog had to pass a separate tracking test in order to earn a U.D. For roughly the first ten years, tracking received one paragraph of description in the regulations, which set out the barest basics of length and age of the track. On the day of the test, the tracklayers were to walk the tracks, deposit the article, and retrace their steps to remove all but the two starting flags. By 1938, it was added that the tracklayer could not wear rubber-soled shoes, and the dog had to be on a 30—40 foot leash and work without help from the handler. By 1943, the tracklayers were required to follow the track, deposit the article, and walk directly off the course.

In 1947, tracking was made a separate class, and more detail began to appear in the regulations: The tracklayers were required to wear leather-soled shoes until they deposited the article, whereupon they were to put on a pair of rubbers and walk off the course at a right angle. The article was to be a leather glove or wallet. Finally, the dog was permitted one additional chance to take the scent between the starting flags, provided he had not passed the second flag. It is obvious from the changes in the regulations that there must have been considerable discussion of how a track was to be properly laid by the tracklayer. Tracking and advanced tracking regulations were destined eventually to swell, from the original single paragraph of description in 1936, to some eight pages—the length of the entire rule book in 1936!

In December of 1966, another Obedience Advisory Committee meeting was called by the AKC. Among other things, the committee recommended that prizes for the four official placings be awarded only to dogs that earned qualifying scores; that the fencing for obedience rings be the same as that provided for the breed rings; and that no tags or ornaments be hanging from the dogs' collars. Further, it was at this point that the wooden article was eliminated from the Scent Discrimination exercise, because the dog had already retrieved a wooden article (the dumbbell) in the Open class.

The Seek Back exercise had been in the Utility class from the very beginning of obedience, but had come under attack from time to time over the years. It was argued that this was not really a scenting exericse because of the limits imposed by the size of the ring. The 1966 committee elected to recommend that the Seek Back exercise be eliminated in favor of the Directed Retrieve. This exercise entailed having three gloves placed across the end of the ring and having the dog, as directed by the judge, retrieve one of the three. Directed Retrieve was approved by the AKC and appeared in the 1969 regulations, although to this day the Seek Back is advocated as valuable training for the beginner in tracking.

Until this time, if a dog in the Long Sit or Long Down exercise maintained his position for three-quarters of the time allotted, he would receive a qualifying score, although with a penalty. The 1966 committee strongly recommended that, in order to qualify, the dog should maintain the required position for the full length of time imposed by the exercise, and this change was approved for the 1969 revision. Other changes included clarifications in the scoring and working of the dogs, and clear distinctions between commands and signals.

The 1966 advisory committee recommended that the Scent Discrimination exercise be moved to follow the Signal exercise, and this was approved on January 1, 1975. It also recommended that the AKC revise the examination of judging applicants and more closely observe judges when they presided over their rings. It was suggested that a handbook for judges be provided, and this was accomplished

An Obedience exhibition in Rockefeller Plaza during National Dog Week, c. 1950.

James Dearinger, Director of Obedience at the American Kennel Club, and Mrs. Helene Whitehouse Walker, who was honored for her fifty years of service to Obedience in 1983.

in 1972 when the first *Guidelines for Obedience Judges* was issued. Finally, the committee felt a great need for clinics or classes to educate judges, but this was not to come about until 1975, when the Obedience Department inaugurated the judges' educational seminars program.

Obedience competitors, from the beginning and continuing to this day, have worked toward "legs," as they are commonly called, and when a third leg is won for a particular class, a title certificate is awarded by AKC. (It should be noted that for the first two years, only two legs were required for a title. In 1950, the additional requirement was made that the three legs had to be earned under three different judges; from 1938 to 1949, "at least two different judges" was the rule.) Throughout the years, obedience enthusiasts have recommended a championship title competition in the hope that this recognition would single out the exceptional competitor. On July 1, 1977, a championship program was inaugurated, and just twenty-three days later, Moreland's Golden Tonka U.D., a Golden Retriever, earned her Obedience Trial Championship—the first "O.T.Ch." She was owned and handled by Russell H. Klipple of Parker Ford, Pennsylvania.

As early as 1947, and encouraged by obedience advisory committees, the tracking fraternity urged AKC to approve a more advanced type of tracking test that would test a dog's ability to track a person over a course that had aged for at least three hours and for about twice the distance required by the Tracking Test. This advanced test, called Tracking Dog Excellent, was approved by the AKC in 1979 and became effective on March 1, 1980. The first T.D.X. dog was a Dachshund, Gretel Von Bupp Murr, U.D., T.D.X., who passed the Tracking Dog Excellent Test on March 15 of that year. This dog was owned and handled by George Richards of Sun City Center, Florida.

The growth in the sport of obedience has been phenomenal. In 1936, perhaps 200 dogs were entered in the eighteen licensed tests, with a total of thirty-three C.D.'s and three C.D.X.'s awarded to 9 different breeds. In 1983 there were over fourteen hundred trials, with roughly 104,000 dogs competing. Over eleven thousand titles were earned by dogs of 121 different breeds. The Obedience Regulations has grown from eight pages in 1936 to fifty-nine at present, but the basic structure of the sport and many of the exercises remain the same today as when first approved. In September 1983 the Board of Directors of The American Kennel Club adopted a resolution of gratitude and appreciation to Mrs. Helene Whitehouse Walker—who continues to reside in Mount Kisco, New York—on the occasion of the fiftieth anniversary of obedience in America.

12

Field Trials

by A. Hamilton Rowan, Jr.

Tests for dogs in the field were developed to allow hunting dogs to compete with one another with the object of improving their performances in the field. It is generally agreed that these tests originated in England in 1866.

In order to pick up the thread in this country, we turn to a wounded Civil War soldier named P. H. Bryson from Memphis, Tennessee. He was released after the war ended and permitted to go home to die so that he might have a decent burial. When he reached home, his family physician advised him to buy a shotgun and a bird dog and get as much exercise as possible. In time he recovered, became a dedicated sportsman, and, through the sporting journals of the time, began to advocate the holding of dog shows in the United States.

Bryson formed the Tennessee Sportsmen's Association and organized a combined Dog Show and Field Trial held on October 7 and 8, 1874. The only breeds represented at the show on the first day were Pointers and Setters, and the entries totaled ninety-five. The old soldier's Setter, "Maud," was awarded Best in Show.

Fourteen Pointers and Setters competed in the field trial on the second day. The winner was an all-black Setter, and the results are recorded in volume 1 of the National American Kennel Club's Stud Book.

The National American Kennel Club, forerunner of The American Kennel Club, supported both bench show and field activities, although the majority of its members were field-trial oriented. It also sponsored a stud record, which was placed in the hands of Dr. Nicholas Rowe for compilation. Dr. Rowe was the first president of that club, editor of the sporting paper, *The Field,* and a strong supporter of all efforts to bring the pure-bred dog into greater prominence. The initial volume of this stud book appeared in 1878 and reported shows and trials from 1876.

An English Springer Spaniel flushing a pheasant. Allen Peck photo

Not until 1884 did Dr. Rowe, at his own expense, produce volumes 2 and 3, giving them immediately to the fledgling American Kennel Club. Shortly after accepting Dr. Rowe's gift, the AKC published volume 4 of the set, which now contains more than 25 million registration entries after Dog Number 1 in volume 1, an English Setter named "Adonis."

Thus, volume 1 of the National American Kennel Club's Stud Book, by virtue of Dr. Rowe's generosity, also became volume 1 of The American Kennel Club's Stud Book, and contains records dating to 1876, a full eight years before AKC's founding in 1884.

Having determined when the first recorded testing of dogs in the field took place in America, it becomes illogical to follow the development of the sport of field trials without breaking down the sport into its four component parts, each of which is based upon the hunting characteristics of the breeds involved:

1. *The scenting or trailing hounds* pursue the cottontail rabbit or hare at trials either in packs or in pairs or braces. They include:
    Bassets
    Beagles
    Dachshunds

2. *The pointing breeds* assist the hunter in the field by stopping or pointing the very moment they scent the presence of a game bird, permitting the hunters to walk past their dogs on point and flush the birds into the air. They include:
    Brittanys
    Pointers
    German Shorthaired Pointers
    German Wirehaired Pointers
    English Setters
    Gordon Setters
    Irish Setters
    Vizslas
    Weimaraners
    Wirehaired Pointing Griffons

3. *Flushing dogs* are expected to search for feathered game within gunshot range of the hunter. When game is located, they must flush the bird into the air and retrieve it on command if it is shot. They include:
    Clumber Spaniels
    Cocker Spaniels
    English Cocker Spaniels
    English Springer Spaniels
    Field Spaniels
    Sussex Spaniels
    Welsh Springer Spaniels

4. *Retrievers* do just what their name implies—fetch or retrieve from both water and land all game shot by the hunter. They include:

Chesapeake Bay Retrievers
Curly-Coated Retrievers
Flat-Coated Retrievers
Golden Retrievers
Irish Water Spaniels
Labrador Retrievers

Several other national dog organizations in this country also license formal field trials and award their own championships. However, only in AKC licensed competition can a dog be awarded the title of Dual Champion. In order to achieve this AKC title, a dog must complete the requirements for both a Field and a Show Championship. The existence of this coveted title will always set AKC events apart from those of other dog organizations. The Dual Championship title also serves as an incentive for sportsmen to breed dogs capable of doing equally well on the bench and in the field.

The six sections following this introduction to field trials will concentrate on a brief history on AKC's involvement with each of these divergent field sports.

Beagle Field Trials

(Edited and written by A. Hamilton Rowan, Jr., from material submitted by Robert A. Bartel and Robert F. Slike.)

Beagle field trials, a sport found only in the United States and Canada, started with this announcement in the *Sunday Boston Herald* on October 26, 1890: "A group of Beagle owners would hold a Beagle field trial in Hyannis, Massachusetts, in a fortnight." This group called themselves the National Beagle Club of America, and the advertised trial was held on November 4, 1890, with eighteen entries— fifteen dogs and three bitches.

Shortly thereafter, this group applied for membership in The American Kennel Club, which was then just six years old. They were denied because a group of show enthusiasts, known initially as the American English Beagle Club, already held membership.

The men in the National Beagle Club refused to give up. Finally, in May 1891, the American Beagle Club (formerly the American English Beagle Club) merged with the National Beagle Club. The new group called itself The National Beagle Club, and it became the parent club for the breed. At that time, the AKC was completely show oriented, and an interesting sidelight on the club's admission to AKC membership was the AKC's strong objections to the parent club's involvement in both field trials and shows. H.F. Schellhass, then president and AKC delegate of the National, told the AKC: "This club was formed for improvement in the field and on the bench of the Beagle hound in America, and will enter the AKC with its constitution unchanged, if it enters at all." The AKC dutifully backed off.

Today the sport of field trials for Beagles has something to offer any Beagle owner who can compete with his hound in any one of five different kinds of trials. The most popular trials are those in which the hounds compete by sex in pairs, or *Braces,* in pursuit of the cottontail rabbit. They can also compete in *Small Packs* of up to nine hounds, either with or without being tested for gun-shyness. In the northern tier of states, where the varying, or "snowshoe," hare is found, Beagles may be trialed in *Large Packs,* where a pack of thirty to sixty hounds or more in a single class is not uncommon. Lastly, there are the traditional *Formal Packs,* which are either privately owned or supported by subscription from local Beagle devotees.

Three Formal Packs were entered at the National Beagle Club's meet in 1896. Today, twenty-eight such packs are registered with that club. They are hunted as three-couple (6), four-couple (8), and eight-couple (16) packs. At a Formal Pack field trial, each pack is judged as a unit or team, and its performance is measured

against that of other packs entered in the trial. The packs are foot handled, with the Huntsman and his (or her) assistants, called Whippers-in, all resplendent in green jackets, white pants, knickerbockers or skirts, and black velvet caps. Packs are identified by the uniquely colored piping on the Huntsman's jacket.

The ultimate competition for the Formal Packs is held annually at the Mecca for all beaglers—the National Beagle Club's Institute Farm in Aldie, Virginia— with all competition still under AKC sanction.

Participation in the sport of Formal Pack beagling has always been limited to people with means. With the popularity of the Beagle, a new concept emerged in the early 1900s. Americans became interested in the development of an individual hound that could trail the hare or rabbit effectively and efficiently without the assistance of variously endowed pack mates. Beagles, selectively bred with this concept in mind, were referred to by the pack men as "singles." To this day, it is not unusual to hear this term on the running grounds of the National Beagle Club when reference is made to Beagles run in Braces.

In a sense the merits of a Formal Pack were to be discovered by *testing,* the traditional method of evaluating the abilities of working dogs, sporting dogs, and hounds. But rather than putting them to *tests,* most Americans always preferred to

The first Field Trial of the National Beagle Club. Courtesy National Beagle Club

put dogs in competition on a head-to-head basis. In fact, the AKC Beagle Field Trial Rules and Standard Procedures states it this way in the foreword:"The holding of field trials at which pure-bred dogs may be run in competition . . . has been found to be the best method by which the progress which has been made in breeding can be shown.''

Early beaglers became aware that industrialization and development for business and housing were reducing the availability of hunting and training grounds. The purchase of land by Beagle clubs was encouraged and even mandated by the AKC. In contrast to field trials for breeds in which domestically raised game can be released for the trial, the Beagle field trial is limited to the pursuit of a quarry that must be acclimated to the terrain. Beaglers became ardent conservationists. Natural food and cover programs on the Beagle club grounds became necessary to maintain a natural supply of rabbits for training and trialing. In many instances, clubs reclaimed marginal land; soil fertility was measured and improved; and the term "rabbit farming" became the byword at any progressive Beagle club. Today more than four hundred Beagle clubs either own or lease land in excess of 150 acres each.

The building boom that followed World War II introduced hazards to Beagles intent on the chase. Too often the rabbit could take them across a new road or superhighway. Most clubs were forced to fence their land for the safety of the hounds. This, of course, also enclosed the rabbits, who then developed running traits quite unlike their "wild" cousins outside the enclosures.

In order to get hounds that could effectively trail the "enclosure" rabbit, houndmen bred for a slower, more precise working dog. Gradually, the old, one-on-one competition was replaced by an appreciation of the "style" in which the field-trial Beagle tracked a rabbit. This was significant in light of the fact that nearly 90 percent of the four hundred clubs holding AKC licensed trials were running Brace events. At these trials the hounds whose "style" most impressed the judges were given the ribbons. Through selective breeding, the Beagles used at field trials and run in Braces became slow and meticulous tracking specialists.

However, the rabbit hunter, still the most numerous of all who take wild game in the United States, found that the slow "stylish" field-trial Beagle was totally undesirable as a hunting dog. By the early 1970s, the need developed for a real gundog, or hunting Beagle. This movement gathered momentum, and its breeding programs reflected the trend to hark back to the early days.

Meanwhile, the situation was somewhat different for those northern clubs that ran their hounds in Large Packs on hares. They continued to pride themselves justifiably on producing hunting Beagles and believed that their trials showed the Beagle to such an advantage.

The promoters of the "gundog" or "hunting Beagle," however, did not believe that the Large Pack was the most acceptable method to pursue the cottontail rabbit. Instead, they chose to use a running standard that was already in the AKC Rules. This was the Small Pack in which hounds are run on rabbits in packs of from

A ''small pack'' of Beagles. A. H. Rowan photo

A nice brace of Field Trial Beagles. A. H. Rowan photo

four to seven hounds, with the judges selecting the outstanding performers to be run in a second series and then finally in a Winners Pack. To prove beyond a doubt that they were competing with "hunting Beagles," the AKC in the late 1970s permitted the additional testing of their hounds for gun-shyness and searching ability in what became known as the Small Pack Option, the fifth and newest type of competition for Beagles. By the end of 1983, 8.75 percent of all Beagle clubs were conducting licensed and sanctioned trials in this manner.

With the sport of Beagle field trials so diversified, and with traditions dating back almost one hundred years, how could the AKC cope with its administration of the five distinctive competitive standards for Beagle trials, recognizing that pure-bred Beagles are the objects of competition in all five standards? It took a unique mechanism.

In order to understand this administrative evolution, the reader must know that an AKC Member parent club for any breed, such as the venerable National Beagle Club of America, has not only the responsibility to approve the dates of the events held by local clubs for its breed but also to propose the standards by which its breed is judged in conformation and performance.

In 1936 the National Beagle Club voted to abrogate part of its responsibilities as a parent club and ceased granting consent for field-trial dates. Instead they recommended that the AKC appoint a ten-member Advisory Committee from among the delegates of the Beagle AKC member clubs whose purpose would be to advise the AKC's Board of Directors on the matter of granting licenses for Beagle field trials. A member of the AKC's executive staff was to chair this Advisory Committee.

And so for fifty years a Beagle Advisory Committee (BAC) had been responsible for advising the AKC's Board of Directors on meeting the challenge of the administration of the sport of Beagle field trials. Evolution has played its part, and there have been some significant changes in the BAC's structure. For instance, since 1962 it has been a committee of twelve members, eleven of whom each represent some forty Beagle clubs from across the nation. The twelfth committee member belongs to the National Beagle Club of America. An AKC executive still chairs the meeting. The system has worked well.

FIRST AKC BRACE TRIALS FOR BEAGLES

November 4, 1890	*National Beagle Club Hyannis, Massachusetts	(18 starters)
November 1, 1893	Northwestern Beagle Club Whitewater, Wisconsin	(10 starters)

November 6, 1893 **New England Beagle Club   (21 starters)
                    Oxford, Massachusets

          1896 **Central Beagle Club   (15 starters)
                    Waynesburg, Pennsylvania

  * Current AKC member parent club
 ** Current AKC member club

Basset Hound Field Trials

**(Edited and written by A. Hamilton Rowan, Jr., from material submitted by
Marjorie Skolnick.)**

It is generally acknowledged that the first Basset Hounds came to America from
France. George Washington's friend Lafayette sent him hounds for pack hunting in
America, and these hounds were probably the so-called Old Virginia Bench-
Legged Beagles. Other imports in the early nineteenth century were obtained from
France, but some also came from British packs, especially the Walhampton Pack.
Gerald Livingston imported from the Walhampton Pack in the 1920s forming his
well-known Kilsyth Pack. At the same time, Loren Free of Ohio also imported
from the Walhampton Pack to form his Shellbark Pack. During the 1930s, another
Ohioan, Carl Smith, acquired the Starridge Pack, and when economic conditions
improved, he was able to supply a new demand for hunting Bassets.

The American Kennel Club registered Bassets in 1885 and recognized them as
a breed in the United States in 1916. After AKC recognition of the Basset Hound
Club of America in 1937, show and field-trial activities grew and spread rapidly.
The first Basset field trial was an AKC-sanctioned trial held at Hastings, Michigan,
on October 24, 1937, by the then newly formed Basset Hound Club of America. It
attracted seven Bassets. The hounds were run in Braces (pairs) under the AKC rules
and procedures already in use for Beagle trials.

Soon thereafter, two AKC-licensed Basset field trials a year were held in
Michigan, Ohio, or Pennsylvania, with a growth to about thirty to forty entries per
trial. By 1964, ninety-seven Bassets had fulfilled the requirements for the Field
Championship title. The sport spread rapidly to New York State, Massachusetts,
New Jersey, Maryland, Kentucky, Illinois, California, and Texas, with many trials
attracting over one hundred entries. Today some twenty Basset Hound clubs hold
thirty-eight trials each year, and the Basset Hound Club of America gets the best of
the Bassets together each spring and fall for a national event.

There have been only nine Dual Champion Bassets over the years. The first,
Dual Ch. "Kazoo's Moses the Great," won his second of the Champion titles in
1964.

The Gallery at an AKC Dachshund Field Trial. A. H. Rowan photo

Although it is not an AKC-recognized sport, the hunting of Basset Hounds in Formal Packs remains a viable interest in America and receives encouragement from the Basset Hound Club of America. Early packs that no longer exist included the Kilsyth, Starridge, Shellbark, Brandywine, Stockford, and Coldstream packs.

Eleven Basset packs were active in 1983 and included the Ashland, Sandanona, Tewksbury Foot, Three Creeks, Winward, Boniwell, Skycastle French, South Illinois, Wayne DuPage, Tantivy, and Timber Ridge packs.

Dachshund Field Trials

(Edited and written by A. Hamilton Rowan, Jr., from material submitted by George C. Wanner.)

In the early 1930s, the short-lived U.S. Dachshund Field Trial Club held the first organized field trial for Dachshunds. The hounds were put to ground in artificial rabbit burrows and were judged by rules brought over from Germany.

In 1935, under the leadership of the renowned and respected Dachshund fancier Laurence A. Horswell, the Dachshund Club of America, the parent club for the breed, held its first trial at Lamington, New Jersey, under revised rules tailored

for American competition. It remained the only club holding field trials for Dachshunds until the Dachshund Club of New Jersey held its first trial in 1966. Thus,
with only one trial each year to attend, by far the greatest challenge for any
Dachshund owner was to keep his field trial prospect alive long enough to earn the
twenty-five points for its Field Championship title.

Today eight clubs hold some ten trials each year in Connecticut, New York,
Ohio, California, New Jersey, and Pennsylvania.

The AKC Rules for Dachshunds specify that the judging be based on the
following standard of performance:

> In all Stakes the principal qualifications to be considered by the Judges are good
> noses, courage in facing punishing coverts, keenness, perseverance, obedience
> and willingness to go to earth. Should a rabbit lodge in any earth, or run through
> any drain large enough for the Dachshunds to enter, the dogs should, of course,
> be expected to enter without hesitation; and failure to do so should automati-
> cally render them ineligible for first award, even though their performance was
> in all other respects outstanding.

Since Dachshund trials must be held on live rabbits or hare, they are always held on
the grounds of an existing Beagle club where game is usually plentiful. Like
Beagles, the Dachshunds compete in Braces (pairs), and the dogs both seek and
pursue their game with obvious delight. However, unless the scent is particularly
''hot'' or the quarry is in sight, most Dachshunds run mute.

All varieties and sizes of Dachshunds—Longhair, Wirehair, and Smooth—and both Standard or Miniature compete in the field on an equal eligibility basis. At a trial, a Dachshund is a Dachshund regardless of coat or size, and all varieties have done their share of winning over the years. The AKC record books also show that seven Dachshunds have achieved the ennobled designation of Dual Champion, thereby proving to all breeders that function can follow form, or vice versa.

Pointing Breed Field Trials

The distinction of being the first to hold a field trial of any canine persuasion in America belongs to the group of dogs that point their game—the Pointing Breeds.

In 1884, eight years after the British held their first field trial, the first-recorded trial in America was held near Memphis, Tennessee, when H. C. Pritchard's Setter, "Knight," became the immortalized first winner.

Dr. Nicholas Rowe, the same nineteenth-century sportsman who played such a vital role in the founding of The American Kennel Club, maintains a sure place of honor in the history of trials for the Pointing Breeds—then only for Setters and Pointers. In 1876, Dr. Rowe bought the *Chicago Field,* changing it to the *American Field* some five years later—a style under which it is still published today as America's oldest continuous sporting journal.

While trials for Setters and Pointers grew rapidly under the aegis of the *American Field,* particularly in the Southern states where these two breeds were (and still are) referred to as "bird dogs," it was not until 1924 that a written record existed for a Pointing Breed trial under AKC license. This event was held by the English Setter Club of America on their grounds in Medford, New Jersey, which they still own and use for trials.

Seven years were to elapse before AKC recorded another Pointing Breed trial, when a joint trial was held in October, 1931, by the Gordon Setter Club of America and the Irish Setter Club of America at the Owen Winston estate in Gladstone, New Jersey.

Coming out of the Depression years of the 1930s and through the years of World War II, AKC trials for Pointing Breeds never exceeded ten in any year, and in several years only two were held.

The end of World War II, however, brought a dramatic upsurge in the number of Pointing Breed trials. The American servicemen had been to Europe, and those hunters among them had seen, first hand, the efficacy of the now so-called "Continental" breeds, which include the German Shorthaired and Wirehaired Pointers, Weimaraners, Brittanys, Vizslas, and Wirehaired Pointing Griffons. These were all marvelous, utilitarian breeds that put game on the tables of those American hunters who were fortunate enough to own a specimen.

An Irish Setter on point, with its handler. A. H. Rowan photo

Break-away at a Pointing Breed Trial. A. H. Rowan photo

The traditional, competitive American spirit, however, brought the "Continental" breeds into popularity in the American field-trial game—although at nowhere near the sophisticated level of competition that had always been maintained from the previous century in the Pointer/Setter trials held under the so-called minimum requirements of the *American Field*.

In the 1950s, the handling of Pointing Breed dogs at AKC trials by professional trainers marked a major turning point in the quality of performance that was required in order to win.

From their beginning (and unlike the trials held by the *American Field* for Setters and Pointers), AKC trials did not permit the handling of the dogs from horseback. The professional trainers, many of whom had gained experience in American field trials, felt that this restriction was highly detrimental to the improvement of the performance of their dogs, and they campaigned actively against this aspect of the AKC regulations. Thus, in 1966, the AKC Standard Procedure for Pointing Breed trials was amended to permit the optional handling of dogs from horseback—an action now generally regretted. Having overcome that alleged restrictive barrier, the popularity of competing in AKC trials for Pointing Breeds doubled in twenty years to over 450 trials per year, with more than 35,000 dogs competing annually.

In 1965, taking a cue from the successful administration of Beagle trials, the first of a series of four Pointing Breed Advisory Committee meetings was held at the AKC offices to recommend rule and procedure amendments to AKC's Board. A representative from each of the nine Pointing Breed parent clubs made up the committees, which were chaired by an AKC executive staff member.

AKC Pointing Breed trials are today experiencing the same problems that beset Beagle and Retriever trials during the past six years. The sophistication of

modern trial competition created a void for the myriad of hunters with Pointing Breed dogs who were either unwilling or unable to pay the price in time and money in order to be successful in the sport of field trials. Therefore, as AKC moves into its second century, it is predictable that a program will soon be developed and implemented by AKC to allow Pointing Breed dogs to be tested under standards of performance that are truly characteristic of hunting afoot.

The following additional milestone dates have been important in the development of field trials for Pointing Breeds at AKC:

FIRST AKC-LICENSED POINTING BREED TRIALS BY BREED

1924	English Setter Club of America
	Medford, New Jersey
October, 1931	Gordon Setter Club of America/Irish Setter Club of America
	Joint trial held at Owen Winston estate,
	Gladstone, New Jersey
November, 1943	American Brittany Club
	Ravenna, Ohio
May, 1944	German Shorthaired Pointer Club of America
	Anoka, Minnesota
November, 1953	American Pointer Club
	Fairfield, Connecticut

A handler inspects his string of Brittanys. A. H. Rowan photo

September, 1955   Weimaraner Club of America
                   Fort Lewis, Washington
November, 1962   Vizsla Club of America
                   New Sharon, Iowa
April, 1963   German Wirehaired Pointer Club of America
                   First licensed trial, Ingleside, Illinois

FIRST AKC NATIONAL AND NATIONAL AMATEUR CHAMPIONSHIP STAKES BY ELIGIBLE BREEDS

October, 1953   German Shorthaired Pointer Club of America
                   at Volo, Illinois
                   National Champion—"Dandy Jim V Feldstrom" (M)
                   O/Clark Lemley, M.D.
December, 1957   American Brittany Club at Carbondale, Illinois
                   National Champion—Fld. Ch. "Towsey" (M)
                   O/Thomas Black
October, 1966   German Shorthaired Pointer Club of America
                   at Denver, Colorado
                   National Amateur Champion—Withheld
November, 1966   American Brittany Club at Carbondale, Illinois
                   National Amateur Champion—Fld. Ch. "Towsey's Bub" (M)
                   O/M. D. Nelson
December, 1976   Weimaraner Club of America at Ardmore, Oklahoma
                   National Champion—Fld. Ch. "Unserhund Von Sieger" (M)
                   O/Mr. and Mrs. William J. McGinty
                   National Amateur Champion—Fld. Ch. "Fran's Dee Dee Von
                   Heiser" (F) O/R. H. and K. J. Snyder
October, 1977   Vizsla Club of America at Fort Ord, California
                   National Champion—Fld. and Amateur Fld. Ch. "Randy
                   Duke" (M) O/Bart Boglioli
                   National Amateur Champion—"Mehagian's Peppy
                   Paloma" (F) O/Marge Mehagian
October, 1979   Irish Setter Club of America at Rend Lake, Illinois
                   National Champion—Fld. and Amateur Fld. Ch. "Ramblin'
                   Red Banshee" (M) O/Randy Kubacz
                   National Amateur Champion—Fld. Ch. "Ivor Glen
                   Dinah" (F) O/Mike Jones

Retriever Field Trials

The AKC Rules for Retriever Trials state that the word ''Retriever'' includes the several breeds of Retrievers and/or Irish Water Spaniels. Continuing, it says that field-trial clubs formed to improve any one of the several Retriever breeds may hold field-trial stakes in which *one or more* of the Retriever breeds may compete. The organization of this sport, therefore, did not follow AKC's traditional breed concept because all-retriever breed clubs were allowed, in order to foster all-retriever breed competition.

In 1983, 119 clubs held 201 licensed trials for all Retriever breeds across the United States. In addition, the American Chesapeake Club and the Golden Retriever Club of America each held a ''National'' trial for their respective breeds; and National and National Amateur Championship Stakes were held for those relatively few qualified Retrievers by the two national clubs formed specifically to put on these events annually.

Considering the fact that the first Chesapeake Bay Retriever was registered in 1878, six years before AKC's founding, it is hard to believe that the still burgeoning popularity in Retrievers began only some fifty years ago in America. Labs and Goldens were not accepted in the Stud Book until 1917 and 1925 respectively. It is also startling to note that only 64 Retrievers were registered in 1926. In 1983 this figure was to be 124,785, with 67,389 of these Labs, placing them third in breed registration ranking.

The fortunes of the Retriever breeds in America, and the Labrador in particular, were tied to the fortunes of wealthy, Eastern estate owners who, accustomed to shooting in Scotland, began to import Labs from the British Isles in the late 1920s and early 1930s. Since the imports were strictly hunting dogs, the owners saw no reason to register their imports with AKC.

And along with the dogs came young Scottish gamekeepers and kennel men to train them.

Noted American Retriever owners of the late 1920s and early 1930s and their ''imported'' trainers included:

Hon. W. Averell Harriman	Tom Briggs and Jim Cowie
Jay F. Carlisle	Dave Elliot
Mr. and Mrs. Marshall Field	Douglas Marshall
Robert Goelet	Colin MacFarlane and Jock Munro
Dr. Samuel Milbank	Lionel Bond

1931 saw the organization of the Labrador Retriever Club, with Mrs. Marshall Field as its first president. On December 21 of that same year, it put on the first field trial for Retrievers in America on the eight-thousand acre Glenmere Court estate of Robert Goelet in Chester, New York—deliberately holding it on a Monday so that

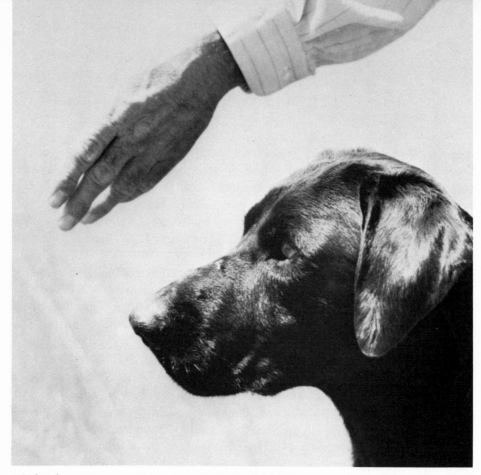

A Labrador Retriever set to retrieve. A. H. Rowan photo

it would not attract a gallery. The George Foley Dog Show Organization of Philadelphia managed the event for the few dozen wealthy competitors. Although the program states that it was held under AKC and Labrador Retriever Club rules, the accounts of the trial indicate clearly that it was run under British rules. Mr. and Mrs. Field took first and second placements respectively in the Open All-Age Stake. W. Averell Harriman won the American-Bred Stake.

The trials that followed continued through the 1930s in the hunting tradition of the British rules until increased entries and the development of sophisticated training methods assured the impracticality of British trialing procedure in America. Controlling the dogs by whistle, voice, and hand commands (handling) revolutionized the sport, starting in the 1940s. Today's tests for Retrievers, in spite of the dictates of the AKC rules, no longer represent practical hunting situations.

With the current popularity of the Retriever breeds as superb hunting companions, both in duck marsh and in pursuit of upland game, came a growing desire from a large group of non-trialers to have an organized activity where their Retrievers could be tested under simulated hunting situations. In 1983, the North American Hunting Retriever Association, the parent association for this new sport, developed the necessary set of regulations and field procedures, and these received

AKC Board approval. The first AKC-sanctioned Hunting Retriever Field Test was held in Richmond, Virginia, in February 1984 and drew an entry of over two-hundred Retrievers.

And so with the addition of this new activity for Hunting Retrievers, and with the ever-expanding sport of field trials for the Retriever breeds still vibrantly popular, the future for a dramatic increase in participation in these two AKC field activities is almost assured.

The following additional milestone dates have been important in the development of field trials for Retrievers:

1932	First trial held by the American Chesapeake Club for Chesapeakes only
1935	First Chesapeake Bay Retriever Field Champion: "Skipper Bob"—O/Harry T. Conklin
1936	First Labrador Retriever Field Champion: "Blind of Arden"—O/W. Averell Harriman
1939	First Golden Retriever Field Champion: "Rip"—O/H. Paul Bakewell III
1940	First trial held by the Golden Retriever Club of America for Goldens only.
1941	First National Championship Stake for Retrievers, held at Penniman's Point, Quogue, Long Island, New York. Ch. "King Midas of Woodend,"—Golden Male, O/E. W. Dodge.
1953	Amateur Field Championships first available for Retrievers.
1957	First National Amateur Championship Stake for Retrievers, held at Park Rapids, Minnesota. 1954 NFC-Amateur Field Ch. "Major VI," Lab Male, O/Mrs. F. M. Horn.

Spaniel Field Trials

(Edited and written by A. Hamilton Rowan, Jr., from material submitted by Evelyn Monte Van Horn.)

American sportsmen used Spaniels for hunting game birds and waterfowl long before there were Spaniel field trials. The Cocker Spaniel, recognized by The Kennel Club of England in 1892, had no trouble gaining stature in the United States as a hunting dog. The breed even had a sponsoring club early in the game—the American Spaniel Club, a strong organization founded in 1881, which eventually took all the hunting Spaniels—the Clumber, the Sussex, the Irish Water Spaniel, the Field, and the Springer Spaniel—under its wing.

The first stakes for Cocker Spaniels were held at Verbank, New York, in 1924 by the Hunting Cocker Spaniel Field Trial Club of America, a club that was largely the creation of Mrs. Ella B. Moffit, a well-known sportswoman from Poughkeepsie, New York.

The name Hunting Cocker Club was changed to Cocker Spaniel Field Trial Club of America and the catalogue of its trial on October 28—29, 1931, shows that the judges were David Wagstaff and Captain Paul A. Curtis. Other luminaries of the Spaniel world who officiated as guns or stewards included Ralph C. Craig, Henry Ferguson, Elias Vail, Dr. Samuel Milbank, and H. E. Mellenthin, breeder of Dual Ch. "My Own High Time" and of the famous "My Own Brucie."

The English Springer Spaniel breed, which had become eligible for AKC registry in 1910, started to gain in popularity as an effective hunting dog in the early 1920s, ever since Freeman Lloyd, a respected gundog journalist of his day, wrote glowingly of this "rare" new breed's ability as a hunter and retriever.

There was never any conflict between the Cocker people and the Springer people. From the beginning, trials held by the Cocker clubs included stakes for Springers. Likewise, Springer clubs throughout the country held Cocker stakes, and American and English Cockers competed in the same stakes without breed distinction.

Field trials were the perfect showcase for the Springer. The first field trial for Spaniels in the United States took place late in 1924 at Fishers Island, New York.

There was always a "bench show," or conformation judging, held in conjunction with the early trials at Fishers, and it was judged by a show judge. This was dropped in later years, but there still exists the Horsford Dual Challenge Cup, presented in 1926 by William Humphrey of Shrewsbury, England, for the "Best Looking, Best Working Dog" in the trial. The trial judges now select the winner. Other impressive trophies of long standing are the British Challenge Cup and the International Gun Dog League of England Challenge Cup.

With English Springer Spaniels competing in Spaniel trials, it was only natural that 1926 should see the founding of that breed's parent club, the English Springer Spaniel Field Trial Association—the only AKC breed parent club to carry a field-trial connotation in its name.

The Depression years and World War II caused an alarming decline in Spaniel trials between 1934 and 1945; but it was a rekindled interest in field trials for Cocker Spaniels that led the way to inspired activity in Spaniel trials. For nine years there was a National Championship for Cocker Spaniels, the last one being held in 1962 at Amwell, New Jersey. The last field-trial stake for Cocker Spaniels was held in 1965.

The game little Cocker Spaniel had become the darling of the dog-show world, where, in misguided innocence, the natural hunting instincts of most Sporting Breed dogs are bred-out on the notion that function follows form. With no pool of Cockers having functioning genes available in America for breeding, the Cocker became a modern-day, field-trial dinosaur—another man-made, huntless sporting dog.

Fortunately, the English Springer Spaniel did not suffer the same fate as the Cocker, because the basic pool of functioning genes for the breed remained intact in England. Nevertheless, once again, breeding for form in the American show ring produced an entirely different dog from the specimens found on the modern English Springer Spaniel field-trial circuit.

The following additional milestone dates have been important in the development of field trials for Spaniels in America:

1947   First National Championship Stake for English Springer Spaniels was held by the English Springer Spaniel Field Trial Association at Crab Orchard Lake, Herrin, Illinois, with 32 starters. "Russett of Middlefield," bitch, O/H Dr. C. G. Sabin, Portland, Oregon, was the first National Champion.

1953   First National Championship for Cocker Spaniels was held by the American Spaniel Club, Herrin, Illinois. "Camino's Cheetah," O/ H. C. McGrew, Fortuna, California, was the first National Champion.

1960   Amateur Field Championships first available for Spaniels.

1963   First National Amateur Championship Stake for English Springer Spaniels was held by the English Springer Spaniel Field Trial Association at Hazard Farms, Wilmington, Ohio, with 52 starters. "Pam's Aphrodite of Camden," bitch, O/ George Webster, London, Ontario, Canada, was the first National Amateur Champion.

THE WHITE HOUSE

WASHINGTON

November 13, 1984

I am delighted to send my warm greetings to all
those gathered to celebrate the 100th anniversary
of the American Kennel Club.

Helping dog lovers throughout the nation to
organize shows and trials guided by uniform
standards of breeding and registration, your
fine organization has a reputation as being a
dog's best friend. I commend you for your
devoted efforts to promote proper pet care
and a better appreciation of our canine
companions.

Nancy joins me in congratulating you on this
important milestone, and we send you our best
wishes for continued success in the years
ahead.

Ronald Reagan

13

The
American Kennel Club
Centennial Show
and Obedience Trial

by Roger A. Caras

It was entirely appropriate that the American Kennel Club should mark its birthday with a dog show. It was only the second show the AKC has ever directly produced—the last one was in 1926—but since so many of the dogs registered at 51 Madison Avenue are at least part-time show dogs, (and certainly just about all of the dogs registered have show dogs in their background), it was a fine and proper way to mark the occasion.

The show, held on November 17 and 18, 1984 at the massive Philadelphia Civic Center, was officially labeled the AKC Centennial Dog Show and Obedience Trial. Over eight thousand dogs were entered, which made it the largest dog show ever recorded in the United States. When combined with the specialty shows on Friday, the day preceding, and the Philadelphia Kennel Club Dog Show on the following Monday, it created the largest canine weekend in the whole world, with somewhere between fourteen thousand and fifteen thousand dogs involved. Getting a hotel room anywhere near the Civic Center that weekend was about as tough as getting a seat in the U.S. Senate.

Anyone entering the center on the upper level from Civic Center Boulevard could only describe the experience as mind-boggling. A handsome AKC display rose up straight ahead, a post office offering first-day cachets and special commemorative sheets stood to the left, and the escalators to and from the lower level were on the right. It was after you stepped onto those moving stairs that the full impact of

Charles A. T. O'Neill - Executive Vice-
President and Show Chairman
(Grace Satriale)

what the AKC and Show Chairman C. A. T. O'Neill had wrought was felt. Below, swirling in some kind of massed, self-contained chaos were people and dogs by the thousands. It was like a descent into another world—an ultimate world of dogs. Thousands of local doglovers and just plain curious Philadelphians joined the exhibitors, handlers, and the seemingly endless battalions of well-wishers who had come to see the impossible come true. What was impossible? The very idea that any kind of order could conceivably emerge from that many people, animals, vending booths, food stalls, officials and security personnel. It wasn't that the show differed so drastically from any other dog show, certainly not from the annual Westminster Kennel Club Dog Show at Madison Square Garden in New York, it was just that it was four to five times larger than anything anyone has ever seen in the Western Hemisphere. "Surely," one thought going in, "they have taken on too much. It has to sink itself with its own weight." The glory and perhaps the miracle of November 17th and 18th is that that did not happen. It worked, from eight in the morning 'til eleven at night, on two consecutive days, it worked.

If you assemble approximately 8075 dogs from all over North America it stands to reason that some pretty nice dogs will show up and they did. Every dog fancier in the United States seemed to have the same idea, Philadelphia in 1984 was offering what had to be considered the chance of a lifetime, for every human enthusiast there and certainly for every dog—one that probably won't come again until another century has passed. So they came with the best they had—the exhibitors, the handlers, and their friends—to face the toughest roster of judges that could be assembled. If anyone ever wants to compile the supreme court of dog-show judges they can simply check the premium list of the AKC's 100th birthday show: William W. Brainard, Jr.; Mr. and Mrs. James Edward Clark; Chester Collier, chairman of the Westminster Kennel Club Show; Melbourne T. L. Downing; Mr. and Mrs. Robert S. Forsyth; William L. Kendrick; Dr. W. Edward McGough; Maxwell Riddle; Mrs. Augustus Riggs IV; Langdon L. Skarda; Henry H. Stoecker; and many, many more—121 judges in all—of equal stature and reputation. The people who help give the dog fancy its dignity and its quality came from all over the continent to appraise the dogs that represented the other half of the equation. It was an unbelievable forty-eight-hour spectacle that the AKC and Show Chairman C. A. T. O'Neill had wrought—a massive display of sportsmanship, charm, and just plain show-biz excitement. Not everyone's favorites won their class, much less their breed or group, but it was quality against quality being judged by the best every time a steward gave the signal for an event to begin.

At nine o'clock on Saturday morning, the judging of the Toy Group, the Working Dogs, the Herding Dogs and the Non-Sporting Group began. Coming from the three benching halls, from their hundreds of benching slots, the Affenpinschers entered Ring 19, the Akitas Ring 3, the Bearded Collies Ring 10, and the Lhasa Apsos Ring 26. Some of the more massive entries had started coming in at eight-thirty: the 181 Dalmatians, the 144 Rottweilers, and the 163 Yorkshire Terriers. The largest breed entry, 214 Doberman Pinschers, got off at nine. The classes rolled on in a no-nonsense progression, and one distinguished entry after another began the climb up the slippery side of the dog show pyramid. This was not a show where a hair could be out of place or a step mis-taken. The best were pitted against the best under the eyes of the most discerning. To add just that little extra touch of pressure the crowds around every ring for every event included some of the most knowledgeable dog fanciers in the United States or Canada.

Coming down the escalator from the street level one looked down on what may have appeared to be massed confusion. As you moved through the crowds of dogs and people, however, the confusion became less a factor than the electricity. The intensity that makes any dog show an exciting event was multiplied in Philadelphia ten-fold. The irony that also marks every dog show was no less in evidence—the more electric the atmosphere, the more fun people seem to have, and that feeling is inevitably conveyed to the dogs. The dogs themselves seemed more intent than ever to please the people who meant the most to them.

It wasn't long before the best-of-breed winners began to emerge, shaping the groups that would be judged that evening. Affenpinscher Ch. Puff Von Apache Rauchen was selected by Frank T. Sabella out of an entry of seventeen. Italian Greyhound Ch. Mira Hill N Dale D'Dasa emerged from an impressive entry of thirty-four selected by Raymond V. Filburn, Jr. Toy Poodle Broad Bay Just in Time, out of an entry of forty-eight, was picked by Mrs. William Kendrick. The toys were picked one by one, nineteen stunning little dogs that would parade that night seeking to complete the next giant step, a group win.

It was the same kind of progression with the Non-Sporting Breeds. Out of seventy-six Standard Poodles, judge Dr. Jacklyn E. Hungerland selected Ch. Valhalla Jacquelyn. Out of the thirty-eight Schipperkes judge Joseph E. Gregory

Setting Up - About 7:00 A.M.   (Jim Callea)

Roger Caras (Grace Satriale)

Same day — 11:00 A.M. (Jane Donahue)

*Mrs. Mandy Cronin and the Bedlam
Beagles* (Jane Donahue)

Thomas J. Crowe, Superintendent (Grace Satriale)

Mrs. Amelia Rogers and the Timber Ridge Bassets (William Gilbert)

Mrs. Nan R. Ayling, AKC Vice-President (Grace Satriale)

Robert G. Maxwell, Vice-President and Controller, discussing business with Mrs. L. Stewart Cochrane and Mr. John Hauser, Superintendent (Grace Satriale)

M. Josephine Deubler, D.V.M., Centennial Show Judge and Member of Local Show Committee (Grace Satriale)

put up Ch. Skipalong's Jelly Side Down. The entries were exceptionally large and distinguished, and ringside experts crowded in and second-guessed every decision made. In that sense, even this massive affair was at heart just another dog show— just ever so much grander.

By evening all the classes in the first four groups had been completed, and out of 674 Non-Sporting Dogs, 13 best-of-breeds remained; out of 546 Herding Dogs, 15 were left; and out of 1,117 Working Dogs, 19 survived the judging to face group competition. Nineteen toys would represent the 799 Toy entries that same night. An incredible 3,136 dogs had been meticulously examined by fifty-nine judges, while they in turn were being just as meticulously examined themselves by thousands of spectators, some of whom had never even been to a dog show before. It was, by anyone's standards, a remarkable mix. A sense of humor and comfortable shoes helped.

On that same day, starting at eight in the morning, six judges put the obedience entries through their paces, and some remarkable performances were recorded.

On Saturday evening, following the Field Trial Program, the group judging began. This reporter had the honor of announcing the groups and can honestly say he has not often seen dogs of such quality assembled. Mrs. Augustus Riggs IV faced the Working Group to begin the final selection process. The field was distinguished and the task a difficult one, but the Working Group went to a Doberman Pinscher, Ch. Brierpatch's Christmas Dream, a five-year old who rose above 177 entries shown in the breed.

The Toy Group was judged next, Melbourne T. L. Downing presiding. Maltese Ch. Keoli's Small Craft Warning, one of thirty-two in that breed judged that day, took the group and went on line for the main event the next evening.

Henry H. Stoecker judged the third of Saturday's groups, the Non-Sporting, and after apparently agonizing over the field of thirteen, settled on a Bichon Frise, Ch. Camelot's Brassy Nickel. The little champion had a lot of fans in the audience and seemed to know it.

The last group, judged late in the evening on Saturday, was the Herding Dogs. Langdon L. Skarda had a field of fifteen distinguished dogs, and as is generally the case, the group attracted a great deal of attention, virtually all of it partisan. It was no great surprise that one of the greatest German Shepherd Dogs in memory won the group, Ch. Covy Tucker Hills Manhattan. It was by no means ever certain that he would win—not with the field he faced—but the honor was a logical extension of his already spectacular career.

And so ended evening Number 1. There was no one present whose feet did not hurt. Dogs, crates, grooming benches, thermos jugs, camp chairs, and assorted human and canine maintenance paraphernalia were loaded into scores of vans and rigs occupying every conceivable parking spot. The professional handlers and their helpers, with anywhere from several to a good many dogs to worry about, had the toughest time of all. Somehow, though, the evening wound down. Exhibitors, handlers, groomers, judges, and officials made their way to their hotels, while the thousands of Philadelphians who had attended found their transportation of choice and went home. The Civic Center was suddenly quiet, with the sounds of brooms and oversize vacuum cleaners the loudest noises of all. Thousands of human voices and the barking of over three thousand excited dogs drifted away in the brisk night air. It was over, Day One, the opening round. Shortly after dawn it would all begin again, the remarkable task of judging the veritable legion of dogs of high quality.

Sunday, shortly after sunup, the vans and cars began arriving. In a matter of a couple of hours, with the twenty-eight rings set as they had been the day before, 1,017 hounds of twenty-four breeds, 647 terriers of twenty-five breeds and, 1,334 sporting dogs of twenty-six breeds would be in position to be winnowed down by fifty-one judges, while Junior Showmanship and Obedience judging went on in yet other rings. Same huge halls, same vast crowds, different dogs, same boat. Of the 2,998 dogs assembled on Sunday, only 3 could climb the ladder to face the 4 survivors of the preceding day. Everyone involved in the show itself settled in for another long and exciting event, as thousands of Philadelphians began streaming into the aisles between the rings and into benching areas to view the contenders. "What kind of a dog is that?" was a question asked thousands of times by people exploring the dog world. The AKC Centennial turned out to be not only the dog show of the century but a major spectator attraction in a city thoroughly conditioned to such superlatives as *biggest*, the *best*, and the *only*.

In Ring 1 at 8:30 A.M., Lt. Col. Wallace H. Pede faced off the first of 159 Borzois to be seen that day. He selected Ch. Lanel's Lobachevski to go forward to the evening's big events.

A little later in the morning, in Ring 27, a remarkable assembly of forty-two Bloodhounds was judged by Mrs. Curtis M. Brown. Ch. Baskerville's Sole Heir, a notorious ham, who sings to the audience in return for their applause, took the breed, and so it went through the twenty-four breeds. The newest of the recognized hound breeds, the Ibizan and the Pharaoh, were represented by eighteen and sixteen entries, respectively—a remarkable showing. For many people, it was the first chance to observe these ancient breeds, at least in numbers that would allow a comparison to be made. Otter Hounds, so often missing at smaller shows, had sixteen of their kind on hand for the competition.

Simultaneously with the hounds, the Terrier and Sporting Groups were judged. Mrs. Helen Gay minutely examined 136 Golden Retrievers, always one of the most popular breeds at any show, and gave the breed win to Ch. Libra Malagold Coriander. Dr. Arthur B. Ferguson judged the quality of 66 English Cocker Spaniels and decided on Ch. Amawalk Perrocay Qeqertaq. The Sporting Dogs in general constituted one of the most distinguished groups ever assembled in this country.

The 647 terriers were hardly less exciting. Mrs. Mareth K. Kipp had thirty-four Airedales to consider and finally selected Ch. Finlair Tiger of Stone Ridge, while James A. Boland chose Colored Bull Terrier Ch. Banbury Benson of Bedrock to represent that variety in the group that evening.

In each breed and variety, in each of Sunday's three groups, the judging went forward relentlessly. As smiling and happy as the owners and handlers appeared to be, as cordial and obliging as the judges and stewards certainly were, the show was winding up for the climax and the tension, although contained, was certainly felt. A win of any kind at this landmark show was important not only to one dog or bitch but also to its offspring and its kennel's name. A ribbon or trophy earned in Philadelphia that weekend would be a part of the history of dogdom in America. That thought was never far from anyone's mind, certainly not anyone for whom the dogs are a way of life or at least a major hobby.

By late in the evening 3 dogs out of 2,998 were left; an Irish Terrier, a Bloodhound, and a Golden Retriever. The terrier, Ch. Tralee's Rowdy Red, selected for the breed win by judge Dennis M. Barnes, had been as popular a choice as the other two in their breeds earlier in the day. The groups were judged by E. W. Tipton, Jr. (Sporting Group), Maxwell Riddle (Hound Group) and Michele L. Billings (Terrier Group). They followed a field trial exhibition and the Junior Showmanship Finals judged by Robert S. Forsyth. The Junior Showmanship winner was Penelope A. Bender showing a 15 inch Beagle.

And then there were seven: a Golden Retriever, a Bloodhound, a Doberman Pinscher, an Irish Terrier, a Maltese, a Bichon Frise and a German Shepherd Dog. One of them would go on to become the winner of the biggest dog show and one of the most distinguished events of any kind recorded by the dog fancy in North America. Other dogs were already home, others were on planes and trains, others in vans heading out to almost every state and province. But the mighty seven remained behind. William L. Kendrick had been waiting perhaps less than patiently in his hotel room and would not come to the Civic Center. He had not seen a catalog (and wouldn't until the show was over) and had not been told who the dogs would be or even what their breeds were. He probably had made some educated guesses as to what might be waiting for him, but no news had been allowed to pass his way.

There wasn't a dog in the huge arena that didn't have its champions in the audience. The individual breed fanciers, of course, had much to gain in pride if not in the value of the puppies their own dogs would produce in future years. Even people whose interests lay in different breeds than the seven represented on the floor had enthusiasm for their own group. The individual dogs had their fans. The atmosphere was charged as one might expect. But only one person could make the decision, William L. Kendrick. As experienced in the way of dog shows and judging as he is, he no doubt felt special pressure that night, and after allowing the anticipation to build—perhaps ignoring the individual cheering sections and probably not listening to the applause from all sides as each dog was moved and checked—he made his judgment. There were many people who were disappointed, but no one could fault his choice. German Shepherd Dog Number 6, Ch. Covy Tucker Hills Manhattan, one of the most distinguished representatives of the recently constituted Herding Group ever seen in this country, took the ribbon and silver trophies. The great show was over, and all that was left now were memories. For many, that was reward enough.

In recounting the events of any dog show, much less the biggest one of all, only a few names of dogs and judges can be even mentioned. I admit here to random sampling in mentioning names to give a sense of reality to all of those splendid dogs that did not get near the top of the pyramid in Philadelphia and to all of the judges who labored through the classes and best-of-breed selection so that the groups could be formed.

We have used a lot of numbers in this brief summary and that, too, is an inevitable hazard of reporting on a historical event: How many votes were cast? How many people were polled? How many dogs were judged? But, although they were not judged during those two days in Philadelphia, love and faith were elements at least as important as any other. Dogs, the first animals man domesticated and, for perhaps two hundred centuries, has made his favorite companion animal— out of about 2 million animal species—were given their day in November 1984 in Philadelphia; in fact, two very exciting days that will be remembered always by all who were there and recounted repeatedly to those who were not.

Show Committee (composed of the Directors of the American Kennel Club), American Kennel Club Centennial Dog Show and Obedience Trial, November 17, 18, 1984. Seated, Left to right: *Charles A. T. O'Neill (Executive Vice President, AKC, and Show Chairman), William F. Stifel (President, AKC), William Rockefeller (Chairman of the Board, AKC), John S. Ward (Treasurer, AKC, and Obedience Trial Chairman).* Standing, left to right: *Robert C. Graham, Alfred E. Treen, John A. LaFore, Jr., Haworth F. Hoch, David C. Merriam, W. Nelson Sills, E. Irving Eldredge, and Louis Auslander.*

Electric display atop the Philadelphia Electric Company's main offices in central Philadelphia, commemorating the Centennial Show as one of its distinctive events of the year.

The "moment of truth"—seconds before Judge William L. Kendrick indicates his choice for Best in Show, William F. Stifel, Charles A. T. O'Neill, and William Rockefeller (of the American Kennel Club) and J. A. MacDougall (Chairman of the Board, The Kennel Club, London, England), anxiously await his decision. To their left are the Best in Show Trophies—Best in Show Rosette, the AKC solid gold medallion, the antique sterling silver trophy from The Kennel Club (London, England), and in the background the antique silver tray donated by The Canadian Kennel Club (Toronto).

Charles A. T. O'Neill, William F. Stifel, Dr. Richard Meen (President of the Canadian Kennel Club) presenting the silver tray; Mr. William L. Kendrick, BIS Judge, presenting the BIS Rosette; James Moses, handler for owners Shirlee Braunstein and Jane Firestone, handling the canine who went for the gold and got it, Ch. Covy Tucker Hills Manhattan, German Shepherd; William Rockefeller presenting the AKC solid gold medallion; and J. A. MacDougal presenting their antique silver trophy.

Appendices

Presidents of the American Kennel Club

Major James M. Taylor

Major James M. Taylor was one of that small group of men who met in Philadelphia on September 17, 1884, to take some action concerning the state of the sport of dogs in America. Major Taylor's extensive activities in this and other related sports gave him a clear view of the situation. He knew that there was cheating at dog shows, such as the substitution of one dog for another. He was aware of the frequent intimidation of judges. He also realized that a reliable stud book was needed. At that Philadelphia meeting The American Kennel Club began.

It may have seemed to him at the time that this was only another one of his manifold activities on behalf of sport. His name appears frequently in the publication *American Field,* during this period. It reports the adoption of the AKC constitution and the election of Taylor as AKC president in its issue of November 1, 1884. (This took place on October 22, 1884.) Taylor is identified as a representative of the Cincinnati Bench Show Association.

American Field of October 10, 1885, reports on a meeting of the National Sportsmen's Convention at Saint Louis on September 29, 1885. Major Taylor appears to have been prominent in the proceedings. He made a speech in favor of outlawing spring shooting in order to preserve game birds and animals by giving the young a chance to grow to maturity. Thus, we gather that Major Taylor was active in bench shows and in field sports; he also seems to have been ahead of his time in the area of conservation. The infant AKC enjoyed the benefit of his prominence and prestige when he became its first president.

His presidency extended approximately fourteen months. On December 16, 1885, Major Taylor's resignation was accepted. Elliot Smith was unanimously elected as The American Kennel Club's second president. Underneath these events is a history of disagreeing factions in the AKC too complex and obscure to be fully comprehended nearly a century later. However, the record is clear on certain points. We know that Major Taylor continued to serve The American Kennel Club in various capacities for the rest of his life. He was a delegate from various clubs over the years. He represented the Kansas City Kennel Club between December 1890 and April 1892. In May 1893, he became the delegate of the Saint Louis Kennel Club, continuing through January 1895. Beginning in February 1895, he represented the Columbus Fanciers' Club. He remained as its delegate through March 1909, the year before his death. The pages of the *Gazette* attest to the faithfulness with which he attended and took part in AKC meetings.

In 1894, 1895, and 1896, Major Taylor was a member of the Advisory Committee, a forerunner of the AKC Board of Directors. He took an active part in the work of this committee. For instance, in 1894, he was a member of a committee of the AKC that was to confer with representatives of the Canadian Kennel Club concerning an agreement for cooperation between the two organizations. At one time, he offered to resign from the Advisory Committee because illness was preventing him from carrying out his duties temporarily. His resignation was not accepted.

Years before The American Kennel Club was founded, Mr. Taylor was a busy judge, both at bench shows and at field trials. He judged at the Westminster Show a number of times. He was still active in the first decade of the twentieth century, his well-known tall, bearded figure seen at shows in Boston, Rutherford, New Jersey, and other cities. He judged numerous breeds, mainly sporting dogs and hounds.

An adequate picture of James Taylor's career must include his work as a sporting journalist. Articles by him appeared in various sporting publications for many years. But his most important achievement was *Field Trial Records of Dogs in America,* published in 1907.

The book begins with a set of biographical essays about prominent field sportsmen of the day. These are full of courtly compliment and ornate prose. Today they are of interest mainly because they are so very representative of their period.

But when we approach the statistical section of the book, we find accuracy and completeness, an astonishing accomplishment for one man. Here are field-trial records extending from 1874 through the first half of 1907. Owners, dogs, sires and dams, handlers, prizes—all are included. Later students of the subject have found the book virtually free from error.

Major Taylor died at his home in Rutherford, New Jersey, on September 1, 1910.

Elliot Smith

Elliot Smith became The American Kennel Club's second president in December 1885. He served all of 1886 and part of 1887. He was one of the group that met in Philadelphia in 1884 to begin the work that resulted in the founding of The American Kennel Club. On the original slate of officers, he was first vice president.

We know that, when his presidency ended, he remained active in AKC affairs. He represented several dog clubs as delegate, beginning with the Pacific Kennel Club, during 1889. From February 1896 through January 1897, he was the delegate of the Westminster Kennel Club. He then became the delegate of the Oakland Kennel Club for a very brief period.

On September 17, 1894, a luncheon party was held at Delmonico's to celebrate the tenth anniversary of The American Kennel Club. One of the toasts offered was to the former officers of the club. Elliot Smith made a gracious response to the toast, and incidentally gave some insight into the period of his presidency. In part, he said: "Everything was novel; we had no example to follow nor avoid. Everyone had a different view to be discussed."

The Westminster Kennel Club shared Smith's time and energy with the AKC. Each year from 1892 to 1896, he was a member of its Bench Show Committee. In 1896, he was show chairman. Also, he was a member of Westminster's board of governors during the same years, 1892 through 1896.

At the present time, little personal information remains concerning the AKC's second president. Records show he was a native of Brooklyn. In 1887, Mrs. Elliot Smith showed a sable and white Collie at Westminster. This adds a bit of detail to his portrait; he was married, and it is reasonable to presume that he liked Collies.

William H. Child

In 1887 and the early part of 1888, William H. Child was President of The American Kennel Club, after having been second Vice President and then first Vice President.

Less information has survived concerning this third AKC President than about any of the others. He was a native of Philadelphia. He served as AKC delegate from the Philadelphia Kennel Club between February 1891 and November 1891. Soon thereafter, his name faded from AKC records, except that he continued to own a registered kennel name, Oakview, for some years. Otherwise, time has obscured the details of his life.

August Belmont, Jr.

August Belmont, Jr., was the second child of August Belmont and Caroline Perry Belmont. His mother was the daughter of Commodore Matthew Perry, who opened Japan to Western trade. His father had come to the United States in 1837 at the age of twenty-four as an agent of the House of Rothschild. He was on his way to Cuba on Rothschild business, but he never got there. Grasping immediately the financial possibilities of the panic of 1837, he opened a small office on Wall Street with almost no capital. He represented himself as the agent of the Rothschilds; he secured their approval of the venture afterward. Operating brilliantly on behalf the Rothschilds and for himself as well, he was soon a millionaire.

Though this first August Belmont had stopped formal schooling at fourteen to sweep and polish the Rothschild offices, he had extraordinary intelligence and discrimination. He became an art collector, an opera patron, a notably successful breeder of thoroughbred race horses. He admired the political system of his adopted country enough to devote time and money to political activity.

Thus, August Belmont, Jr., had a heritage of business and public service. When he became the fourth President of The American Kennel Club in 1888, he was the head of the great international banking firm that his father had founded. But he addressed the problems of this young organization as though nothing else required his attention.

In 1888, The American Kennel Club was in its fourth year of existence. August Belmont had come to it as a dog lover and breeder of Fox Terriers. He found an organization both small and unformed. An official 1886 report shows a balance of $49.15 in the club treasury. The nature and extent of the club's operation had not as yet been defined. Some dog fanciers even assumed that it would be a gentlemen's social club, a place for leisurely eating, drinking, and talk. But August Belmont apparently had from the beginning a clear-eyed perception of what the organization must become. He directed it steadily toward the goal.

He suggested that a publication chronicling official actions of the AKC was needed. And so the *Gazette* was begun in 1889. President Belmont personally guaranteed five thousand dollars each year for five years against possible losses.

The club has always been proud that not a penny of the President's money needed to be used.

Mr. Belmont supervised the incorporation of The American Kennel Club in 1906. A special charter was secured from New York State in 1908, setting out clearly the club's right to regulate dog shows and the stud book. He also negotiated with organizations in other countries, particularly Canada and Great Britain, setting up reciprocal relationships with them.

When August Belmont, Jr., resigned as President in 1916, because he could no longer devote the necessary time to AKC business, the AKC was recognizable as the organization existing today. It supervised the sport of pure-bred dogs throughout the United States. It was financially solid. Its integrity was respected.

Mr. Belmont's tenure of twenty-eight years has never been approached since. He died in 1924. His second wife, whom he married in 1910, survived until 1979, when she died at the age of one hundred. She was the former Eleanor Robson, a young actress prominent on the British stage when she married August Belmont. Thus her interest was almost inevitably directed toward the performing arts. Over the years, as she metamorphosed into the imperious grande dame of New York society, she devoted much money and attention to the needs of the Metropolitan Opera. She was the greatest factor in that company's survival during the Depression.

Through August Belmont, Jr., the AKC is linked to a fascinating and significant era in the social history of America.

Hollis H. Hunnewell

Hollis Horatio Hunnewell became the fifth President of the AKC after the departure of August Belmont, Jr., in 1916. He came from an old Massachusetts family whose lives reflected respect for the traditions of a gracious and solidly established way of life. He himself bore a name that belonged to his father before him and was passed down to his son. The family was based on an estate in the town of Wellesley. It was famous for its beautiful, extensive gardens.

In accordance with another respected tradition, the young man attended Harvard; he graduated in 1890. He was then able to pursue his personal interests, which were those of a sportsman. However, he was not a dilettante.

In the amusing book, *Life With Father,* Clarence Day remembers his own forceful father advising him with a misquotation from Scripture: ''Whatsoever thy hand findeth to do, do thy damnedest!'' It was some such principle that Horatio Hunnewell followed. One of his hobbies was the indoor court game of racquets. He became a nationally known player. He built the first squash court in the United States on the Hunnewell estate in Wellesley.

The other consuming interest in his life was the sport of dogs. He began early to breed Fox Terriers. Two years after his graduation from college, in 1892, he was granted the registered kennel name Hill Hurst. He became the Secretary of the American Fox Terrier Club in 1898, and its AKC delegate in 1899. He remained its Delegate for the rest of his life.

During those years, Mr. Hunnewell occupied many positions with the AKC. Some of these sound unfamiliar to us today, dating as they do from a time when the AKC was differently organized. He was, for example, President of the Associate Subscribers of AKC in 1899. In 1901, he was an AKC Vice President, and in 1909, first Vice President. His committee assignments were numerous. He had a reputation for faithful attendance at meetings, where the tasks essential to a complex operation,must be patiently performed.

August Belmont, Jr., withdrew as President in 1916 after twenty-eight years of service. Two decades of experience had prepared Horatio Hunnewell for what must have been the somewhat daunting prospect of succeeding Mr. Belmont. His presidency was capable and orderly, representing a smooth transition to a new era. He resigned in 1921 because of poor health; he died the following year. He was survived by his second wife, two daughters, and a son.

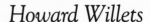

Howard Willets

The Willets family first came to America from England in 1638, a generation after the Pilgrims landed. They settled on Long Island, in an area that has since become part of the borough of Queens, a comfortable middle-class section of New York City. Today, Willets Point Boulevard runs adjacent to Shea Stadium and the site of two world's fairs.

Howard Willets, the sixth President of The American Kennel Club, was born in New York on April 6, 1861. He spent his life in the city and in Westchester County, a suburban area to the north. He attended Friends School in Brooklyn. Immediately afterward, he began his business career as a commission merchant. His partnership in Willets and Company began in 1885; it lasted until his death more than a half century later. His business interests were extended steadily, to include firms such as a Colorado coal company.

Howard Willets had an abiding interest in animals, encompassing horses, cattle, and dogs. He purchased the famous 250-acre Gedney Farms estate in Westchester County in 1898 from the Gedney family. There he maintained his herd of prize Jersey cattle. He raised dogs and harness horses. Gedney Farms became his registered kennel name in 1904. Mr. Willets might often be seen in those days driving a carriage and horses, with Dalmatians running under the coach, both horses and dogs bred at Gedney Farms. It was a prized local spectacle.

He was also an expert horseman. He owned the world's champion high jumper, Heatherbloom.

Mr. Willets began his association with the AKC at the time it was founded. He held various positions with the organization, culminating in the Presidency in 1921. He served until 1923, when he found that his personal responsibilities did not permit him to devote what he considered adequate time to his duties. He continued as a delegate, however.

Howard Willets died in 1938, at the age of 77. At that time, his home was on a piece of property that had originally been part of Gedney Farms; the farms had long since been converted into a successful residential subdivision. His second wife,

Elyse Young Willets, survived him. She had been associated with the AKC in 1923, when they were married. One of his sons, J. Macy Willets, also served as an AKC delegate.

John E. De Mund, M.D.

The only President of The American Kennel Club who was a physician was the seventh, Dr. John Emmons De Mund. His term lasted from 1923 to 1932. Documents of that time refer to his uncommon decisiveness and energy. With his help, the AKC managed to survive the first terrible years of the Depression without disaster.

Dr. De Mund was also prominent in a significant court case initiated by the AKC while he was President. It sued an Illinois organization calling itself The American Kennel Club. The defense was that the New York charter of the AKC (which had been secured by the foresight of August Belmont, Jr.) was valid in New York, but nowhere else. The Illinois court found for The American Kennel Club in 1924; it enjoined the Illinois organization from imitating The American Kennel Club in any way, including the use of its initials, seal, and certificates. This landmark decision confirmed the legal right of the AKC to regulate the registration and showing of pure-bred dogs all over the United States.

John E. De Mund was born in 1866 in the village of New Utrecht, now part of Brooklyn, New York. His father, Dr. Frederick Cornell De Mund, was also a well-known physician. The son was graduated from Rutgers College and from the College pf Physicians and Surgeons of Columbia University. He practiced medicine between 1890 and 1912. For some years, he was a member of the staff of the New York Eye and Ear Hospital, as an otolaryngologist.

In 1912, Dr. De Mund retired from medical practice to devote himself to his other interests, particularly pure-bred dogs and yachting. He was a delegate of the Russian Wolfhound (later known as the Borzoi) Club of America for many years.

He was second Vice President and first Vice President of the AKC before becoming President.

As chairman of the Brooklyn Yacht Club, Dr. De Mund sponsored one of the first-long distance ocean races for small craft. He himself sailed several times on the American challengers in the Lipton Cup yachting races.

A startling cloak-and-dagger touch is added to Dr. De Mund's biography by his activity during World War I: he was a secret agent for the United States Department of Justice.

He died on November 11, 1933, of a heart attack. He was survived by his wife, Elizabeth Little De Mund.

Charles T. Inglee

The eighth President of The American Kennel Club was Charles Topping Inglee. He was born in Brooklyn, New York, on December 18, 1877. As a child, he was what an earlier generation called "delicate." Because of his poor health, he spent a lot of time in the country, reaping the benefits of fresh air and sunshine. There he became interested in dogs.

He owned his first gundog when he was twelve. He showed dogs for the first time at a Long Island Kennel Club show in a skating rink in Brooklyn in 1895. These were English Setters. But he soon turned his attention to Gordon Setters. No breeder has been more closely identified with a particular breed of dog than Charles Inglee was with the Gordon Setter.

He did not introduce it to America; this was done by Daniel Webster, who, with a friend, acquired a pair from the Scottish Duke of Gordon in 1842. But he bred Gordons so successfully at his Inglehurst Kennels that he became known as "The Father of the American Gordon." He founded the Gordon Setter Club of America and was its delegate to the AKC during the 1920s.

By 1928, Mr. Inglee was second Vice President of The American Kennel Club. He became first Vice President in January 1932, and President in September 1932. Soon after, there was an extensive reorganization of the administration. Mr. Inglee resigned the presidency after five months in office. He took the newly created post of Executive Vice President, a position he held until his death on April 3, 1941.

Charles Inglee's business career centered in real estate. He was married to Eunice Baker and had one daughter, Jean. She became the wife of the artist Edwin Megargee, famous for his precise and sensitive drawings of dogs. Those who have visited the AKC library in New York City may have noticed the beautiful AKC bookplate, which was drawn by Edwin Megargee.

Russell H. Johnson, Jr.

Russell Hampden Johnson, Jr., was President of The American Kennel Club from 1933 to 1940.

He was a Pennsylvanian, born in 1878, the son of Dr. and Mrs. Russell H. Johnson. His education was at private schools in the Philadelphia area. After that, he entered the firm of Lawrence Johnson and Company, dealers in hides and goatskins. The business had been founded by his two uncles. Russell Johnson, Jr., was associated with it for the remainder of his life, for many of those years as president. He was married to the former Natalie M. Sauveur and had two daughters.

His love of pure-bred dogs began early; this has almost always been true of persons who have become prominent in the sport. Someone who visited the home of another AKC President when the future dignitary was a boy recalled shuffling along a floor " ankle deep in puppies." Mr. Johnson was never without a dog from the age of four. He owned, bred, and showed Airedale Terriers, Fox Terriers and other Terrier breeds as a very young man. He also developed into a respected judge of terriers.

His first official relationship with The American Kennel Club commenced in 1905. In that year, he became a delegate representing the Wissahickon Kennel Club; he continued to do so until his death. He became a director of the AKC a few years later, then second Vice President in 1932, first Vice President in 1933, and finally President in the same year.

A powerful, impressive figure, he was also devoted to active sports. As a boy, he played football at school. A few years later, he became an amateur rowing enthusiast. He was a well-known oarsman in four-oared and eight-oared shells. When he gave that up, he coached rowing crews.

At one time, he bred Jersey cattle. However, fine Terriers had priority. He had an active kennel for which he would travel to England to acquire promising dogs. These trips were made every year for over twenty-five years. He was a member of The Kennel Club (England). Participants in the sport of dogs from all over knew him and were his friends.

His term as ninth President ended abruptly on August 18, 1940, when he died of a heart attack. He has the sad distinction of being the only AKC President to die while in office.

Dudley P. Rogers

The lifespan of Dudley Pickman Rogers, tenth President of The American Kennel Club, extended over nearly a century. He was born on October 8, 1875, at Oakhill, Peabody, Massachusetts, and died on October 4, 1972, four days before his ninety-seventh birthday. He was born and bred a New Englander, with his existence centered in Massachusetts.

He attended Salem High School and the Hopkinson School. He was a member of Harvard's Class of 1896.

By the early years of the twentieth century, the name of Dudley P. Rogers was becoming familiar in the world of pure-bred dogs. He owned Brecknock Kennels, where he raised Sealyham Terriers. He showed several notable Sealyhams during the 1920s. He became the AKC delegate of the Eastern Dog Club in September 1925. In that same month, he was elected to the AKC Board of Directors; he remained an AKC director until his retirement in 1951, except for a brief period in 1931-1932, when the board was reorganized. He was also secretary of the Eastern Dog Club from 1925 to 1931, secretary-treasurer of the American Sealyham Terrier Club from 1928 to 1930, and for many years president of the Westminster Kennel Club.

After Russell H. Johnson, Jr., died in office, Mr. Rogers was called upon to take his place. He served as AKC President from 1940 to 1951.

At various times, he was a member of the firm of William A. Russell and Brothers, Boston, and a director of the Webster and Atlas National Bank and the American Locker Company.

His diverse concerns are reflected by membership in such organizations as the City Club of Boston, the Harvard Club of New York City—and the American Sheep Breeders Association. He was a dairy farmer and breeder of livestock in his late years; he enjoyed a sort of semiretirement at Danvers, Massachusetts, where he owned the Wetherfield Farm and Dairy.

Mr. Rogers married Mary Gertrude Sutton Russell, who predeceased him. He had a stepdaughter and a stepson.

William E. Buckley

William E. Buckley, eleventh President of The American Kennel Club, held the office from 1951 to 1968, the longest tenure in the club's history, with the single exception of August Belmont, Jr.,'s twenty-eight-year term.

Mr. Buckley was born January 23, 1900. He attended the Massachusetts

Institute of Technology and graduated from Trinity College at Hartford, Connecticut, in 1922. At Trinity, he was elected to Phi Beta Kappa. He received a law degree from Harvard Law School.

Early in life, his interest in dogs, particularly terriers, became evident. He owned his first Airedale Terrier when he was fourteen. By the time he became AKC President, he was already president of the Airedale Terrier Club of America. He and Mrs. Buckley owned Marbuck Kennels, where Airedales were the principal breed. But Wire Fox Terriers were also bred at the kennel. And the Buckleys owned other terriers on occasion such as Kerry Blues and Scottish Terriers.

Mr. Buckley was also president and director of the Suffolk County Kennel Club. He became AKC delegate from the Westbury Kennel Association in 1944. He was elected an AKC director in 1947, becoming President in 1951.

A unique contribution to the world of dogs, as well as to the American war effort, was made by William Buckley during World War II. In 1942, he organized Dogs for Defense. This was a voluntary civilian agency that encouraged dog owners to offer their dogs to the armed services, where the animals were trained for various kinds of war work. Mr. Buckley took charge of solving the inherent legal complexities. He continued as legal director and trustee until the organization could be dissolved after the war was over. It is considered by many persons that the prestige of dogs was much enhanced by their valuable war services given through Dogs for Defense.

During the many years of his work for the AKC and other organizations, Mr. Buckley was busy with his career as a distinguished attorney, a member of the Wall Street law firm, Buckley and Buckley. Finally, in 1968, the pressure of his law work made him resign from the presidency of The American Kennel Club.

William E. Buckley died on November 9, 1975.

Alfred M. Dick

In 1968 Alfred M. Dick became the twelfth President of The American Kennel Club. He assumed the post when William E. Buckley retired after serving in the presidency of the AKC for seventeen years.

Mr. Dick first joined the staff of the AKC as a field representative in October 1947. His performance in the position was such that he won the prestigious Gaines "Man of the Year" award in 1950. In 1951, the year that John C. Neff became Executive Vice President, he became Executive Secretary. They served together until Mr. Neff's retirement in 1964. At that time, Mr. Dick became Executive Vice President. Thus, he stepped into the Presidency in 1968 after seventeen years as an AKC officer.

His long relationship with pre-bred dogs began with his interest in the Dachshund. He became an exhibitor and subsequently a judge of the breed. In 1946, the Dachshund Club of America made him its delegate to the AKC. Later, he represented the Golden Gate Kennel Club and then the Tucson Kennel Club as delegate. In addition, he was at various times secretary of the Dachshund Club of America, President of the Kennel Club of Philadelphia, and an active member of the Bryn Mawr Kennel Club.

Alfred M. Dick was born in Philadelphia. After education in local schools, he attended the University of Pennsylvania. When he graduated, he entered the field of investment banking. There he made his career—until Dachshunds and the world of pure-bred dogs turned a hobby into a full-time preoccupation.

Mr. Dick retired from the presidency of the AKC in 1971. After retirement, he maintained his interest in pure-bred dogs by continuing to attend dog shows as often as possible.

John A. Lafore, Jr.

John A. Lafore, Jr., was born on May 25, 1905, in Bala, Pennsylvania. He attended the University of Pennsylvania as well as Swarthmore College. In 1933, he was married to Margaret Dexter Read, who shared his abiding interest in dogs.

Mr. Lafore was a Lieutenant Commander in the United States Navy during World War II. Afterward, he became active in political affairs. He served four consecutive terms in the Pennsylvania State Legislature, from 1950 to 1957. In 1957, he was called upon to fill the unexpired term of a member of the United States House of Representatives for the 13th District of Pennsylvania, and was then re-elected to serve a full term as Congressman. He was a member of the Congressional Ways and Means Committee.

In addition, he maintained a career in business. He was president of the Kellett Aircraft Corporation of Willow Grove, Pennsylvania, and financial Vice President of Day and Zimmerman, Philadelphia.

Even while he was busy in community service and business, Mr. Lafore became more and more involved in the world of pure-bred dogs. He and Mrs. Lafore began to breed Collies. In 1956, their attention became focused on the Keeshond. His varied dog-club affiliations reflected his growing interest. He was at various times, district director of the Collie Club of America, a first Vice President and President of the Keystone Collie Club, a Director of the Keeshond Club of America, and President of the Keeshond Club of Delaware Valley. In addition, he was a Director of the Chester Valley Kennel Club.

As early as 1953, Mr. Lafore was a delegate to The American Kennel Club, representing the Devon Dog Show Association. He became a member of the AKC Board of Directors in 1963. The board elected him Executive Vice President in 1968, and then President of the AKC in 1971.

Under his leadership, a definitive step was taken to cope with the avalanche of paperwork that threatened to engulf the AKC. This was a result of the huge spurt in registrations and show activity that occurred after World War II. The computerization of American Kennel Club records began.

Mr. Lafore also guided another movement toward the future, as women delegates from member clubs were accepted, and, at last, the AKC had its first woman Vice President.

John A. Lafore, Jr., retired in 1978. However, in *Pure-Bred Dogs/American Kennel Gazette,* those persons given to nostalgia might still see the name of the genial, competent man who had been the AKC's thirteenth President listed as Delegate and Director. When Mr. Lafore retired as President, he did not retire from service to The American Kennel Club.

William F. Stifel

William Frederick Stifel was elected the fourteenth President of The American Kennel Club on March 14, 1978.

Mr. Stifel joined the AKC staff as a part-time typist in August, 1957, and became a full-time employee three weeks later. He became Supervisor of the Show Plans and Show Records departments, and served in this capacity until 1964, when he was elected Executive Secretary. In 1976, he became Executive Vice-President and in 1978 was elected President. He was elected to the Board of Directors in 1977.

He was Chairman of the Beagle Advisory Committee from 1969 to 1977.

Mr. Stifel was born on June 6, 1922, in Toledo, Ohio. He studied at Western Reserve Academy and at Harvard University. During World War II, he served in the United States Coast Guard. He was married to Carolyn Graham in 1957; they have two daughters.

He is a member of the Westminster Kennel Club, the Westchester Kennel Club, and the Greater St. Louis Training Club, of which he is AKC Delegate. He served as Delegate of the San Francisco Dog Training Club from January, 1970, through December, 1971.

In 1982, Mr. Stifel received the Fido Award as Man of the Year from the Gaines Dog Research Center. The citation singled out his work in lifting The American Kennel Club to ''greater heights than ever before,'' and, specifically, ''his direction in bringing about major changes in the judge selection process and the standards for judges.''

Mr. Stifel represented The American Kennel Club at the first World Conference of Kennel Clubs held in London in 1978 and at the Second World Congress of Kennel Clubs in Edinburgh in 1981. He was Chairman of the third World Congress of Kennel Clubs, which was hosted by The American Kennel Club in Philadelphia in 1984.

Mr. Stifel was also founding President of The American Kennel Club Foundation, which, in 1980, established the Dog Museum of America.

B

AKC Directors

Chairmen of the Board

Alexander Feldman 1972-1977   **Haworth Hoch** 1979-1982

August Belmont 1977-1979   **Hon. William H. Timbers** 1982-1984

William Rockefeller 1984-

Below is a list of persons who have served as Directors of The American Kennel Club, together with a record of the clubs that they have represented as Delegates.

The Board of Directors was created in its present form in November 1906. From the AKC's founding in 1884 until March, 1897, the governing body was known as the Advisory Committee. Between March, 1897, and November, 1906, the governing body was the Executive Board.

The dates in parentheses after each name represent the years during which the person was a member of the AKC Board of Directors or one of the two predecessors noted above. Dates before 1897 show the individual was a member of the Advisory Committee. Dates between 1897 and 1906 refer to service on the Executive Board. Dates of 1906 and after refer to the Board of Directors.

Information on delegates comes from the AKC *Gazette,* which began publication in January 1889, with a personal financial guarantee from President Belmont. Delegate records for the first five years of the club's existence are not available any longer.

The names of AKC Presidents are starred.

(Each Tenure as delegate reflects the listing in the AKC Gazette rather than the actual date of election or resignation.)

Ackerman, Irving C. (1906-1907) Southwestern Kennel Club, Sept. 1906-Aug. 1912.

Albright, Andrew, Jr. (1910-1911)Monmouth County Kennel Club, Dec. 1909-Nov. 1911.

Allen, Samuel G. (1921-1925; 1929-1931) New York State Fair Dog Show, Nov. 1919-April 1925; Pointer Club of America, June 1929-Feb. 1931.

Anthony, James L. (1889-1893) Southern Field Trial Club, Jan. 1889-March 1890; Associate Members, April 1890-May 1893.

Appleton, James W. (1900-1916) National Beagle Club, May 1900-Oct. 1915.

Arnold, Walter. (1928-1931) Golden Gate Kennel Club of San Francisco, June 1928-July 1931. (Name changed to Golden Gate Kennel Club, Jan. 1929).

Auslander, Louis. (1984-   ) International Kennel Club of Chicago, June 1982-

Ball, Ancel H. (1906-1910) Pointer Club of America, May 1903-Nov. 1910.

Barclay, William L. (1909-1930) Airedale Terrier Club of America, May 1904-Nov. 1933.

Barrie, Caswell. (1926-1953) Oakland Kennel Club, May 1920-Feb. 1933; Hudson County Kennel Club, June 1933-March 1942; Minnesota Field Trial Association, April 1942-June 1946; Sahuaro State Kennel Club, Oct. 1946-Feb. 1954.

Bates, John G. (1906-1915; 1917-1922) Cedarhurst Kennel Club, Jan. 1906-Jan. 1910; Western Fox Terrier Breeders Association, May 1910-April 1914; Irish Terrier Club of America, May 1914-April 1922.

Bearse, Frederick A. (1930-1931) Boston Terrier Club of America, May 1924-Nov. 1945.

Belmont, August. (1968-1980) American Chesapeake Club, May 1964-Jan. 1981.

*Belmont, August, Jr. (1889-1916) Massachusetts Kennel Club, May 1909-Jan. 1914; Golden Gate Kennel Club of San Francisco, May 1914-Oct. 1922.

Belmont, Raymond. (1912-1916) Butterfly Branch Show Association, Sept. 1910-April 1912; Manchester Terrier Club, May 1912-Aug. 1912; American Foxhound Club, Sept. 1912-April 1914; Western Fox Terrier Breeders Association, Dec. 1914-Oct. 1915; National Beagle Club, Dec. 1915-April 1917.

Bernheimer, Charles D. (1911-1912) Associate Members, Feb. 1892-Jan. 1893; Southern California Kennel Club, Dec. 1895-Feb. 1898; North Jersey Kennel Club, Sept. 1910-Nov. 1911; Monmouth County Kennel Club, Dec. 1911-Aug. 1912.

Billings, W. C., M.D. (1923-1927) Englewood Kennel Club, May 1922-Aug. 1923; California Airedale Terrier Club, Oct. 1923-June 1936.

Bixby, Henry D. (1925-1936; 1943-1956) Scottish Terrier Club of America, June 1917-March 1948; Norwich Terrier Club, April 1948-March 1957.

Bleistein, George. (1907-1909) Buffalo Kennel Club, May 1903-Jan. 1917.

Blessing, Thomas A. (1963-1967) English Springer Spaniel Club of Michigan, June 1956-Dec. 1968.

Bloodgood, Hildreth K. (1897-1918) Associate Members, Feb. 1897-Jan. 1901; American Spaniel Club, Dec. 1902-Feb. 1918.

Boger, Edwin L. (1914-1925) Bulldog Club of America, Dec. 1909-Aug. 1925.

Brookfield, J. H. (1906-1909) Airedale Terrier Club of New York, May 1905-May 1909.

Brooks, Edward. (1894-1901; 1906-1913) New England Kennel Club, Dec. 1892-Nov. 1902; Ladies' Kennel Association of Massachusetts, April 1905-Jan. 1909; New England Kennel Club, Feb. 1909-Jan. 1911; Ladies' Kennel Club of California, Jan. 1911-Nov. 1913.

Brown, Hubert R. (1923-1928) Irish Terrier Club of America, Sept. 1922-March 1936.

Brownell, John A. (1951-1955) New England Dog Training Club, Oct. 1947-Feb. 1955; July 1970-June 1972.

Buchanan, Joseph A. (1914-1928) Philadelphia Bulldog Club, Dec. 1912-Aug. 1928.

*Buckley, William E. (1947-1968) Westbury Kennel Association, March 1944-Feb. 1969.

Burnhome, Clement M. (1930-1945) Lynn Kennel Club, Sept. 1921-Feb. 1945.

Burns, W. Chalmers. (1952-1963) Saw Mill River Kennel Club, April 1944-April 1963.

Cadwalader, Thomas. (1924-1928) Pacific Coast Collie Club, Dec. 1924-Feb. 1929.

Caesar, Harry I. (1936-1945) Monmouth County Kennel Club, Oct. 1935-March 1943; English Springer Spaniel Field Trial Association, April 1943-Sept. 1952.

Campbell, L. W. (1906-1909) Brunswick Foxhound Club, Feb. 1903-Nov. 1912. (Originally Brunswick Fur Club. Changed name Jan. 1905.)

Carnochan, Gouverneur M. (1897-1898; 1902-1907) Metropolitan Kennel Club, Dec. 1896-May 1898; Duquesne Kennel Club of Western Pennsylvania, Feb. 1899-March 1907.

Carruthers, Thomas H. III. (1936-1953) Cincinnati Kennel Club, Oct. 1932-March 1971.

Cleveland, Reginald M. (1919-1921) Shepherd Dog Club of America, Feb. 1919-Aug. 1924.

Codman, William C. (1907-1910) Bulldog Club of America, Sept. 1903-Dec. 1909; Rhode Island Kennel Club, Dec. 1897-April 1915.

Collier, Chester F. (1985-   ) San Francisco Dog Training Club, June 1972-

Collins, John F. (1913; 1916-1926) Long Island Kennel Club; Feb. 1909-Jan. 1926.

Conlan, Raymond J. (1956-1964) New England Beagle Club, June 1953-Feb. 1964.

Creuzbaur, R. W. (1918-1926) Irish Setter Club, May 1910-April 1923; Coronado Kennel Club, May 1923-May 1926. (Name changed to Coronado-San Diego Kennel Club, Dec. 1924.)

Croker, Richard, Jr. (1909-1910) Colorado Kennel Club, Sept. 1905-May 1913. (Name changed to Colorado Kennel and Intermountain Terrier Club during 1910. Returned to original name during 1911.)

Cromwell, H. B. (1893-1896) Collie Club of America, Dec. 1889-Aug. 1890; Westminster Kennel Club, Feb. 1892-Jan. 1895.

Cutler, Samuel R. (1909-1918) Revere Kennel Club, July 1906-Jan. 1918.

Dale, Joseph M. (1906-1909) Long Island Kennel Club, May 1903-Dec. 1906; Asbury Park Kennel Club, Oct. 1907-Dec. 1909.

*De Mund, John E., M.D. (1909-1913; 1916-1932) Russian Wolfhound Club, Sept. 1904-Nov. 1933. (Became Russian Wolfhound Club of America, Feb. 1927.)

Denby, Garvin. (1926-1931) Bay Kennel Club of Santa Cruz, May 1926-Sept. 1933.

De Ronde, Dr. John D. (1930) Pacific Coast Collie Club, Oct. 1929-Nov. 1930.

*Dick, Alfred M. (1967-1971) Dachshund Club of America, July 1946-March 1951; Golden Gate Kennel Club, July 1966-Sept. 1970; Tucson Kennel Club, Oct. 1970-Oct. 1971.

Drake, Craig F. R. (1906-1910) Mascoutah Kennel Club, May 1893-Jan. 1910.

Duncan, William Cary. (1927-1945) Irish Setter Club of America, May 1925-Nov. 1945.

Dwight, Edwin W. (1910-1911) Bay State Co-operative Bench Show Association, Feb. 1909-Jan. 1911.

Earle, William P. (1906-1907) Associate Subscribers, Jan. 1905-Jan. 1907.

Ebbets, William E. (1930-1936) Shepherd Dog Club of America, Sept. 1924-Nov. 1936. (Name changed to German Shepherd Dog Club of America, June 1931.)

Eddy, Spencer. (1919) Associate Delegates, Feb. 1919-Jan. 1920.

Edson, R. Stuart. (1909-1912) Collie Club of America, Feb. 1906-April 1912.

Eldredge, E. Irving. (1978-1985) Irish Setter Club of America, July 1967-March 1985.

Emery, William B. (1903-1909) New England Kennel Club, Dec. 1902-Jan. 1909.

Emmons, N. F. (1926-1930) Bull Terrier Club of America, May 1921-May 1930.

Eskrigge, Frank T. (1930-1931) Middlesex County Kennel Club, Feb. 1921-May 1948.

Feldman, Alexander. (1964-1977) Great Dane Club of America, July 1956-Oct. 1963; Saw Mill River Kennel Club, Nov. 1963-March 1983.

Flammer, George A. (1931) New Jersey Beagle Club, March, 1928-July 1941.

Fleitmann, Henry T. (1914-1919) American Sealyham Terrier Club, Sept. 1913-Nov. 1917; June 1932-May 1936.

Foote, H. T. (1898-1902) Toledo Kennel Club, Dec. 1890-Nov. 1891; Associate Members, Dec. 1892-Jan. 1897; Metropolitan Kennel Club, May 1898-Jan. 1902; Atlanta Kennel Club, May 1902-Feb. 1904; Scottish Terrier Club of America, May 1906-Feb. 1907.

Ford, W. Fred. (1930-1931) Greyhound Club of America, Oct. 1929-Feb. 1934.

Gamewell, John A. (1923-1931) Ladies' Kennel Association of Massachusetts, Feb. 1923-March 1931.

Gillette, Abram D. (1906-1909; 1913) Champlain Kennel Club, Sept. 1905-Jan. 1910; Lehigh Valley Kennel Club, Dec. 1911-Nov. 1913.

Gilliland, C. L. (1921-1924) Delaware County Kennel Club, Sept. 1920-Jan. 1925.

Glass, Dr. Alexander. (1929-1931) English Setter Club of America, May 1927-June 1931.

Goodsell, P. Hamilton. (1924-1932) Westchester Kennel Club, Dec. 1921-April 1926; New York State Fair Dog Show, May 1926-May 1932. (In April 1928, name changed to New York State Fair.)

Graham, Robert C. (1972-   ) Central New York Kennel Club, Oct. 1959-Oct. 1978; Tampa Bay Kennel Club, Nov. 1978-

Graham, Walter J. (1927-1931) Westbury Kennel Association, May 1926-May 1927; Coronado-San Diego Kennel Club, Sept. 1927-Feb. 1930; Queensboro Kennel Club, June 1930-Dec. 1932; Oakland Kennel Club, Oct. 1933-Aug. 1936.

Greer, George. (1910-1925) Westchester Kennel Club, Feb. 1907-Jan. 1920; American Spaniel Club, Feb. 1920-May 1940.

Gurnee, W. S., Jr. (1913) Santa Clara County Kennel Club, Feb. 1911-Jan. 1914.

Halpin, Lt. Comdr. Thomas M. (1945-1949) Chicago Collie Club, Oct. 1928-July 1958.

Harriman, O. Carley. (1917-1919) Great Dane Club of America, May 1916-Aug. 1917.

Hartman, George H. (1945-1952; 1957-1964) American Fox Terrier Club, July 1937-June 1942; St. Louis Collie Club, Jan. 1943-Sept. 1945; Kennel Club of Philadelphia, Oct. 1945-Feb. 1964.

Hartmann, Thomas W. C. (1927-1928) International Toy Poodle Club, Dec. 1913-Dec. 1928.

Heaney, Rev. F. J. (1924-1926) Oakland and Alameda County Kennel Club, Sept. 1923-Jan. 1926. (Became Oakland Kennel Club, 1925.)

Hitchcock, Wilbur Kirby. (1926-1930) Akron Kennel Club, May 1925-Feb. 1928; Old English Sheepdog Club of America, March 1928-Nov. 1947.

Hoch, Haworth F. (1970-1984) Mississippi Valley Kennel Club, April 1966-

Hooley, A. G. (1910-1918) Piping Rock Kennel Club, Dec. 1909-April 1914; Associate Delegates, Feb. 1914-Jan. 1918.

Hooley, George B. (1921-1927) New Jersey Beagle Club, Feb. 1919-Oct. 1927.

Hritzo, Dr. Robert J. (1985-   ) Mahoning-Shenango Kennel Club, June 1973-

Hungerland, Dr. Jacklyn E. (1985-   ) Del Monte Kennel Club, March 1976-

*Hunnewell, Hollis H., Jr. (1896-1921) American Fox Terrier Club, March 1896-Jan. 1922.

Hunt, Douglas L. (1952) Birmingham Kennel Club, Jan. 1943-Aug. 1952.

Hunt, Richard H. (1909-1910) French Bulldog Club of America, May1905-April 1910.

Hutchinson, William J. (1925-1928; 1932-1933) Englewood Kennel Club, Dec. 1923-Sept. 1930; Ladies' Kennel Association of America, June 1932-Sept. 1936.

*Inglee, Charles T. (1925-1941) Gordon Setter Club of America, Dec. 1924-April 1941.

Jacobberger, H. Fred. (1964-1979) Nebraska Kennel Club, Oct. 1954-July 1979.

*Johnson, Russell H., Jr. (1909-1940) Wissahickon Kennel Club, May 1905-Aug. 1940.

Keasbey, Rowland P. (1906-1923) San Francisco Kennel Club, Dec. 1902-Dec. 1909; Bergen County Kennel Club, Dec. 1909-Jan. 1912; Spaniel Breeders' Society, Sept. 1912-Nov. 1915; Pacific Coast Cocker Spaniel Club, May 1915-April 1923.

Kelly, Charles A. (1918-1927) Colorado Kennel Club, Sept. 1916-July 1927.

Keyes, Charles W. (1913-1917) Wisconsin Kennel Club, Dec. 1905-Jan. 1917.

Kinney, Morris. (1916-1919; 1921-1923; 1925-1926) Garden City Kennel Club, Sept. 1916-Jan. 1919; Westchester Kennel Club, Sept. 1920-Nov. 1921; Old English Sheepdog Club of America, May 1922-Oct. 1927.

Knight, Edward Dana. (1942-1946) Tri-State Kennel Association, July 1941-Jan. 1959.

Kobler, Henry B., M.D. (1929-1931) Devon Dog Show Association, Feb. 1927-May 1932; Capital City Kennel Club, March 1933-May 1945.

Korbel, Anton B. (1950-1954) Golden Gate Kennel Club, Oct. 1947-Nov. 1950; Sun Maid Kennel Club of Fresno, Sept. 1950-Jan. 1957.

Kramer, Adolph F. (1944) Chicago Bulldog Club, June 1936-Oct. 1944.

Kunca, Adolph F. (1970-1978) Trenton Kennel Club, Nov. 1963-June 1974; Bedlington Terrier Club of America, July 1974-

*Lafore, John A., Jr. (1963-   ) Devon Dog Show Association, Jan. 1954-

Lauder, George, Jr. (1909-1915) Scottish Terrier Club of America, Feb. 1907-May 1909; West Highland White Terrier Club, Sept. 1909-Dec. 1915.

Lawrence, Effingham. (1918-1919) West Highland White Terrier Club, Sept. 1916-Jan. 1922.

Lederer, Alison M. (1915-1916) Colorado Kennel Club, Aug. 1913-Aug. 1916.

Lloyd, Francis G. (1916-1921) Associate Delegates, Feb. 1916-Sept. 1920.

Lord, Franklin B., Jr. (1909-1910) Welsh Terrier Club of America, Sept. 1907-April 1915; Westminster Kennel Club, June 1930-Sept. 1945.

Lothrop, Samuel K., Jr. (1977-1979) Standard Schnauzer Club of America, July 1972-April 1979.

Lundeen, J. Wen. (1952-1960) Atlanta Kennel Club, July 1944-Feb. 1967.

McKean, Q. A. Shaw. (1917-1929) Western Fox Terrier Breeders' Association, May 1916-Oct. 1940.

Maclay, Alfred B. (1912-1922) Dalmatian Club of America, May 1909-April 1937.

MacMonnies, Wallace. (1928-1932) Chow Chow Club, May 1926-May 1932.

Meade, James E. (1918-1921) Seattle Kennel Club, Dec. 1916-Jan. 1921.

Megargee, S. Edwin, Jr. (1928-1931) Los Angeles Kennel Club, Sept. 1927-Sept. 1929; Louisiana Kennel Club, June 1930-March 1958.

Merriam, Hon. David C. (1979-   ) Bull Terrier Club of America, Nov. 1978-

Merritt, Thomas W. (1953-1970) Midwest Field Trial Club, April 1941-June 1971.

Metz, William A. (1977-1979) Mid-Del-Tinker Kennel Club, April 1976-July 1979.

Milbank, Samuel, M.D. (1933) Welsh Terrier Club of America, May 1922-Sept. 1945.

Mohr, Howard K. (1929-1931) Pacific Coast Boston Terrier Club, Sept. 1927-Dec. 1931.

Moore, Dwight, (1906-1913) Associate Delegates, Jan. 1905-Jan. 1914.

Morris, Monson. (1906-1909; 1927-1931) Rockland County Industrial Association, Sept. 1905-Jan. 1908; Irish Wolfhound Club of America, May 1927-Jan. 1931.

Morse, Tyler. (1912-1917) Old English Sheepdog Club of America, May 1910-April 1922.

Mortimer, James. (1906-1913) Ladies' Kennel Association of America, Sept. 1900-Sept. 1915.

Murr, Louis J. (1930-1931) Pasadena Kennel Club, Jan. 1929-Dec. 1938.

Muss-Arnolt, G. (1906-1909) Pointer Club of America, May 1892-Dec. 1893; Great Dane Club of America, Jan. 1898-Dec. 1904; American Dachshund Club, Jan. 1905-Aug. 1910.

Neff, John C. (1946-1977) Skokie Valley Kennel Club, July 1942-June 1946; Irish Setter Club of America, July 1946-Sept. 1965; Hawaiian Kennel Club, Oct. 1965-Nov. 1982.

Neilson, C. Frederick. (1917-1923) California Airedale Terrier Club, May 1916-Jan. 1923.

Ober, Harold. (1921-1929) Associate Delegates, Sept. 1921-Jan. 1924; Pacific Cocker Spaniel Club, Feb. 1924-Feb. 1935.

Offerman, Theodore. (1914-1921; 1926-1931) Scottish Terrier Club of America, May 1905-April 1906; American Pomeranian Club, May 1909-Aug. 1921; Airedale Terrier Club of New York, Feb. 1923-March 1937.

Ogilvie, William E. (1949-1953) International Kennel Club of Chicago, July 1940-April 1969.

Oldham, E. M. (1895-1897) American Spaniel Club, Sept. 1891-Aug. 1897.

O'Neill, Charles A. T. (1971-   ) Doberman Pinscher Club of America, May 1965-

Osgood, Dr. F. H. (1909-1914) Boston Terrier Club, Jan. 1905-Jan. 1913; Lynn Kennel Club, Feb. 1913-Feb. 1914.

Palmer, M. Mowbray. (1910-1917) Greyhound Club of America, May 1909-April 1910; Golden Gate Kennel Club of San Francisco, May 1910-April 1912; Collie Club of America, May 1912-March 1914.

Parker, Howard P. (1953-1963) St. Bernard Club of America, October 1949-April 1963.

Perry, Dr. J. Frank. (1889-1894) Associate Members, April 1889-Jan. 1892; Keystone Kennel Club, Jan. 1893-Jan. 1894.

Peters, Harry T. (1906-1907) Westminster Kennel Club, Dec. 1904-Sept. 1907.

Post, George B., Jr. (1909-1910) Southern Beagle Club, Sept. 1905-Jan. 1910.

Price, J. Sergeant, Jr. (1907-1912; 1919-1929) Atlantic City Kennel Club, Dec. 1903-Nov. 1911; Delaware State Fair, Nov. 1919-Nov. 1921; Kennel Club of Atlantic City, Dec. 1921-April 1925; Kennel Club of Philadelphia, May 1925-March 1940.

Proctor, William Ross. (1946-1968) American Sealyham Terrier Club, Dec. 1917-April 1922; Del Monte Kennel Club, April 1939-July 1947; American Sealyham Terrier Club, April 1947-March 1971.

Proctor, W. Ross. (1916-1921) Welsh Terrier Club of America, May 1915-April 1922.

Rauch, William. (1907-1924) Westminster Kennel Club, Sept. 1907-Nov. 1925.

Reick, William C. (1892-1894) St. Bernard Club of America, Sept. 1892-Jan. 1896.

Remick, Major J. Gould. (1945-1953) Cardigan Welsh Corgi Club, July 1939-March 1956.

Rickel, Cyrus K. (1955-1963) Fort Worth Kennel Club, Oct. 1952-Jan. 1972.

Rieger, Harry G. (1924-1930) Gwynedd Valley Kennel Club, Sept. 1920-Dec. 1938.

Ritchey, Daniel P. (1922-1925) Toy Spaniel Club of America, Sept. 1921-Oct. 1925.

Rockefeller, William. (1979-   ) Tucson Kennel Club, Feb. 1958-March 1970; Westminster Kennel Club, April 1970-

Rockefeller, William A. (1958-1972) Bedlington Terrier Club of America, July 1950-Oct. 1973.

Rockefeller, William G. (1903-1915) Associate Delegates, Feb. 1903-Jan. 1916.

Rodman, Charles W., Jr. (1901-1903)Dog Owners' Protective Association of Cincinnati, Dec. 1899-Jan. 1902; Chicago Kennel Club, Feb. 1902-Nov. 1903.

*Rogers, Dudley P. (1925-1952) Eastern Dog Club, Sept. 1925-Sept. 1954.

Rogers, William B. (1933-1943) West Highland White Terrier Club of America, March 1928-Feb. 1944.

Rutherfurd, Winthrop. (1907-1912) Associate Delegates, Feb. 1907-Jan. 1912.

Savage, Clarence L. (1972-1977) Santa Ana Valley Kennel Club, Jan. 1967-Dec. 1976; Kennel Club of Beverly Hills, Jan. 1977-Jan. 1978.

Sawyer, W. H. (1912-1913) Nassau County Kennel Club, Dec. 1911-Jan. 1914.

Schellhass, Hermann F. (1896-1899) National Beagle Club, Jan. 1889-Nov. 1899.

Scribner, Charles A. (1946-1950) Cairn Terrier Club of America, July 1945-Feb. 1952.

Scudder, Townsend. (1919-1923) Ohio Valley Kennel Club, Feb. 1919-Jan.

1923; Southampton Kennel Club, June 1932-July 1939.

Sedgwick, Robert, Jr. (1914) Greyhound Club of America, May 1913-April 1914.

Sills, A. Nelson. (1980-   ) Labrador Retriever Club, April 1980-

Sinnott, John. (1916-1920; 1923-1927) Devon Dog Show Association, Dec. 1913-Jan. 1927.

Smalley, William L. (1928-1951) Japanese Spaniel Club of America, June 1928-Feb. 1933; Mid-Jersey Field Dog Club, June 1933-July 1945; Plainfield Kennel Club, Aug. 1945-Oct. 1955.

Smith, B. S. (1906-1915) Welsh Terrier Club of America, Dec. 1900-June 1907; Associate Subscribers, Feb. 1907-Jan. 1914.

Smith, Chetwood. (1906-1921) New England Beagle Club, May 1906-Jan. 1922.

Steiner, Richard P. (1964-1974) Longshore-Southport Kennel Club, May 1962-Dec. 1969; San Mateo Kennel Club, Jan. 1970-

Stewart, Harry B., Jr. (1954-1958) Cairn Terrier Club of America, Oct. 1952-Aug. 1962.

Stewart, Ralph C. (1912-1930) Erie Kennel Club, Feb. 1911-March 1930.

*Stifel, William F. (1977-   ) San Francisco Dog Training Club, Jan. 1970-Dec. 1971; Greater St. Louis Training Club, July 1977-

*Taylor, Major James M. (1894-1896) Kansas City Kennel Club, Dec. 1890-April 1892; St. Louis Kennel Club, May 1893-Jan. 1895; Columbus Fanciers' Club, Feb. 1895-March 1909.

Tennant, Col. W. Brydon. (1926-1940) Cairn Terrier Club of America, May 1925-Dec. 1940.

Terhune, Albert Payson. (1922-1925; 1928-1930) Ladies' Kennel Association of Massachusetts, Dec. 1921-April 1922; Collie Club of America, May 1922-Nov. 1924; Puget Sound Kennel Club, Dec. 1924-April 1930.

Terry, Thomas H. (1889-1895) Collie Club of America, Jan. 1889-Nov. 1889; Westminster Kennel Club, Dec. 1889-Jan. 1892; Associate Members, June 1893-Jan. 1895; Westminster Kennel Club, Feb. 1895-Jan. 1896.

Tharp, Harold B. (1953-1957) Hossier Kennel Club, April 1951-Dec. 1958.

Thorndike, John R. (1916-1917) Irish Terrier Club of America, May 1915-April 1917.

Timbers, Hon. William H. (1968-1984) Ox Ridge Kennel Club, Jan. 1966-

Trachtman, Hilbert I. (1969-1971) Suffolk County Kennel Club, Jan. 1951-April 1978.

Treen, Alfred E. (1979-1985) Waukesha Kennel Club, April 1969-

Tucker, William R., Jr. (1922-1923; 1933-1945) West Highland White Terrier Club, Feb. 1922-Jan. 1924; Manchester Terrier Club of America, Oct. 1932-March 1940; Kennel Club of Philadelphia, April 1940-March 1945.

Untermyer, Alvin. (1910-1913) Fairfield County Kennel Club, Feb. 1909-Feb. 1913.

Van Court, Albert E. (1966-1970) Ventura County Dog Fanciers' Association, Jan. 1954-June 1968; Kennel Club of Beverly Hills, July 1968-April 1970.

Van Schaick, Edwin J. (1906-1909) Portland Kennel Club, Jan. 1906-Jan. 1915.

Van Schaick, Singleton. (1906-1913) Irish Terrier Club of America, May 1898-June 1913.

Vita, Marcel. (1898-1909) American Spaniel Club, Sept. 1897-Aug. 1902; Spaniel Breeders' Society, Sept. 1902-Aug. 1912.

Wall, J. S. (1921-1924) Associate Subscribers, Feb. 1921-Feb. 1924.

Wallace, Mahlon B., Jr. (1940-1944) Mississippi Valley Kennel Club, June 1932-March 1966.

Ward, Harold R. (1941-1946) Minneapolis Kennel Club, Oct. 1936-June 1948.

Ward, John S. (1974-   ) Old Dominion Kennel Club of Northern Virginia, Feb. 1960-Dec. 1969; Mount Vernon Dog Training Club, Jan. 1970-

Warren, Bayard. (1923-1924) American Sealyham Terrier Club, Jan. 1922-May 1932.

Watson, James. (1895-1898) American Spaniel Club, Sept. 1889-April 1891; Southern California Kennel Club, May 1891-Aug. 1895; Collie Club of America, Oct. 1895-April 1902; Colorado Kennel Club, Sept. 1902-Feb. 1904; Seattle Dog Fanciers' Association, Jan. 1905-Sept. 1907.

Webster, Charles D. (1963-1969) Newfoundland Club of America, July 1954-June 1971.

Webster, Frederic S. (1895-1897) Washington City Kennel Club, Jan. 1889-April 1894; Northwestern Beagle Club, Sept. 1894-Jan. 1897.

Werber, Charles H., Jr. (1953-1966) Beverly Hills Kennel Club, July 1945-June 1949; (name changed to Beverly-Riviera Kennel Club, May 1948); Scottish Terrier Club of America, July 1949-June 1970.

West, George S. (1913-1925) Eastern Dog Club, May 1913-August 1925.

*Willets, Howard. (1906-1929) Associate Subscribers, Feb. 1904-Dec. 1904; San Mateo Kennel Club, Feb. 1906-Sept. 1936.

Willets, J. Macy. (1914-1928) New London Kennel Club, May 1911-April 1916; Spaniel Breeders' Society, May 1916-Oct. 1940.

Williston, Samuel H. (1960-1964) California Airedale Terrier Club, July 1957-April 1964.

Wilmerding, A. Clinton. (1895-1903; 1910-1916) New Jersey Kennel Club, Jan. 1889-May 1891; Associate Members, Feb. 1893-Jan. 1903; Santa Cruz County Kennel Club, Feb. 1910-Jan. 1915; Plainfield Kennel Club, Feb. 1915-Dec. 1916; Rochester Dog Protective Association, March 1933-Dec. 1953.

Wise, Hon. John S. (1889-1893) Virginia Field Sports Association, Jan. 1889-Dec. 1893.

Wolcott, William Prescott. (1915-1930) Manchester Terrier Club, May 1913-Aug. 1921; Whippet Club of America, Sept. 1921-May 1924; Brockton Agricultural Society, Sept. 1924-May 1930.

Wood, Charles R. (1913-1923) Gwynedd Valley Kennel Club, Feb. 1911-Nov. 1916; Newfoundland Club of America, Dec. 1916-June 1927.

Woodward, Edwin S. (1923-1924) Pinehurst Kennel Club, Sept. 1922-Dec. 1925.

Member Clubs

NAME OF CLUB	ELECTED	DROPPED
Afghan Hound Club of America	1940	current
Airedale Terrier Club of America	1901	current
Airedale Terrier Club of New York	1901	1901
	1905	1946
Akron Kennel Club	1921	1958
Akron Poultry and Kennel Club	1893	1894
Alameda County Sportsman's Association	1894	1897
Alaskan Malamute Club of America	1953	current
Albany Dog Club	1916	1918
Albany Kennel Club	1889	1890
	1946	current
All-Breed Training Club of Akron	1954	current
Allegheny County Agricultural Society	1939	1945
Altoona Kennel Club	1905	1909
American Bedlington Terrier Club	1896	1898
American Belgian Tervuren Club	1980	current
American Bloodhound Club	1958	current
American Bouvier des Flandres Club	1971	current
American Boxer Club	1935	current
American Brittany Club	1936	current
(Brittany Spaniel Club of North America until 1944)		
American Brussels Griffon Association	1982	current
American Bullmastiff Association	1964	current
American Chesapeake Club	1918	current
American Dachshund Club	1896	1910
American English Beagle Club	1889	1889
American English Setter Club	1901	1902
American Field Trial Club	1889	1890
American Foxhound Club	1912	current

American Fox Terrier Club	1886	current
American Gordon Setter Club	1889	1890
American Lhasa Apso Club	1974	current
American Maltese Association	1969	current
American Manchester Terrier Club	1938	current
(American Toy Manchester Terrier Club until 1958)		
American Mastiff Club	1889	1897
American Miniature Schnauzer Club	1933	current
American Pet Dog Club	1889	1901
American Pointer Club	1938	current
American Pomeranian Club	1900	current
American Pug Club	1897	1900
American Scottish Terrier Club	1895	1897
American Sealyham Terrier Club	1913	current
American Shetland Sheepdog Association	1929	current
American Shih Tzu Club	1981	current
American Spaniel Club	1889	current
American Whippet Club	1930	current
Anderson Kennel Club	1936	current
Androscoggin Kennel Club	1892	1894
Anthracite Kennel Association	1907	1908
Arizona Kennel Club	1917	1918
Arkansas Kennel Club	1951	current
Asbury Park Kennel Club	1906	1909
Asheville Kennel Club	1937	current
Atlanta Kennel Club	1900	1904
	1906	1907
	1916	current
Atlanta Obedience Club	1971	current
Atlantic City Kennel Club	1902	1912
Augusta Kennel Club	1977	current
Aurora Kennel Club	1902	1904
Austin Kennel Club	1900	1901
	1947	current
Australian Terrier Club of America	1977	current
Back Mountain Kennel Club	1949	current
Badger Dog Club	1918	1923
Badger Kennel Club	1956	current
Baltimore County Kennel Club, Inc.	1939	current
Baltimore Kennel Association	1896	1899
Bar Harbor Kennel Club	1902	1909
Basenji Club of America	1957	current
Basset Hound Club of America	1937	current
Battle Creek Kennel Club	1966	current
Bay Kennel Club of Santa Cruz	1925	1933
Bay State Cooperative Bench Show Association	1903	1911
Bay State Kennel Club	1902	1903
Bay State Kennel Club of Southern California	1913	1919

Beaver County Kennel Club	1956	current
Bedlington Terrier Club of America	1936	current
Belgian Sheepdog Club of America	1925	1935
	1949	current
Berks County Kennel Club	1929	current
Bergen County Kennel Club	1907	1912
Bernese Mountain Dog Club of America	1981	current
Bexar Field Trials Club	1891	1894
Bichon Frise Club of America	1984	current
Binghamton Industial Exposition	1895	1897
	1902	1922
Birmingham Kennel Club	1916	1930
	1935	current
Blennerhassett Kennel Club	1980	current
Bloodhound Club of America	1895	1921
Bloomington Kennel Club	1899	1900
Blue Grass Kennel Club	1891	1894
Border Terrier Club of America	1980	current
Borzoi Club of America	1904	current
(Russian Wolfhound Club of America until 1936)		
Boston Terrier Club of America	1893	current
Branford Driving Park Kennel Club	1904	1904
Briard Club of America	1935	current
Bridgewater Kennel Club	1923	1925
Brockton District Kennel Club	1905	1911
Brockton Fair Kennel Club	1919	1958
(Brockton Agricultural Society until 1950)		
Bronx County Kennel Club	1920	current
Brookhaven Kennel Club	1984	current
Brunswick Foxhound Club	1894	1949
Brunswick Fur Club	1894	1905
Brussels Griffon Club of America	1915	1920
	1932	1938
Bryn Mawr Kennel Club	1903	1911
	1921	current
Buckeye Beagle Club	1920	current
Bucks County Kennel Club	1945	current
Buffalo Kennel Club	1890	1897
Bulldog Club of America	1890	current
Bulldog Club of New England	1946	current
Bulldog Club of Philadelphia	1912	current
Bull-Mastiff Club of America	1935	1942
Bull Terrier Breeders' Association	1905	1910
Bull Terrier Club of America	1897	current
Bull Terrier Club of San Francisco	1906	1906
Burlington County Agricultural Society	1892	1895
Burlington County Kennel Club	1950	current
Butler County Kennel Club	1949	current

Butterfly Bench Show Association	1896	1900
Cairn Terrier Club of America	1917	current
California Airedale Terrier Club	1910	current
California Cocker Club	1909	1910
California Collie Clan	1897	1899
(California Collie Club until 1946)	1945	current
California Kennel Club	1890	1896
California Scottish Terrier Club	1913	1918
California State Poultry and Kennel Association	1896	1899
Camden County Kennel Club	1934	current
Canobie Kennel Club	1906	1907
Canonsburg Kennel Club	1904	1905
Canton Kennel Club	1917	1930
Cape Cod Kennel Club	1982	current
Capital City Kennel Club	1900	1902
	1922	1945
Capital Dog Training Club of Washington, D.C.	1949	current
Cardigan Welsh Corgi Club of America	1935	current
(Cardigan Welsh Corgi Club until 1961)		
Carolina Dog Training Club	1975	current
Carolina Kennel Club	1938	current
Catonsville Kennel Club	1949	current
Cedarhurst Kennel Club	1905	1909
Cedar Rapids Kennel Association	1951	current
Central Beagle Club	1896	1897
	1905	current
Central City Kennel Club	1890	1894
Central Florida Kennel Club	1948	current
Central Iowa Kennel Club	1973	current
Central New York Kennel Association	1909	1922
Central New York Kennel Club	1909	1921
	1928	current
Central Ohio Kennel Club	1949	current
Chain O'Lakes Kennel Club	1953	current
Champlain Kennel Club	1901	1921
Charleston Kennel Club	1938	current
Chattahoochee Valley Exposition Company	1889	1890
Chattanooga Kennel Club	1953	current
Chesapeake Bay Dog Club	1890	1892
Cheshire Kennel Club	1957	current
Chester Kennel Club	1906	1909
Chester Valley Kennel Club	1950	current
Chicago Bulldog Club	1936	current
Chicago Collie Club	1909	current
Chicago Pet Dog Club	1900	1902
Chihuahua Club of America	1923	current
Chow Chow Club	1906	current
Cincinnati Kennel Association	1904	1918

Cincinnati Kennel Club	1890	1893
	1922	current
Cincinnati Sportsman's Club	1885	1890
City of the Straits Kennel Club	1893	1899
Clermont County Kennel Club	1983	current
Cleveland All-Breed Training Club	1948	current
Cleveland Bench Show Association	1887	1890
Cleveland Fanciers' Club Company	1911	1917
Cleveland Kennel Club	1890	1904
Cocker Spaniel Breeders Club of New England	1933	current
Cocker Spaniel Club of California	1898	1898
Collie Club of America	1887	current
Colorado Kennel Club	1901	current
Colorado Kennel and Intermountain Terrier Club	1909	1911
Colorado Springs Kennel Club	1979	current
Columbia County Agricultural Society	1901	1903
Columbia County Kennel Club	1894	1896
	1922	1927
Columbia Kennel Club	1970	current
Columbus Fanciers Club	1889	1897
Columbus Kennel Club	1909	1910
Conemaugh Valley Kennel Club	1907	1910
Connecticut State Kennel Club	1889	1889
Continental Kennel Club	1889	1889
Contra Costa County Kennel Club	1949	current
Coshocton Kennel Club	1902	1904
Corn Belt Kennel Club	1954	current
Cornhusker Kennel Club of Lincoln, Nebraska	1956	current
(Cornhusker Kennel Club until 1972)		
Coronado Kennel Club	1923	1925
Coronado-San Diego Kennel Club	1925	1930
Coulee Kennel Club	1963	current
Council Bluffs Kennel Club	1919	1919
	1983	current
County-Wide Dog Training Club	1983	current
Crotona Collie Club	1906	1912
Dachshund Club of America	1895	current
(includes American Dachshund Club and Badger Dog Club)		
Dalmatian Club of America	1905	current
Danbury Fair	1893	1950
(Danbury Agricultural Society until 1946)		
Dandie Dinmont Terrier Club of America	1910	current
Dayton Dog Training Club	1972	current
Dayton Kennel Club	1938	current
Delaware County Kennel Club	1935	current
Delaware State Fair	1915	1921
Delaware and Susquehanna Poultry and Pet Stock Association	1890	1893
Delaware Valley Kennel Club	1912	1916

Del Monte Kennel Club	1938	current
Del Sur Kennel Club	1971	current
Deseret Agricultural and Manufacturing Society	1905	1907
Des Moines Kennel Club	1935	current
Des Moines Poultry and Pet Stock Association	1893	1898
Detroit Kennel Club	1916	current
Devon Dog Show Association	1913	current
(Devon Kennel Club until 1914)		
District of Columbia Kennel Club	1906	1909
Doberman Pinscher Club of America	1921	current
Dog Fanciers Association of Oregon	1946	current
Dog Owners Training Club of Maryland	1947	current
Duluth Kennel Club	1969	current
Duquesne Kennel Club of Western Pennsylvania	1890	1931
Durham Kennel Club	1953	current
Dutchess County Kennel Club	1928	1930
Eastern Beagle Club	1918	1975
Eastern Collie Breeders Association	1915	1919
Eastern Dog Club	1911	current
Eastern German Shorthaired Pointer Club	1940	current
Eastern States Exposition	1935	1953
Elm City Kennel Club	1920	current
Elmira Poultry and Pet Association	1889	1889
El Paso Kennel Club	1938	current
El Pismo Beach Kennel Club	1918	1922
Empire Beagle Club	1913	current
Englewood Kennel Club	1904	1905
	1922	1947
English Cocker Spaniel Club of America	1946	current
English Setter Association of America	1931	current
(English Setter Association until 1953)		
English Setter Club of America	1906	1931
(English Setter Club until 1911)		
English Springer Spaniel Club of the Central States	1936	current
English Springer Spaniel Club of Michigan	1940	current
English Springer Spaniel Club of Ohio	1937	1959
English Springer Spaniel Field Trial Association	1926	current
English Springer Spaniel Field Trial Club of Illinois	1941	current
Erie County Society for the Prevention of Cruelty to Animals	1896	1899
Erie Kennel Club	1906	current
Eskimo Dog Club of America	1929	1959
Evansville Kennel Club	1950	current
Fairfield County Kennel Club	1907	1912
Fairfield County Hunt Club	1930	1937
Fanciers Association of Indiana	1906	1911
Farmington Valley Kennel Club	1956	current
Fayetteville Kennel Club	1984	current
Finger Lakes Kennel Club	1949	current

First Company Governor's Foot Guard Athletic Association	1928	current
First Dog Training Club of Northern New Jersey	1947	current
Forsyth Kennel Club	1953	current
Fort Lauderdale Dog Club	1956	current
Fort Orange Poultry, Kennel, and Pet Stock Association	1913	1915
Fort Schuyler Kennel Club	1889	1889
Fort Worth Kennel Club	1937	current
Framingham District Kennel Club	1939	current
Franklin Kennel Club	1905	1909
Franklin Oil City Kennel Club	1903	1905
Frederick County Agricultural Society	1903	1905
Fredericksburg Kennel Club	1948	1960
Freeport Poultry and Pet Stock Association	1891	1893
French Bulldog Club of America	1897	current
French Bulldog Club of New York	1911	1930
Furniture City Kennel Club	1974	current
Galveston County Kennel Club	1973	current
Garden City Kennel Club	1916	1919
Genesee County Kennel Club	1937	current
Genesee County Agricultural Society and Kennel Club	1905	1907
Genesee Valley Kennel Club	1939	current
Georgia Poultry and Pet Stock Association	1889	1896
German Shepherd Dog Club of America	1913	current
(from 1918-1931, Shepherd Dog Club of America)		
German Shorthaired Pointer Club of America	1940	current
German Wirehaired Pointer Club of America	1973	current
Giant Schnauzer Club of America	1979	current
Gladstone Beagle Club	1937	1963
Golden Gate Kennel Club	1910	current
(Golden Gate Kennel Club of San Francisco until 1929)		
Golden Retriever Club of America	1938	current
Gordon Setter Club of America	1890	1890
	1924	current
Grand Rapids Kennel Club	1954	current
Grand River Kennel Club	1963	current
Great Barrington Kennel Club	1941	current
Great Dane Club of America	1889	current
Greater Lowell Kennel Club	1983	current
Greater Miami Dog Club	1950	current
Greater St. Louis Training Club	1957	current
Great Pyrenees Club of America	1935	current
Green Mountain Dog Club	1969	current
Greenville Kennel Club	1950	current
Greenwich Kennel Club	1933	current
Greyhound Club of America	1909	current
Hackensack Kennel Club	1920	1923
Harbor Cities Kennel Club	1923	1964
Harrisburg Kennel Club	1938	current

Harrisburg Society for the Prevention of Cruelty to Animals	1921	1924
Hartford Kennel Club	1887	1892
Hartford Show Association	1906	1913
Hatboro Dog Club	1983	current
Haverhill Kennel Club	1903	1904
	1908	1937
Hawaiian Kennel Club	1937	current
Heart of America Kennel Club	1951	current
Hermitage Kennel Club	1892	1893
Hollywood Dog Obedience Club	1956	current
Hollywood Kennel Club	1925	1926
Holyoke Kennel Club	1962	current
Hoosier Kennel Club	1927	current
Hoosier Poultry & Kennel Association	1900	1902
Hornell Kennel Club	1887	1906
Hornellsville Kennel Club	1904	1905
Houston Kennel Club	1935	current
Hudson County Kennel Club	1917	1942
Huntingdon Valley Kennel Club	1922	current
Huntington Kennel Club	1954	current
Huron Hills Kennel Club	1953	1959
Hutchinson Kennel Club	1961	current
Idaho Capital City Kennel Club	1981	current
Illindio Kennel Club	1893	1902
Illinois Capitol Kennel Club	1938	current
(Illinois State Fair Kennel Club until 1951)		
Illinois Valley Kennel Club of Peoria	1951	current
Indianapolis Obedience Training Club	1946	current
Indiana State Poultry Association	1890	1894
Ingham County Kennel Club	1943	current
Inland Empire Kennel Association	1947	current
Intermountain Kennel Club	1928	current
International Kennel Club of Chicago	1900	current
International Toy Poodle Club	1913	1943
Interstate Fair Kennel Club	1905	1906
Interstate Poodle Club	1940	1957
Irish Setter Club of America	1896	current
(Irish Setter Club until 1897)		
Irish Terrier Club of America	1897	current
Irish Water Spaniel Club of America	1943	current
Irish Wolfhound Club	1911	1912
Irish Wolfhound Club of America	1926	current
Islip Kennel Club	1913	1916
Italian Greyhound Club of America	1959	current
Jacksonville Dog Fanciers' Association	1950	current
Jacksonville Kennel Club	1923	1936
Japanese Chin Club of America	1912	current
(Japanese Spaniel Club of America until 1977)		

Jaxon Kennel Club	1944	current
Jersey City Kennel Club	1903	1914
Joliet Kennel Club	1898	1901
Kalamazoo Kennel Club	1954	current
Kanadasaga Kennel Club	1956	current
Kansas City Kennel Club	1926	1947
K-9 Obedience Training Club of Essex County, New Jersey	1948	current
Keeshond Club of America	1935	current
(Keeshond Club until 1955)		
Kenilworth Kennel Club of Connecticut	1980	current
Kennel Club of Atlantic City	1916	1955
Kennel Club of Beverly Hills	1942	current
(Beverly Riviera Kennel Club until 1964)		
Kennel Club of Buffalo	1928	current
(Buffalo Kennel Club until 1931)		
Kennel Club of Northern New Jersey	1940	current
Kennel Club of Pasadena	1907	current
(Pasadena Kennel Club until 1965)		
Kennel Club of Philadelphia	1913	current
Kennel Club of Riverside	1937	current
(Riverside Kennel Club until 1965)		
Kern County Kennel Club	1949	current
Kentucky Kennel Club	1897	1898
Kentucky State Fair Kennel Club	1918	1923
Keystone Beagle Club	1905	1906
Keystone Kennel Club	1892	1895
Kiwanis Club of Hartford	1923	1924
Kodak City Kennel Club	1913	1913
Labrador Retriever Club	1936	current
Lackawanna Kennel Club	1927	current
Ladies' Dog Club	1915	current
Ladies Kennel Association of America	1900	current
Ladies Kennel Association of California	1911	1917
Ladies Kennel Association of Massachusetts	1899	1938
Ladies Kennel Club of Southern California	1912	1915
Lake Mohawk Kennel Club	1950	1958
Lake Shore Kennel Club	1947	current
Lakes Region Kennel Club	1976	current
Lancaster Kennel Club	1949	current
Land O'Lakes Kennel Club	1956	current
Langley Kennel Club	1955	current
Lawrence Kennel Club	1904	1905
Lehigh Valley Kennel Club	1912	1912
	1935	current
Lenox Dog Show Association	1925	1925
Lenox Kennel Club	1930	1949
Lenox Horse and Dog Association	1930	1932
Lewiston-Auburn Kennel Club	1976	current

Lexington Kennel Club	1955	current
Livestock Society of America	1896	1896
Long Beach Kennel Club	1928	1934
Long Island Kennel Club	1903	current
Long Island Livestock Fair Association	1889	1893
Longshore-Southport Kennel Club	1944	current
(Longshore Kennel Club until 1951)		
Los Angeles Kennel Club	1917	1958
Louisiana Kennel Club	1923	current
Louisville Kennel Club	1894	1895
	1916	current
Lynn Kennel Club	1905	1945
M.A.A.C. Rod and Gun Club	1896	1904
Madison Athletic Association	1904	1909
Mad River Valley Kennel Club	1959	current
Magic Valley Kennel Club	1954	current
Mahoning-Shenango Kennel Club	1939	current
Maltese Club	1917	1925
Maltese Terrier Club	1909	1917
Manchester Kennel Club	1932	1960
Manchester Terrier Club of America	1912	1952
Manitowoc County Kennel Club	1949	current
Mankato Kennel Club	1937	1942
Marin County Kennel Club	1915	1915
Marin Valley Kennel Club	1912	1912
Marion Kennel Club	1950	current
Marion Ohio Kennel Club	1954	current
Maryland Kennel Club	1910	current
Maryland Society for the Prevention of Cruelty to Animals	1902	1907
Mascoutah Kennel Club	1889	1909
Massachusetts Kennel Club	1889	1894
Mastiff Club of America	1941	current
Maui Kennel Club	1938	1949
McKinley Kennel Club	1951	current
Memphis Kennel Club	1935	current
Memphis Obedience Training Club	1979	current
Menlo Park Kennel Club	1908	1909
Mensona Kennel Club	1973	current
Metropolitan Kennel Club	1896	1904
Metuchen Kennel Club	1906	1908
Merrimack Valley Kennel Club	1902	1903
	1978	current
Miami Valley Kennel Club	1905	1908
Michiana Kennel Club	1948	current
Michigan Kennel Club	1889	1895
Michigan State Fair Dog Club	1922	1929
Mid-Continent Kennel Club of Tulsa	1935	current
Mid-Del Tinker Kennel Club	1975	current

Middlesex County Kennel Club	1912	current
Middlesex East Agricultural Association	1901	1906
Mid-Hudson Kennel Club	1950	current
Mid-Jersey Companion Dog Training Club	1952	current
Midwest Field Trial Club	1940	current
Millers River River Kennel Club	1905	1906
Milwaukee Pet Stock Association	1896	1898
	1900	1900
Miniature Pinscher Club of America	1930	current
Minneapolis Kennel Club	1936	current
Minnesota Field Trial Association	1940	current
Mispillion Kennel Club	1978	current
Mississippi Valley Kennel Club	1906	current
Mississippi Valley Retriever Club	1970	current
Mohawk Kennel Club	1896	1896
Mohawk Valley Kennel Club	1891	1892
	1940	current
Monmouth County Kennel Club	1935	current
Montana Kennel Club	1889	1894
Montgomery County Kennel Club	1911	current
(Gwynedd Valley Kennel Club until 1939)		
Montreal Canine Association	1902	1905
Morris County Kennel Club	1921	1925
Morris and Essex Kennel Club	1929	1963
Mountaineer Kennel Club	1974	current
Mountain States Dog Training Club	1956	current
Mount Vernon Dog Training Club	1969	current
Muncie Kennel Club	1939	current
Nassau County Kennel Club	1911	1953
Nassau Dog Training Club	1952	current
National Beagle Club	1887	current
National Capital Kennel Club	1933	current
National Field Trial Club	1887	1897
National Fox Hunters Association of Kentucky	1913	1918
National Greyhound Club	1890	1900
National Poultry and Bench Show Association	1889	1890
Nebraska Dog and Hunt Club	1945	current
Nebraska Kennel Club	1937	current
Newark Kennel Club	1913	1968
New Bedford Kennel Club	1906	1908
New Bedford District Kennel Club	1915	1927
New England Beagle Club	1895	current
New England Collie Club	1915	1917
New England Dog Training Club	1941	current
New England Field Trial Club	1891	1898
New England Kennel Club	1889	1921
New England Old English Sheepdog Club	1944	current
Newfoundland Club of America	1915	1916

Newfoundland Club of America	1930	current
New Haven Kennel Club	1889	1890
New Jersey Beagle Club	1914	current
New Jersey Kennel Club	1887	1913
New Jersey Kennel League	1893	1897
New Jersey Shore Kennel Club of Monmouth County	1921	1922
New London Kennel Club	1910	1917
New Mexico Kennel Club	1935	1980
Newport Dog Show	1903	1907
Newton Kennel Club	1949	current
(Lake Mohawk Kennel Club until 1958)		
New Orleans Fox Terrier Club	1898	1901
New York State Fair (Dog Show)	1915	1951
New York and New England Poultry and Kennel Club	1891	1893
Niagara Falls Kennel Club	1946	1963
North Dakota Retriever Club	1946	current
Northeastern Indiana Kennel Club	1936	current
Northeastern Wisconsin Kennel Club	1942	1959
Northern California Kennel Club	1912	1913
Northern Hare Beagle Club	1917	1983
Northern Illinois Poultry and Pet Stock Association	1890	1891
Northern Kentucky Kennel Club	1974	current
Northern Ohio Beagle Club	1935	current
Northern Ohio Poultry and Pet Stock Association	1893	1893
North Shore Dog Training Club	1956	current
North Shore Kennel Club	1937	current
North Westchester Kennel Club	1929	1946
Northwestern Beagle Club	1893	1897
Northwestern Boston Terrier Club	1913	1914
Northwestern Connecticut Dog Club	1951	current
Northwestern Kennel Club	1897	1901
Norwegian Elkhound Association of America	1936	current
Norwich and Norfolk Terrier Club	1947	current
(Norwich Terrier Club until 1979)		
Oakland and Alameda County Kennel Club	1913	1925
Oakland County Kennel Club	1943	current
Oakland Dog Training Club	1956	current
Oakland Kennel Club	1897	1898
	1904	current
Oakland Poultry Association	1901	1903
Obedience Training Club of Hawaii	1955	current
Obedience Training Club of Rhode Island	1944	current
Ohio Field Trial Club	1893	1894
Ohio Valley Beagle Club	1938	current
Ohio Valley Kennel Club	1919	1924
Oklahoma City Kennel Club	1935	current
Old Colony Kennel Club	1923	1930
(Old Colony Kennel Club of Taunton, Massachusetts, until 1928)		

Old Dominion Kennel Club of Northern Virginia	1939	current
Old English Sheepdog Club of America	1905	current
Old Pueblo Dog Training Club	1970	current
Olympic Kennel Club	1951	current
Omaha Kennel Club	1891	1901
Onondaga Kennel Association	1923	current
Orange County Agricultural Society	1902	1916
Orange Empire Dog Club	1946	current
Orange Kennel Club	1936	1947
Ox Ridge Kennel Club	1940	current
Ozarks Kennel Club	1979	current
Pacific Coast Boston Terrier Club	1912	current
Pacific Coast Bulldog Club	1940	current
Pacific Coast Collie Club	1914	1932
Pacific Coast Pekingese Club	1917	current
Pacific Coast Pomeranian Club	1918	1930
Pacific Coast Toy Dog Association	1912	1921
Pacific Cocker Spaniel Club	1913	1960
Pacific Fox Terrier Club	1896	1898
Pacific French Bulldog Club	1915	1916
Pacific Kennel Club	1889	1897
Pacific Mastiff Club	1897	1898
Pacific Sheepdog Club	1905	1906
Pan-American Exposition Association	1900	1903
Panhandle Kennel Club of Texas	1957	current
Papillon Club of America	1935	current
Pasanita Obedience Club	1951	current
Passaic County Fish and Game Protection Association	1905	1907
Paterson Kennel Club	1923	1942
Pekingese Club of America	1909	current
Pembroke Welsh Corgi Club of America	1937	current
Penn Ridge Kennel Club	1983	current
Penn State Agricultural Society	1893	1894
Penn Treaty Kennel Club	1950	current
Pensacola Dog Fanciers Association	1949	current
Peoria and Central Illinois Kennel Club	1940	1945
Philadelphia Bulldog Club	1912	1929
Philadelphia Collie Club	1906	1909
Philadelphia Dog Show Association	1899	1912
Philadelphia Dog Training Club	1949	current
Philadelphia Kennel Club	1887	1891
	1894	1899
Philadelphia Pointer Club	1903	1908
Piedmont Kennel Club	1936	current
Pinehurst Kennel Club	1920	1923
Pinetree Kennel Club	1906	1916
Pittsburgh Collie Club	1910	1918

Pittsburgh Kennel Club	1922	1958
Plainfield Kennel Club	1911	1923
(Mid-Jersey Field Dog Club 1928-1945)	1928	current
Pocono Beagle Club	1937	current
Pointer Club of America	1889	1931
Pointer Club of California	1897	1899
Poodle Club, The	1913	1927
Poodle Club of America	1896	1899
	1931	current
Port Chester Obedience Training Club	1947	current
Portland Kennel Club	1893	1897
	1926	current
Poultry and Pet Stock Association	1892	1892
Providence County Kennel Club	1919	current
Pueblo Kennel Club	1903	1905
Pug Dog Club of America	1931	current
Puli Club of America	1977	current
Putnam Kennel Club	1966	current
Queen City Dog Training Club	1952	current
Queen City Kennel Club	1916	1921
Queensboro Kennel Club	1924	current
Queens County Agricultural Society	1896	1896
Ramapo Kennel Club	1969	current
Rapid City Kennel Club	1982	current
Reno Kennel Club	1961	current
Revere Kennel Club	1906	1918
Rhode Island Kennel Club	1887	1887
	1897	current
Rhode Island Poultry Association	1894	1898
	1900	1901
Rhode Island State Fair Association	1894	1897
	1900	1902
Rhodesian Ridgeback Club of the United States	1971	current
Richland County Kennel Club	1982	current
Richland Kennel Club	1953	current
Richmond County Poultry and Pet Stock Association	1889	1889
Richmond Dog Fanciers Club	1953	current
Rio Grande Kennel Club	1937	current
Rio Grande Obedience Dog Club	1955	current
Roanoke Kennel Club	1938	current
Rochester Dog Protectors and Animal Clinic Association	1926	1957
(Rochester Dog Protectors Association until 1942)		
Rochester Exposition Kennel Club	1921	1932
Rochester Kennel Club	1889	1895
	1903	1904
Rockingham County Kennel Club	1969	current
Rockland County Industrial Association	1905	1921
Rockland County Kennel Club	1950	current

Rock River Valley Kennel Club	1943	current
Rubber City Kennel Club	1944	current
Rumson Kennel Club	1913	1929
Sahuaro State Kennel Club	1943	current
St. Bernard Club of America	1898	current
St. Bernard Club of California	1889	1889
	1898	1900
St. Clair Kennel Club	1910	1913
St. Joseph Kennel Club	1950	current
St. Louis Beagle Club	1938	current
St. Louis Collie Club	1902	current
St. Louis Kennel Club	1893	1901
St. Paul Kennel Club	1937	1953
St. Paul and Minnesota Kennel Club	1889	1900
St. Petersburg Dog Fanciers Association	1955	current
Salina Kennel Club	1972	current
Salinas Kennel Club	1914	1915
Salinas Valley Kennel Club	1963	current
Salisbury Maryland Kennel Club	1967	current
Saluki Club of America	1930	current
Samoyed Club of America	1923	current
San Antonio Kennel Club	1921	current
Sandemac Kennel Club	1954	current
Sandia Dog Obedience Club	1960	current
San Diego Kennel Club	1917	1919
San Francisco Dog Training Club	1947	current
San Francisco Kennel Club	1897	1905
San Francisco and San Mateo Agricultural Association	1900	1901
San Gabriel Valley Kennel Club	1950	current
San Joaquin Kennel Club	1937	1968
San Joaquin Valley Poultry and Kennel Club	1896	1897
San Mateo Kennel Club	1904	current
Santa Ana Valley Kennel Club	1953	current
Santa Anita Kennel Club	1939	1945
Santa Barbara Kennel Club	1929	current
Santa Clara Dog Training Club	1979	current
Santa Clara Valley Kennel Club	1950	current
(Santa Clara County Kennel Club until 1965)		
Santa Clara Valley Poultry and Kennel Club	1897	1899
Santa Cruz Kennel Club	1925	current
(Bay of Santa Cruz Kennel Club until 1933)		
Santa Maria Kennel Club	1980	current
Saratoga Poultry and Kennel Club	1893	1895
Saw Mill River Kennel Club	1943	current
Schipperke Club of America	1912	1913
	1929	current
Scottish Deerhound Club	1907	1913
Scottish Deerhound Club of America	1981	current

Scottish Terrier Club of America	1900	current
Scottsdale Dog Fanciers Association	1983	current
Scottsdale Kennel Club	1934	1935
Seattle Dog Fanciers Association	1905	1910
Seattle Kennel Club	1892	1896
(Puget Sound Kennel Club 1922-1939)	1910	1920
	1922	current
Sewickley Valley Kennel Club	1952	1967
Sharon Kennel Club	1903	1907
Sheepshead Bay Kennel Club	1907	1909
Shreveport Kennel Club	1951	current
Siberian Husky Club of America	1946	current
(Siberian Husky Club until 1949)		
Silky Terrier Club of America	1966	current
Silver Bay Kennel Club of San Diego	1936	current
Simsbury Kennel Club	1907	1910
Sioux City Kennel Club	1912	1913
Sioux Empire Kennel Club	1968	current
Sioux Valley Kennel Club	1966	current
Sir Francis Drake Kennel Club	1982	current
Sixth District Agricultural Association	1901	1904
Skokie Valley Kennel Club	1941	current
Skye Terrier Club of America	1938	current
Snohomish County Kennel Club	1912	1914
Soft-Coated Wheaten Terrier Club of America	1983	current
Somerset Hills Kennel Club	1932	current
Sonoma City Kennel Club	1912	1915
Southampton Kennel Club	1914	1948
South Carolina Kennel Club	1890	1892
South Carolina Poultry and Pet Stock Association	1889	1895
Southeast Arkansas Kennel Club	1978	current
Southeastern Iowa Kennel Club	1948	current
Southern Adirondack Dog Club	1953	current
Southern Beagle Club	1905	1910
Southern California Kennel Club	1889	1889
	1897	1898
Southern Collie Club of Memphis	1910	1914
Southern Field Trial Club	1889	1894
Southern Michigan Obedience Training Club	1953	current
Southern Ohio Kennel Club	1906	1908
Southern Tier Kennel Club	1955	current
South Jersey Kennel Club	1955	current
South Side Kennel Club	1910	1912
South Shore Kennel Club	1949	current
South Texas Obedience Club	1947	current
Southwestern Kennel Club	1903	1912
Spaniel Breeders Society	1902	current
Spartanburg Kennel Club	1980	current

Spokane Kennel Club	1905	1907
	1927	current
Sportsmen's Beagle Club	1920	current
Springfield Kennel Club	1929	current
Staffordshire Terrier Club of America	1940	current
Standard Schnauzer Club of America	1925	current
Staten Island Kennel Club	1939	current
Steel City Kennel Club	1950	current
Stock Association	1892	1893
Stockton Kennel Club	1897	1898
Storm King Kennel Club	1927	1939
Suffolk County Kennel Club	1943	current
Sun Maid Kennel Club of Fresno	1949	current
Superstition Kennel Club	1966	current
Susque-Nango Kennel Club	1950	current
Sussex Hills Kennel Club	1968	current
Syracuse Kennel Club	1889	1893
Talbot Kennel Club	1970	current
Tampa Bay Kennel Club	1955	current
Taunton Kennel Club	1905	1908
Tedesco Kennel Club	1906	1906
Tennessee Valley Kennel Club	1938	current
Terre Haute Kennel Club	1937	current
(Terre Haute Chapter Izaak Walton League of America until 1979)		
Terry-All Kennel Club	1974	current
Texas Kennel Club	1898	current
The Germantown Cricket Club Kennel Association	1921	1927
The Fanciers Club	1889	1890
The People's Poultry and Pet Stock Association	1905	1910
Tibetan Terrier Club of America	1984	current
Tidewater Kennel Club of Virginia	1955	current
Toledo Fanciers Association	1889	1890
	1903	1905
Toledo Kennel Club	1935	current
Tonawanda Valley Kennel Club	1949	current
Topeka Kennel Club	1958	current
Town and Country Kennel Club	1951	current
Toy Dog Club of America	1912	1913
Toy Dog Club of New England	1912	1921
Toy Spaniel Club of America	1904	1932
Treasure Island Kennel Club	1938	1949
Trenton Kennel Club	1932	current
Tri-City Kennel Club	1892	1895
	1937	current
Tri-State Kennel Association	1937	current
Troy Kennel Club	1936	current
(Troy Horse Show Association until 1942)		

Tucson Kennel Club	1935	current
(Catalina Kennel Club until 1936)		
Tuxedo Kennel Club	1927	1959
Twin City Kennel Club	1902	1902
(Twin City Kennel Club, Minneapolis, until 1924)	1923	1933
Union County Kennel Club	1939	current
United States Kerry Blue Terrier Club	1926	current
United States Lakeland Terrier Club	1968	current
Upper Suncoast Dog Obedience Club	1982	current
Utah Kennel Club	1907	1912
Utah State Park Association	1907	1907
Valley Fair Kennel Club	1903	1911
Valley Forge Kennel Club	1951	current
Vancouver Exhibition Association	1912	1913
Vancouver Kennel Club	1946	current
Venice of America Kennel Club	1907	1912
Ventura County Dog Fanciers Association	1939	current
Ventura County Kennel Club	1929	1937
Vermont Kennel Club	1899	1906
Vicksburg Fox Terrier Club	1900	1900
Victoria Kennel Club	1897	1899
Virginia Field and Sports Association	1889	1893
Virginia Kennel Club	1936	current
Vizsla Club of America	1971	current
Wachusett Kennel Club	1950	current
Walla Walla Kennel Club	1940	current
Wallkill Kennel Club	1977	current
Washington City Kennel Club	1889	1897
Washington Kennel Club	1910	1930
Washington, PA Kennel Club	1905	1910
Washington State Obedience Training Club	1971	current
Waterloo Kennel Club	1950	current
Waukesha Kennel Club	1968	current
Weimaraner Club of America	1951	current
Welsh Terrier Club of America	1900	current
Westbury Kennel Association	1926	current
Westchester Kennel Club	1906	current
Western Beagle Club	1907	current
Western Bull Terrier Breeders Association	1907	1909
Western Fox Terrier Breeders Association	1907	current
Western French Bulldog Club	1912	1945
Western Pennsylvania Kennel Association	1940	current
Western Pennsylvania Poultry Society	1887	1890
Western Michigan Agricultural and Industrial Society	1892	1893
Western Michigan Kennel Club	1892	1892
Western Reserve Kennel Club	1917	current
West Highland White Terrier Club of America	1909	current
Westminster Kennel Club	1884	current

Westside Dog Training Club	1955	current
West Virginia Exposition and State Fair Association	1900	1904
Wichita Kennel Club	1971	current
Wilmington Kennel Club	1938	current
(Kennel Club of Wilmington until 1948)		
Windham County Kennel Club	1978	current
Winstead Kennel Club	1889	1894
Winston-Salem Dog Training Club	1982	current
Whippet Club of America	1920	1924
Wisconsin Amateur Field Trial Club	1941	current
Wisconsin Kennel Club	1889	1891
	1906	1917
	1922	1933
	1940	current
Wissahickon Kennel Club	1902	1949
Wolverine Beagle Club	1940	current
Wolverine Kennel Club	1905	1909
Woodstock Dog Club	1970	current
Worcester County Kennel Club	1930	current
Worcester Kennel Club	1889	1917
Wire-Haired Pinscher Club	1925	1926
Yakima Valley Kennel Club	1956	current
York Kennel Club	1906	1911
Yorkshire Terrier Club of America	1906	1906
	1958	current
Youngstown Kennel Club	1890	1891

Encyclopedic Appendix

The first portion of this Source Book has been prepared as a running history of the American Kennel Club and the sport of pure-bred dogs in the United States. While this approach enables the reader to follow the development and growth of the sport as a whole over the period of the American Kennel Club's first one hundred years, it also makes it difficult to trace the development of specific aspects of the sport. This divergence of aims has been necessary, because the various rules, regulations, policies, and institutions in place in 1984 were often developed over a period of many years.

A number of key topics have therefore been selected for special treatment in this appendix. An attempt has been made to consolidate all of the pertinent information on each of these subjects, so that it will be possible for the reader to ascertain key facts without having to refer to several different chapters in the source book. In each case we've chosen the best qualified person to write the section.

Dog Shows

Evolution of Variety Groups

There is a natural tendency for human beings to organize and systematize their world. Some of the schemes they develop are arbitrary, while others are quite logical. Things and places need names, and these names have often reflected purposes and places that were readily recognizable. Even the names of dog breeds have a certain descriptive character.

The earliest writers about dogs often listed different kinds of dogs but rarely described them in detail. Most of these works were concerned with the dogs used for hunting. The authors did not bother to write about the shepherd's dog or the peasant's terrier-like dogs until fairly recent times.

Dame Juliana Berners, the author of one of the earliest treatises in English dealing with dogs, listed the dogs she knew in her *Boke of St. Albans* (1480) naming fourteen kinds. Dr. Caius in *De Canibus Britanicis* (1570) developed a classification for dogs by use. Two centuries after Caius, Pye in his *Sportsman's Dictionary* classified dogs by color.

It wasn't until the advent of dog shows in England in the late 1850s that it became apparent that a system was needed to group dogs with similar characteristics. The men who started the first dog shows were primarily fanciers of Pointers and Setters, so the shows were open only to those breeds, and classification was simple. Competitions involving Foxhounds were held at country fairs. Tavern shows featured terriers and toy breeds.

Gradually, dog shows for all the various kinds of dogs became common. Until the formation of the Kennel Club in 1873 in England, there was no recognized authority to set uniform regulations for dog shows. It even took that organization a while to come up with a system.

The first and most logical division was to separate the sporting dogs from those not used for hunting. Incidentally, the Fox Terriers were often included with the gun dogs. However, not all clubs followed the same classification. For example, in 1860, the Birmingham show used "Division I and Division II Non-Sporting Dogs." Sometimes clubs used "Sporting Dogs" and "Dogs Not Used in Field Sports." The first show held by the Kennel Club was not divided at all.

After the American Civil War, dog shows made their appearance in the United States and tended to follow the English system. The first dog show in America was held in 1874 and was limited to Pointers and Setters. In 1876 a dog show was held in Philadelphia as part of the nation's centennial celebration. The Philadelphia Kennel Club was invited to hold a dog show in

Fairmount Park. It was so well received that a group of sportsmen met later that year and formed the Westminster Kennel Club, planning to hold its first show in New York the following year.

When the American Kennel Club was established in 1884, the Westminster Kennel Club had already been holding shows for seven years. It had its own catalog format that was not necessarily the same from year to year. Other clubs patterned their catalogs after Westminster's, or else acted independently.

It should be remembered that in the early years of the AKC, rule changes were made as problems arose and as situations developed. Nothing was done without a great deal of thought and deliberation. The early sporting press reported on the lively debates about proposed rule changes. For instance, there was much controversy when it became mandatory in 1888 for a dog to be registered or listed with AKC in order to be shown at AKC shows.

While some show catalogs began to divide breeds into Sporting and Non-Sporting groupings, difficulties still arose. In the April 1901 issue of the *Gazette,* G. Muss-Arnolt, the well-known artist, wrote a letter asking AKC to address the problem since a dog had been entered as Non-Sporting in one show and as Sporting in another.

The Stud Book used those two divisions in Volumes IV, V, VI, and VII. Later editions, from 1891 to 1914, reverted to strict alphabetical order. The following year, two volumes appeared, one for Sporting and one for Non-Sporting. In 1916 and 1917, alphabetical order was resumed. From 1918 until April 1924, the two divisions were used again. It was back to the alphabet in May 1924, which held until October 1933, when six groups were designated:

Group 1. Sporting Dogs
Group 2. Sporting Dogs (Hounds)
Group 3. Working Dogs
Group 4. Terriers
Group 5. Toy Dogs
Group 6. Non-Sporting Dogs

However, show classification and catalog order did not follow the same path to these six familiar groups as the *Stud Book* did. As a matter of fact, it took some time before catalog size was standardized. In 1909, major revisions were made in the rules, and for the first time, the rules spelled out the size and arrangement for both show catalogs and premium lists. The divisions were:

Large Dogs
Medium-Size Dogs
Small-Size Dogs
Cage Dogs

For the most part, the Large Dogs *were* large, with the possible exception of the Eskimo Dog. It is not clear how big that breed was. The Medium Dogs were somewhat of a mixed bag and included the Setters, Pointers, Cocker Spaniels, Poodles, and Bull Terriers. The Small category had most of the Terriers, and a few Toy breeds. The Cage Dogs seemed to fit the description. This arrangement was arrived at because all dog shows were benched and keeping similar-size dogs benched together was more practical.

In the early dog shows, the judging routine was determined by what prizes were being offered. Awards did not go beyond winners or best-of-breed unless a prize was offered. Variety groups could be entered, and usually a fee was charged. However, the dog had to be entered in a regular class also.

The first best-in-show prize was awarded in 1885 to a White Bull Terrier named Count at the Western Connecticut Poultry, Pigeon and Pet Stock Association Show. It wasn't until 1924 that clubs began to offer variety groups, as we now know them, and best-in-show competition on a regular basis. These awards were not published as official until 1925. There were five groups then:

1. Sporting Group
2. Working Group
3. Terrier Group
4. Toy Group
5. Non-Sporting Group

In December 1930, the Sporting Group was divided into Sporting Group and Sporting Group (Hounds). This system underwent two more major changes. In 1937, the Sporting Group (Hounds) became the Hound Group, and in 1983, the Working Group was split into the Working Group and the Herding Group.

The Board of Directors is empowered to rearrange the groups without the delegates' consent. In 1984, a committee was appointed by the Board of Directors to investigate the possible regrouping of the breeds. The report was presented to the Board, which in turn put its recommendations before the delegates. The delegates were asked to decide whether to eliminate varieties within breeds so that only one dog of a breed would be in the group. The proposal was overwhelmingly defeated.

While there is really no perfect classification, the present one seems to fit the needs of the sport and the desires of the fancies in America today.

As mentioned above, until the early 1920s, unless prizes were offered for the best dog in a group or in the show, there was no competition at those levels. However, when such prizes were available to be won, multiple judges officiated, sometimes as many as six. As time went on, in order to avoid ties, it became customary to have an odd number of judges. By 1917, the number was limited to five.

The License Committee, whose duty it was to approve judges and shows, was dissatisfied with the system. These men felt that when three or more judges were involved, there was always the possibility that each would have his own favorite. Thus, the winner could be determined by compromise or by the most persuasive judge rather than by merit.

Basically, the committee felt that judging dogs was such a subjective matter that it was virtually impossible for three or more judges to agree totally about any single animal. In May 1930, the delegates approved the committee's recommendations, and the responsibility of selecting winners in breed, in variety groups, and best-in-show was placed with an individual judge who was selected by the show-giving club.

Roberta Vesley

Field Representatives

In 1945, the Board of Directors of the American Kennel Club appointed a committee of its members to consider an additional executive position or positions to relieve the increasing workload on the executive staff. This committee consisted of J. Gould Remick, Thomas M. Halpin, and George H. Hartman. It was charged with determining the type of individual or individuals that would be needed, and what his or her duties would be. This increase in workload was the result of the dramatic increase in dog activity following World War II. At the September 11, 1945, delegates' meeting, Henry Bixby, the Executive Vice-President, advised that 1946 would see an unprecedented number of shows scheduled and emphasized that, if all paperwork was not received on time, as required under the rules, the mounting pressure might require the American Kennel Club to cancel some of the events. In 1945, there had been 140 all-breed dog shows and 77 specialty shows. However, 1946 saw the total rise to 254 all-breed dog shows (an increase of 81 percent) and 178 specialty shows (an increase of 131 percent).

At the October 1945 board meeting, Mr. Bixby announced the employment of Mr. Chester Hager of Buffalo, New York, as assistant to the executive vice-president. Mr. Hager was to assist Mr. Bixby, relieving him of some of his office duties, while at the same time, doing some field work. Mr. Bixby indicated that the special board committee had also recommended that someone be found to work exclusively in the field. As its first full-time field representative, the American Kennel Club finally selected Mr. Leonard Brumby, Sr., who had been the president of the Professional Handlers' Association. Mr. Bixby reported to the Board in December that Mr. Brumby would start on January 14, 1946, and that he had planned to have him go to the Florida shows and be back in time for the Westminster Kennel Club show. Mr. Bixby also indicated that it was expected that Mr. Brumby would be traveling to shows for three weeks out of every month. Mr. Brumby's work was well received, and an editorial that appeared in the March 1946 issue of the AKC Gazette indicated, ''As the field representative, Leonard Brumby has already done yeoman service in 'spiking' ringside gossip before it had a chance to grow into the vicious rumor stage and in settling differences of opinion on the spot before they got out of hand.''

The concept of having a full-time field representative had been so well accepted by the fancy that, when Mr. Brumby died in office the year following his appointment, the Board immediately sought to replace him. At the September 9, 1947, board meeting, Mr. Bixby reported on a number of applicants for the position of field representative, all of whom had been interviewed. The various prospects were discussed at length, and the Board finally voted to authorize the Executive Vice-President to engage the services of Mr. Alfred M. Dick for the position. Mr. Dick, formerly the president of the Kennel Club of Philadelphia, as well as the secretary of the Dachshund Club of America, was to begin in October 1947. The announcement of Mr. Dick's appointment included the statement: ''It will be his task to try to make available to show-giving clubs throughout the United States the knowledge that he gained while bringing his own club to the highest level it has enjoyed.'' It is indicative of how well the concept of a field representative was accepted that, at the same time Mr. Dick was chosen to replace Mr. Brumby, Mr. Leroy Beardsley was hired as the first full-time field trial field representative.

The position of field representative grew in importance over the years, as the sport grew. The field representative became the eyes and ears of the American Kennel Club throughout the country, keeping it in touch with the fancy. By 1950, there was sufficient dog show activity in the western portion of the country to warrant the hiring of a field representative to attend shows there. Major Bryant Godsol was hired as the first West Coast field representative in 1950. Major Godsol resided in Canoga Park, California, and prior to being named a field representative had been the chairman of the Los Angeles Trial Board. When Major Godsol resigned in 1954, he was replaced by Captain A. C. Berry of San Antonio, Texas, who was to cover dog shows in the West and Southwest.

The number of field representatives on the staff of the American Kennel Club has continuously grown, especially with the great upsurge in dog show activity between 1970 and 1980. In 1970, there were 569 all-breed shows and 599 specialty shows. A total of 597,170 dogs competed in these events in 1970. By 1980, the number of all-breed dog shows had risen to 823 (an increase of 45 percent), the number of specialty shows had risen to 1,238 (an increase of 107 percent), and the number of dogs in competition had risen to nearly 950,000 (an increase of 59 percent).

During this same period, the number of full-time field representatives rose from five in 1970 to fifteen in 1980. The first female AKC field representative, hired in 1973, was Mrs. Irene Nail of Fort Worth, Texas. By 1984, six of the fifteen representatives covering dog shows and obedience trials were women.

By 1984, the field representative had a number of duties to perform in connection with AKC dog shows and obedience trials. Paramount among the duties of the field representatives was the observation of judges. The field representatives interview prospective judges who intend to apply for additional breeds, and the reports of the field representatives are considered by the Board of Directors in approving a judge for additional breeds or additional obedience classes. While the conduct of a dog show is entirely the responsibility of the show-giving club, the field representative would be present at the show to assist the club if needed, and to make recommendations and suggestions to the club as to how the event could be improved. Field representatives have become a fixture on the dog-show scene, and they have played a crucial role in enabling the American Kennel Club to remain as responsive as possible to the pure-bred dog fancy. It is also interesting to note that it is not uncommon for the American Kennel Club to go to the ranks of its field staff to fill key executive positions in the club. One president (Alfred M. Dick) and two vice-presidents (William M. Schmick and W. Terry Stacy) first joined the staff of the American Kennel Club as field representatives.

Individuals who have served as field representatives, along with their years of service, are as follows:

Barton, Mrs. Constance 1975-present

Berry, Captain A. C.   1954 - 1968

Brumby, Leonard, Sr. 1946 - 1947

Burggraaf, William J. 1980 - 1983

Butler, James A. 1966 - 1973

Conrad, Mort   1972-present

Cruz, Mrs. Patricia M. 1978 - 1984

De Arment, Col. Harold G.   1970 - 1970

Dick, Alfred M. 1947 - 1951

Droboty, Stephen W. 1951 - 1953

Effinger, Fred   1978 - 1981

Frey, James M.   1972 -1984

Godsol, Major Bryant 1950 - 1954

Harra, Frank W. 1972-present

Hastings, Robert 1974 - 1977

Hiett, Richard C. 1968 - 1978

Holbrook, William H.   1979-present

Hungerford, Becher W. 1967 - 1973

James, Mrs. Helen Lee 1974-present

Knox, Mrs.   Sydney (Monteleone)   1978-present

Lang, William A. 1953 - 1966

Linn, Willis   1968 - 1969

Marsh, Arthur W.   1965-present

Masley, Dr. John W.   1972 - 1978

Merrill, Mrs. Bettye 1977 - 1980

Nail, Mrs. Irene   1973 - 1978

Radcliffe, Mrs. Kay J. 1983-present

Rich, Jerome M. 1971 - 1973

Roberts, Ronald 1982-present

Savory, Mrs. Anne D.   1984-present

Schmick, William M. 1970 - 1978

Scott, Raymond E.   1984-present

Seiler, John J.   1973-present

Stacy, W. Terry 1981 - 1983

Stebbins, J. Monroe, Jr. 1973-present

Storey, Joseph P. 1959 - 1967

Weaver, Mrs. Lynn   1974-present

W. Terry Stacy

Junior Showmanship

Now in existence for more than fifty years, the Junior Showmanship Classes are among the most competitive events featured at today's dog shows, drawing spectators and exhibitors from all parts of the United States and abroad. The competition, however, was not always as popular and competitive as it is today, and the former Children's Handling Class underwent a great transformation before reaching its present status.

The rise and formation of Junior Showmanship can be attributed to the encouragement, influence, and contributions from some adult members of the dog fancy, as well as the children's increased knowledge of handling skills and their desire to compete. Late in the 1920s, when dog showing was considered to be strictly a "wealthy-man's sport," the idea of involving children in the shows came to the forefront.

Many of the shows of this era were characterized by extreme wealth, including the arrival at the Saturday afternoon gatherings of children and their parents in chauffeur-driven limousines. Although the adults were content to stroll around the show grounds watching the dogs being judged, the younger crowd was not always as enthusiastic.

Children who accompanied their parents to the shows frequently became bored and restless. After all, there was nothing for a young child to do at the shows. It was for this reason that Leonard Brumby, Sr., arrived at the idea of creating a special class *for* the children, thus providing these young showgoers with something of interest and amusement, as well as an educational experience. Soon, Leonard Brumby's idea became a reality that delighted both children and adults. Children had a *purpose* for attending the shows, beyond watching the family dog being judged, and parents were able to relax and enjoy the show. The adults were also pleased to see the "dog show children" acquiring handling skills, grooming techniques, and forming a closer bond between themselves and their dogs. The competition, adopting the name "Children's Handling Class," no doubt provided dog and child alike with socialization and experience in the dog world. Many veterans of the Children's Handling Class eventually took over their parents' kennels; and others became breeders, exhibitors, and judges.

The participation of children at the dog shows appears to have been an East Coast phenomenon at first, involving dog fanciers from Long Island and Westchester County, New York, as well as Southern Connecticut. Since the sport of dog showing originally blossomed in the East, it was natural that the Children's Handling Class would also have its roots here. Although other, more informal competitions are believed to have taken place at an earlier date, the first *recorded* Children's Handling Class was held at the Westbury Kennel Club show on Long Island, New York, in 1932. This competition was made available through the efforts of Mr. Brumby, then a professional handler, as well as an officer and member of the Westbury Kennel Club. The show's premium list offered this new event providing the following class divisions:

Class A: Boys under 14 years

Class B: Girls under 14 years

A year later, at the Westbury Kennel Club's 1933 show, the class divisions for Children's Handling were slightly different. At this time, the club combined boys and girls in one class and, for the first time, there was also an age division. The premium list's announcement included the following classes:

Boys and girls under 15 years of age

Boys and girls under 10 years of age

Junior Showmanship Finals, Westminster Kennel Club 1984 (left to right) Leonard Brumby, Jr.; Judge Mrs. Dorothy Welsh; David Harper, Top Junior Handler; Brad Buttner, last year's winner; Rebecca Gilbert, Crufts winner; and Paul Nigro. (Kneeling Lynn Bosley, Second-place winner; Deborah Jones, Third-place winner; and Andrea Spritzer, Fourth-place winner. (John Ashbey)

The only requirement mentioned was "no unruly dogs," and the promise was made to supply candy for all. This award marked the beginning of one of the many Junior Showmanship traditions that were to follow, offering prizes for all entrants or winners to entice children to compete.

Although Leonard Brumby, Sr., will always be considered the "founding father" of Junior Showmanship, another man played an important role in the growth and development of the competition. This man was George Foley, a show superintendent for many of the large dog shows, who took an interest in Children's Handling. He helped to promote the classes and encouraged the show-giving clubs to include the competition at their events. His influence was obvious since Children's Handling began to flourish on the East Coast with more members of the fancy becoming interested and involved.

Another advancement for the Children's Handling Class was its inclusion in the Westminster Kennel Club show in 1933. This was a first for the competition, and the show's magnitude, along with New York City's exciting Madison Square Garden setting, created a memorable event undoubtedly helping the competition gain prominence. The entry was limited to an extent, enabling only those junior handlers who had earned at least one first place during the year to compete. However, those junior handlers who had won three first places were barred from further competition until after Westminster. Today, eight wins are needed to qualify to compete at Westminster and many junior handlers far exceed that number of wins, thus barring other handlers from competition.

The first winner of the Children's Handling Class at the Westminster Kennel Club show was Joseph P. Sayres, who skillfully handled his Irish Terrier, Ch. Kelvin Glorius, into the winner's circle. On that special day, he took the Grand Challenge Trophy home with him. Sayres remained active in the dog world, later becoming a veterinarian and still has very fond memories of his participation in the Children's Handling Class.

In 1949, the Grand Challenge Trophy was replaced by the Leonard Brumby, Sr., Memorial Trophy for the top junior handler at Westminster. Donated by the Professional Handlers Association (PHA) in honor and memory of the founding father of Children's Handling, this became the most prestigious award in Junior Showmanship and is still presented annually. Once again, another Junior Showmanship tradition that began years ago still continues today.

The selection of judges and the judging procedures was far more casual in the early years than it is today. In fact, there were no special qualifications for the judges and often celebrities and movie stars were asked to officiate. Many of these people had no idea what the competition entailed and at some shows, Superintendent George Foley could be seen quickly trying to explain the Children's Handling Class to a mystified judge. This informality in the selection of judges often led to bad judging, in which a child was selected on "cuteness" rather than on handling ability. It was for this reason that the Professional Handlers Association became involved with the competition, encouraging its members to judge Children's Handling. Soon, *only* professional handlers were permitted to judge the class.

Although the professional handlers were certainly more qualified to judge the Children's Handling Class than celebrities, limiting the judging to them involved a number of problems. First, the name of the judge could no longer be printed in the premium list. This was due to the fact that judges were chosen spontaneously and often had to be changed because the professional handlers had to be in the ring, showing dogs themselves. At his shows, George Foley was again involved with the competition, specifically in the selection of judges. He would go into the crowd and ask a number of professional handlers if they would be willing to judge. Although Foley always managed to find a judge, the handlers were often afraid that accepting the assignment might tie them up, and therefore, they declined. Other handlers felt that it was too difficult to judge children, preferring to avoid dealing with the young competitors *and* their parents.

Over the years, the selection of judges and the judging techniques were frequently discussed matters. In an article published in the September 1949 issue of the *Gazette,* Edward Marvin Harrington pointed out that although having professional handlers judge the Children's Handling Class certainly was a step in the right direction, there was still a great deal of room for improvement in terms of judging techniques. Harrington noted a lack of uniformity in judging procedures, where children were not always required to demonstrate the same number of skills with which to prove their handling capabilities. He also encouraged *creativity* in judging in that a judge might, for example, intentionally move a dog's foot out of proper position to see if the young handler was alert enough to correct the position. Also stressed was the fact that in this particular competition it was the *child,* and not the dog, who was being judged, and such factors as a child's age or precocity were not to be taken into consideration. As was customary in the early stages of Children's Handling, judges and other adult members of the dog fancy were encouraged to support the efforts of the children, offering advice and trying hard to make the competition a valuable learning experience.

In 1951, the Children's Handling Class became known as the Junior Showmanship competition, and even though its roots were around 1932, Junior Showmanship did not receive official recognition from the American Kennel Club until 1971, almost forty years later.

Junior Showmanship was clearly an unusual competition, set apart from other dog show activities by its unique criteria for judging. The original proposal for judging, as it was printed in the April 1971 *Gazette* in order to serve as a general reference to all judges, read as follows:

"The judge must never be influenced by the breed of dog presented, age or size of handler or dog. Only the Junior Handler's ability to present his dog quietly, proficiently, and to its best advantage is to be considered, as well as sportsmanlike conduct. In large classes, it is suggested that those dogs not being examined or gaited be allowed to relax."

In 1974, the American Kennel Club invited *former* Junior Handlers to apply for Junior Showmanship judging status, and in 1977, with the termination of formal licensing of professional handlers, only breed judges and Junior Showmanship Only judges were eligible to officiate.

Children's Handling, which began with a small number of children from the New York area, eventually became a thriving competition. Junior clubs sprang up across the nation, and as the sport of dog showing gained in popularity in different parts of the country, the growth of Junior Showmanship paralleled this interest. Naturally as the popularity of Junior Showmanship grew, the class size increased, creating the need for more class divisions. Eventually, all shows had Novice and Open divisions, which were further divided by age: the Junior class for children at least ten years old and under thirteen years old on the day of the show, and the Senior class for competitors at least thirteen years old and under seventeen years old on the day of the show. Some shows even created more class divisions, separating the boys and girls in each class. Since the mid-1950s, children have also been divided according to their experience in the show ring. Originally, the Novice class was for Junior Handlers who had not won a first place at a licensed or member show, whereas the Open class was comprised of handlers who had at least one win in the Novice class. The winner of the Novice class automatically became eligible to enter and compete in the Open class at the same show. However, since July 1, 1976, Junior Handlers have been required to have three wins in the Novice class in order to compete in Open. At some shows, the winners of each of the four classes (Novice Junior, Novice Senior, Open Junior, Open Senior) compete for a Best Junior Handler award.

Changes in the Junior Showmanship competition have not been limited to rules and regulations. Styles of judging, as well as techniques for handling, have been transformed over the past fifty years. Suggestions on technique, attitude, and ring etiquette have appeared in *Gazette* articles and books periodically since the beginnings of the competition. Junior Handlers have repeatedly proved their handling abilities in the breed and obedience rings, as well as their organizational skills in the formation of Junior Clubs and the staging of their own match shows. Junior Showmanship has become an important addition to many specialty shows, and through the help of some involved individuals, including Paul Nigro, many shows offer a reduced entry fee for Junior Showmanship competitors. In addition, Mr. Nigro created the Puppy Placement Program, which unites Junior Handlers with "dog people," often breeders, who are willing to donate or co-own a dog to be shown. Many clubs and individuals also show their support for the competition by donating annual trophies or offering prizes for the Junior classes at the shows.

Andrea D. Korzenik

Premium Lists

The premium list has always been the primary advertisement for any AKC licensed or member event. However, over the years the American Kennel Club has adopted a number of rules that more clearly specified what had to appear in the premium list, which has served to make this document more uniform for all events.

The Bench Show Rules, which appeared in the 1887 issue of the *AKC Stud Book,* make three specific references to the premium list. They are as follows:

15. A dog to compete in a champion class must have won three first prizes, exclusive of puppy classes and miscellaneous classes, at shows recognized by the American Kennel Club, a list of which must be published in the premium list of each show.

24. The secretary of every show must forward to the secretary of the American Kennel Club a copy of the premium list of the proposed show, which must contain a list of officials under whose management the show is to be held.

25. All club members of this association shall be required in future to pay all regular prizes strictly in accordance with the description given of them in the published premium list.

Where medals are awarded, if they are described as gold or silver, their purity shall be that of United States coin. If manufactured of any other material, no description shall be given of its material; it shall be merely called the club medal.

As the years passed, and the sport grew, the American Kennel Club expanded the rules governing the content of the premium list. It was not until much later, however, that restrictions began to be placed on the actual format of the premium list. For example, the early rules contained no mention of size, nor of the order in which items in the premium list had to appear. There was also no mention of a closing date, although the 1937 rules do specify that at least seven days before an event, the club had to send a breakdown of entries in each breed to the American Kennel Club. The first mention of a closing date was in 1942, when it was specified that entries had to close at least seven days before the show. This limitation was placed on all-breed clubs only, and a stipulation was also made that if the closing date fell on a postal holiday, entries could be accepted if they were received in the first mail on the next day.

Beginning in 1948, the American Kennel Club required that clubs send proof copies of the premium list for examination at least seven weeks before the show. A requirement was also established in 1948 that all premium lists be mailed to prospective exhibitors at least four weeks prior to the show. In order to make premium lists more uniform, a requirement was also adopted in 1948, which established a 6'' by 9'' standard size for premium lists and entry forms. Clubs were also required to include the hours of the opening and closing of the show in the premium list, as well as established exercising periods. By 1952, the closing that had to appear in the premium list was moved up to two weeks for all-breed shows, and clubs were then required to submit a proof of their premium list to the American Kennel Club eight weeks before the show.

In an attempt to save on printing and mailing costs, the American Kennel Club adopted a rule in 1967 that enabled all-breed clubs to utilize the condensed form of premium lists. The content of the condensed premium list was identical with the content and format of a regular premium list, except that the listing of most of the prizes and trophies offered was omitted and included in a separate trophy list, which could be obtained by exhibitors upon request. The condensed form of premium list was adopted by many all-breed dog clubs, and in 1976 the rules were amended to permit clubs other than all-breed dog clubs to utilize this format.

The rules were amended in 1972 to provide that a club had to submit a proof of their premium list to the American Kennel Club at least nine weeks prior to the show. At the same time, the mandatory closing date for an all-breed show was moved up to two and a half weeks in order to allow clubs more time to prepare a catalog.

By 1974, the American Kennel Club was receiving a number of requests from clubs for a reduction in the official size of the premium list. It seemed that most commercial presses either could not accommodate the 6'' by 9'' format or had to charge more for the printing of a premium list in this size because of paper waste. Consequently, later that year the American Kennel Club adopted a rule that made the official size a range between $5^{1}/_{2}$'' by $8^{1}/_{2}$'' and 6'' by 9''.

In 1979, the American Kennel Club announced a trial period, during which it was no longer necessary for clubs to submit premium list proofs. This was done because premium lists had become so standardized that it was felt that the American Kennel Club could oversee them effectively through the establishment of guidelines for clubs and superintendents to follow, with the monitoring done after the premium lists were distributed. The trial period was very success-ful with fewer errors noted in the premium lists that were distributed; and so the requirement for the submission of premium list proofs was permanently eliminated in 1980.

James P. Crowley

Professional Handlers

The practice of securing the services of a professional handler is as old as the sport of pure-bred dogs in this country. However, it was not until 1930 that the American Kennel Club established criteria under which handlers were granted a license to engage in their profession at American Kennel Club dog shows.

A group of professional handlers formed the Professional Handlers' Association (PHA) in 1926. Their first real assembly took place in November 1926 in connection with the American Kennel Club sesquicentennial show in Philadelphia. At that time, Leonard Brumby, Sr., who later became the AKC's first full-time field representative, was named as the first president of the Professional Handlers' Association.

The delegates to the American Kennel Club adopted a rule at the September 3, 1929, delegates' meeting, providing: ''No person shall be eligible to handle dogs for pay or act as agent for pay at any show held under American Kennel Club Rules unless he shall hold a license granted by the said Club through its License Committee.'' This rule was made effective ninety days from the date of the meeting. The License Committee subsequently established fees for handlers' licenses: for public handlers $15 with $5 annual renewal and $10 with a $5 annual renewal for private handlers; assistant handlers were to be licensed at a rate of $5 with a $2 annual renewal. In 1954, the fees for obtaining a license and renewal were eliminated.

Handler's license Number 1 was issued to Harold Correll. A list of the first twenty-six public handlers licensed by the American Kennel Club was published in the January 1930 issue of the AKC Gazette. Thereafter, the AKC periodically published a complete alphabetical list of licensed handlers. In 1931, at the request of the PHA, AKC issued a directive to all clubs that handlers were to be given admission to any AKC show upon presentation of their license card.

In 1965, the American Kennel Club took cognizance of the face that certain individuals had a broader base of experience than others and began to approve some handlers on a limited basis. Previously, an individual receiving a handling license was permitted to handle any breed for pay at a dog show.

For many years, handlers were approved as judges of specialty shows on a show-by-show basis. However, this policy was changed in 1969. At the September, 1968 delegates' meeting, Mr. John Cross, AKC Senior Vice-President, addressed the delegates as follows: "When this practice first started, the handling situation was very different from what it is today. There were far fewer handlers in the field. It was a much smaller field, as everything else in dogs was much smaller than it is today; in the beginning, the majority of handlers in this country had come from the other side of the water, and their background in dogs, in most cases, was one that began in childhood. These men were frequently sons of handlers; sometimes their grandfathers and other members of the family had been handlers. It seemed to be something that almost ran in families. The result was that from infancy, these men had been exposed to dogs and their knowledge in most cases was really profound. These men really were the experts of that day, and it was only natural and understandable that exhibitors should want to get the best experts that there were. This type of background in dogs today is a vanishing thing. There are many more handlers today, and in a good many cases, they have a comparatively brief experience as exhibitors, and then been granted a handler's license or a limited handler's license. Frequently, in the opinion of your Board of Directors, the experience and background of these handlers is not sufficient to warrant approving them to judge specialty shows."

Through the years, the American Kennel Club tried to maintain a regular dialogue with the professional handlers, just as it tried to remain as receptive as possible to input from all segments of the fancy. However, it became apparent very early that there were many problems inherent in the licensing process. By 1950, Henry Bixby, AKC Executive Vice-President advised the PHA that AKC could foresee the possibility of discontinuing licensing. Finally, in 1977, the AKC delegates were advised that the time had come—the American Kennel Club was no longer in the position to handle the licensing of professional handlers adequately. At the July 1977 meeting, Mr. John A. Lafore, Jr., AKC President explained, "We have been receiving applications from a large number of people with limited experience in one or two breeds who are not pursuing handling on a full-time basis, but simply want to supplement their regular source of income or to help defray expenses of showing their own dogs. Since AKC licenses all professional handlers, many feel that AKC has conferred its unqualified stamp of approval on the professional competence of each handler it licenses. Unfortunately, such is not the case, as in the majority of cases, there is no definitive practical means by which such large numbers of applicants can be properly tested and screened."

There was a great deal of debate and controversy concerning this proposal. There was also a great deal of lobbying done by the Professional Handlers' Association and the Professional Handlers' Guild. In response to the lobbying that was being done, Mr. John A. Lafore, Jr., directed a memorandum to all delegates in August 1977, emphasizing again that the current rule requiring the licensing of any individual who handled a dog for pay was virtually unenforceable. He also explained that the discontinuance of licensing would not lead to a loss of control over the activities of handlers, as the constitution and bylaws of the American Kennel Club, as well as the rules, provided that charges must be preferred against "any person" for conduct alleged to be prejudicial.

The matter was presented to the delegates for a vote at its September 1977 meeting. There were 265 delegates present and voting at this meeting, which was an all-time record, exceeding the previous total of 209. Mr. William F. Stifel, AKC Executive Vice-President reiterated the American Kennel Club's arguments with regard to the discontinuance of licensing, and he also addressed the proposals submitted by the Professional Handlers' Association, which would have enacted stricter policies for the licensing of handlers, but which did not address the fact that it was virtually impossible to control the handling of dogs for pay by individuals that were not licensed by the American Kennel Club. The rule changes that were necessary to eliminate the licensing of handlers were adopted by the delegates with 228 votes for the motion and 37 votes against the motion.

W. Terry Stacy

Recording Fees

The concept of a recording fee first arose in 1944. At the December 14, 1943, meeting of delegates, Mr. Dudley P. Rogers, AKC President, made an appeal for suggestions on possible new sources of income, because the American Kennel Club was operating in the red. He implied that perhaps the raising of annual dues for member clubs should be considered. After some discussion, Mr. Richard C. Kettles, Jr., Delegate of the American Boxer Club, did move that the member dues be increased from $10 to $25 per year. This motion was seconded and passed.

At the March 14, 1944, delegates' meeting, Mr. Frank Downing, Delegate of the Pekingese Club of America, made a presentation for the institution of a twenty-five cent recording fee. Mr. Downing pointed out, "The keeping of show records places upon the AKC a burden for which it does not receive ample compensation, i.e., the expenses incurred are not adequately covered by the fees received from the clubs holding member and licensed shows. The said show records are kept primarily for the benefit of all dog clubs and dog fanciers; however, I believe the greatest benefit is derived by the exhibitors." Mr. Downing anticipated that, based on the total of 55,000 dogs entered in events during 1943, the recording fee would provide an annual income of $10,000 to $15,000. Mr. Downing proposed that the recording fee be instituted at the discretion of the Board of Directors of the American Kennel Club. Mr. Downing's motion was seconded and adopted.

For the next five years, a recording fee of twenty-five cents was collected intermittently at the discretion of the Board of Directors. However, at the June 7, 1949, meeting, a rule was adopted making the collection of a recording fee mandatory. While no specific amount was indicated, the fee was kept at twenty-five cents.

At this meeting, Mr. Dudley P. Rogers, President of the American Kennel Club, remarked that the recording fees had become an important part of revenue and that they served to offset the rising costs of club operations. He also pointed out that the club had never offered a pension or retirement plan to its salaried employees and that any revenue increases might well be devoted to meeting that problem.

The recording fee of twenty-five cents was collected until 1954. At the March 9, 1954, delegates' meeting, Mr. John C. Neff, Executive Vice-President of the American Kennel Club, presented an amendment to the rule that again made the collection of a recording fee an option to be exercised at the discretion of the Board of Directors, rather than a mandatory policy. A proposal was adopted so that the Board of Directors was given the authority to impose a recording fee, not to exceed twenty-five cents. More than twenty years passed before it again became necessary to implement the fee. An announcement was made at the December 13, 1977, meeting that it would once more be collected, effective April 1, 1978. Mr. William F. Stifel, then AKC Executive Vice-President, explained that, while the increase of the litter fee to $9 that had been implemented the previous year had helped to meet the 1977 budget, it seemed inescapable that the continuously increasing cost of publishing show results could not be paid for indefinitely by a steadily declining base of registrations. At the September 1982 meeting of delegates, Mr. Stifel, now AKC President, announced that the Board of Directors had recommended an increase in the recording fee to fifty cents and that a rule-change proposal would be presented at that December. He explained that the Board believed one of the most important new areas of investment for the AKC should be the improvement of the overall quality of events. One way this could be done, he suggested, would be to upgrade the quality of judging, an area in which the AKC was becoming actively involved. He emphasized again that an important commitment of both time and money would be necessary. The rule change, raising the recording fee to fifty cents, was approved at the December 14, 1982, delegates' meeting, with the change effective May 2, 1983.

James P. Crowley

Superintendents

The dog show superintendent has been a fixture at AKC events from the very beginning. However, the early rules made little distinction between the professional superintendent and the amateur show secretary. In accordance with Rule XX, effective January 1, 1910, neither was permitted to exhibit in shows at which they officiated. Yet a controversy still arose in 1911 concerning the exhibiting activites of superintendents. A rule change was proposed at the December 19, 1911, delegates' meeting, which read: "Dogs belonging to a kennel in which any of the above officials are in any way connected shall be deemed ineligible for competition."

Apparently, at a show held before this meeting, the show superintendent was the manager of a well-known kennel, and this kennel exhibited at that show. The American Kennel Club had received a number of complaints after this incident, which most probably resulted in the adoption of this new amendment to Rule XX.

The question of actually licensing superintendents first arose in 1913. The Rules Committee of the Board, of which Dr. John E. DeMund, the delegate for the Russian Wolfhound Club of America, was chairman, recommended the licensing of judges, handlers, and superintendents. However, when the necessary rule changes were submitted to the delegates in September 1913, there was a great deal of opposition, led by Mr. James Mortimner, delegate for the Ladies' Kennel Association of America. The main objection to the proposal was that it was not needed. The opinion was expressed that Rule XXIII adequately covered possible misconduct by these individuals. This rule dealt with the suspension of any person found guilty of misconduct of any kind in connection with dog events. The proposed amendment regarding licensing was subsequently put to a vote and defeated.

In May 1916, a committee consisting of H. K. Bloodgood, Dr. John E. DeMund, and George Greer was appointed to codify the AKC bylaws. The proposed new bylaws, which were published in the January 1917 Gazette, called for a standing License Committee, which "shall have the power to issue and revoke Licenses to Judges and Superintendents of shows."

At the same time that the above bylaws were proposed, a new set of rules and regulations were also submitted. Rule XX stated in part, "No person shall be eligible to act as superintendent of any show held under these rules, until he or she shall have been licensed to act in that capacity by the American Kennel Club through its License Committee."

The above changes were approved, and the following notice appeared in the April 1917 issue of the Gazette:

> "JUDGES' AND SUPERINTENDENTS' LICENSE APPLICATIONS
> Applicants desiring to officiate as Judges and Superintendents at shows held under American Kennel Club Rules can now obtain at this office application forms to act in either capacity.
> These forms must be filed with the License Committee for approval, after which cards will be issued granting whichever privilege is desired.
> The License Committee meets the first and third Tuesdays of each month.

The first list of licensed superintendents appeared in the May 1917 issue of the Gazette. The fourteen individuals listed were: Frank W. Barnes, Arthur W. Cates, George A. Cranfield, Miss Rhea K. Egolf, George F. Foley, George W. Gall, R. C. Halsted, Henry G. Hammond, Thomas E.L. Kemp, Bayard H. Moul, Charles E. O'Connor, Wilbur H. Purcell, M. D. Railey, and George Tinto.

From 1917 until 1931, superintending licenses were granted by the License Committee. However, the following notice appeared in the March 1931 issue of the Gazette:

> NO MORE STANDING COMMITTEES
>
> Under the new bylaws adopted by the American Kennel Club, all standing committees have been abolished and the duties formerly performed by these committees will in the future be executed by the Board of Directors. All correspondence formerly addressed to the License Committee, Rules Committee, and other committees, should be addressed direct to the Secretary.

At the beginning of 1985, there were sixty active individuals who had been approved as annually licensed superintendents, serving as the head of a superintending organization or as an employee of such an enterprise. Ninety-six percent of the all-breed dog shows held in 1984 were superintended, as opposed to only 4 percent that were handled by nonlicensed show secretaries.

Hilde Weihermann

Veterinarians

All the early American Kennel Club dog shows had a veterinarian in attendance. The bench show rules published in 1887 contained the following three rules referring to veterinarians:

Rule IX.   Total blindness, deafness or lameness shall absolutely disqualify. If the judge or veterinary surgeon is satisfied that the deafness or lameness is temporary, the dog shall be allowed to compete.

Rule X.   A Dog suffering from mange or any contagious disease shall be disqualified, and forfeit any prize which may have been awarded to it, and shall be removed at once from the show room. The regularly appointed veterinary surgeon shall alone decide as to mange or contagious disease, and his decision must be given in writing.

Rule XI.   A judge may disqualify a Dog which in his opinion has been improperly tampered with, subject to the decision of the veterinary surgeon, should the judge's disqualification not be sustained, the class must be immediately rejudged.

The rules adopted in December 1888 specify: "A recognized veterinary surgeon must be appointed at each show held under these rules. Each dog received at a show must be passed upon by him before being benched." This was expanded upon in 1909, when the following rule to take effect January 1, 1910, was instituted:

Rule XVIII.   Every Show must have a qualified veterinarian, who shall be in attendance before and during the progress of the Show, and no dog shall be benched without having been examined and passed by him or his representative, who shall himself be a qualified veterinarian. He is required to personally inspect the dogs on the benches and the quarters where the dogs are exercised, or crated, before 6 P.M. on the opening of the Show, and at least once during the morning of each day shall examine all dogs and submit a written report to the Bench Show Committee. Dogs suffering from contagious diseases must be removed from the building. The Show Committee shall be empowered, in case the regularly appointed veterinarian shall be incapacitated to serve, to appoint another veterinarian to take his place and act for him in all things. Failing to comply with this rule, the Club shall be liable to suspension.

In February 1917, the word *suspension* was replaced by *discipline,* obviously to allow for a variety of measures, rather than just one option, to ascertain compliance with this rule.

Until December 1957, the rules required that every dog attending a show be examined. An editorial appeared in the November 1956 issue of the *Gazette,* questioning whether this practice was necessary. The editorial asked, "Do the protective advantages of the rule more than offset the delays which each exhibitor will experience at the gate, the responsibilities and expenses which clubs will experience through a proper administration of the rule?" The editorial went on to discuss at some length the pros and cons of the mandatory veterinary examination of all dogs at a show. The subject was raised at the December 11, 1956, delegates' meeting. Mr. Trachman, delegate of the Suffolk County Kennel Club, indicated that the aforementioned editorial had engendered considerable interest and comment and suggested he thought the subject important enough to propose that the next meeting of the delegates be devoted entirely to a discussion of the matter, after transaction of the necessary business of the annual meeting. This motion was seconded and passed. The topic "Examined Shows" was discussed at length at the March 12, 1957 delegates' meeting.

Mr. Buckley, AKC President, announced at the June 11, 1957, delegates' meeting that a rule change would be proposed that would "give a show-giving club the right to choose an 'examined' show, and if a club does not so elect, provisions will be made for attendance of qualified veterinarians throughout the show hours who can be called upon by any exhibitor to examine a dog thought to be sick and who also will render opinions on conditions of dogs when called upon by judges or bench show committees." The amendments making an examined show optional were adopted at the September 10, 1957 delegates' meeting.

The number of clubs that exercised the option of having an examined show continuously decreased after 1957. Finally in January 1985, the provision for examined shows was eliminated from the rules, as none had been held in more than ten years.

There were two key rule amendments adopted during the 1970s concerning the role of the veterinarian at a show. Prior to 1972, a judge could call upon the veterinarian, who had to be in attendance at every show, for an opinion on such matters as lameness or surgical alterations. However, effective January 1972, the judge was expected to make these decisions on his or her own. It was still mandatory for a club to arrange for a veterinarian to be in attendance during the show, but it was not necessary to delay the start of judging if the veterinarian was late or to stop judging when it was discovered that the veterinarian had left the grounds prior to completion of best-in-show.

In September 1977, clubs were given the option of having a veterinarian on call rather than in attendance at unbenched shows. This change was adopted because of the fact that there were very few instances where a veterinarian's services had been required, and if there was any serious problem, the dog probably would still have to be moved to the veterinarian's office for treatment. The requirement of having a veterinarian in attendance has been retained for benched shows. It was felt that the elimination of this requirement from those events could prompt excessive requests for excusals, which without the assistance of a veterinarian could create serious problems for the show committee.

Hilde Weihermann

Club Relations

The Development of Dog Clubs

The meeting of bench show associations was held in Philadelphia on September 17, 1884, with thirteen clubs present, for the purpose of organizing a national association. The meeting was reconvened at Madison Square Garden in New York on October 22, 1884. At that meeting it was voted to call the association *The American Kennel Club,* and Article I of its constitution provided that all regularly organized clubs or associations of the United States and British American provinces, under whose auspices bench shows or field trials of dogs were held, or which had been formed wholly or in part for the purpose of holding bench shows or field trials, would be eligible for membership. The constitution also provided for the members of the association to be represented at each meeting by delegates whose appointments would be certified in writing by the secretaries of several member clubs, with these certificates delivered to the Secretary of the association. Delegates were not required to be members of the club or clubs they represented. Article XII stipulated that clubs eligible for membership be proposed by a member of the executive committee and elected by that committee. Two negative votes excluded the candidate. The executive committee was comprised of the president, vice-presidents, secretary, and treasurer, as well as one representative of each club of the association. In accordance with Article II of the bylaws, the executive committee appointed from its members a committee on credentials, whose duties included investigating the qualifications of candidates for membership and reporting same to the executive committee.

Under the rules governing clubs effective January 1, 1910, active members of the American Kennel Club were eligible to hold shows under the rules of the License Committee, and clubs or organizations not a member of the American Kennel Club could be licensed to hold a show. The committee would not approve applications where show dates conflicted, unless it was shown conclusively that the granting of such application would not work to the detriment of the clubs. Member clubs were not charged a fee for their first event in each calendar year but paid $15 for each additional event. Nonmember clubs paid a $15 fee for every event held.

The License Committee, at its March 1930 meeting, adopted rules and regulations governing sanctioned matches. Clubs could hold matches under Plan A, Plan B, Plan C, Plan D, or Plan E.

Under the bylaws adopted in 1930, all standing committees were abolished and their duties assumed by the Board of Directors. An amendment adopted at the February 1933 meeting provided that all clubs or associations that held at least three dog shows or field trials in consecutive years under the rules of the American Kennel Club and all specialty clubs formed for the improvement of any breed or related breeds of pure-bred dogs would be eligible to become members of the American Kennel Club. Beginning in July 1946, all-breed clubs were required to conduct at least two Plan A matches before conducting licensed shows, and in July 1947, the identical criteria were applied to specialty clubs and obedience clubs.

The American Kennel Club now comprises over four hundred member organizations and issues licenses to more than two thousand clubs for the holding of dog shows, obedience trials, field trials, and tracking tests. There are four types of clubs for which accreditation to conduct sanctioned matches is considered: specialty, all-breed, obedience, and tracking. Specialty clubs are devoted to serving the interest of a particular breed, further, there are some breeds for which field-trial competition is offered. All-breed clubs serve the interests of fanciers of all breeds, while obedience clubs serve enthusiasts who are interested in the obedience aspect of the sport. The purpose of tracking clubs is to demonstrate the dog's ability to recognize and follow human scent and to use this skill in the service of mankind.

The formation and organization of a dog club is generally a spontaneous gesture on the part of interested breeders, exhibitors, and dog owners who reside in a given area or, in the case of a national specialty club, in all portions of the United States. The approach usually taken in connection with the formation of a local club is the calling of an organizational meeting of those individuals residing in the immediate area. At the meeting, temporary officers are elected from those present to oversee the group's operation until such time as regular elections are held in accordance with a constitution and bylaws under which the club would be governed. A committee is appointed to propose a constitution and bylaws to the membership for adoption. In addition, a meeting schedule and location are decided upon, and an individual is appointed to keep records of the club's development. After these matters are finalized, the actual existence and operation of the group is in the hands of its membership.

Before any serious thought is given to the possibility of a group's being placed on AKC's records for the holding of informal (Plan B/OB) sanctioned matches, certain requirements must be met. First, while the AKC is prepared to assist new clubs, encouragement will not be forthcoming to new clubs formed to serve the sport in the area of an existing club. Dissatisfaction with an existing club is not sufficient reason to form a new club in the same area. Second, while membership is to be unrestricted as to residence, the club's primary purpose is to be as representative as possible of the breeders, exhibitors, and dog owners in its immediate area. Thus, consideration will not be forthcoming for clubs organized on statewide, regional, or sectional bases. Third, the club's name should identify its geographic range of activity—the area from which the overwhelming majority of the club's membership is drawn—yet be readily recognizable to fanciers in other parts of the country. Fourth, new clubs should demonstrate ongoing viability by establishing a record of meetings and activities and one election under their bylaws over at least a year's period of time. Fifth, a club must demonstrate to the satisfaction of the AKC that there is sufficient interest in the membership and area to warrant accreditation as a sanctioned-match-giving club. A certain minimum amount of interest must be demonstrated. Fanciers should recognize that, unfortunately, there are areas that simply cannot support dog clubs and that there are breeds for which sufficient interest cannot be demonstrated on a local level.

All new club presentations are reviewed by an AKC staff committee. If approved, the club is notified. Clubs not yet sufficiently organized and developed are informed, with an explanation. Clubs should not submit applications until their eligibility to do so is established and the club so notified. Often, clubs are disappointed because AKC approval is not granted after commitments have already been made.

Sanctioned matches serve many purposes. For new clubs they are a means for club members to learn the details and mechanics of a dog show, obedience trial, field trial, or tracking test. For fanciers, matches represent an opportunity for inexperienced dogs to get valuable experience. In some respects matches are the classrooms of tomorrow's exhibitors and judges. AKC presently approves two types of sanctioned matches: an informal Plan B/OB match and the more formal Plan A/OA match. Within one week of a sanctioned B/OB match, the club is required to submit a report of the event. Within one week of a sanctioned A/OA, the club should not only submit a report of the event but also all judges' books, entry forms, premium lists, and a catalog marked to show all awards.

Specialty clubs must hold a "program" of Plan B matches over a minimum period of at least eighteen months. All-breed and obedience clubs must hold a "program" of Plan B/OB matches over a minimum period of at least two years. Tracking clubs must conduct at least one informal tracking/tracking dog excellent match. Clubs may hold Plan B matches as frequently as is considered feasible. When a newly sanctioned club has conducted a "program" of informal matches over the required time period, a presentation for advancement to Plan A/OA sanctioned matches may be submitted. Holding an all-breed show or an obedience trial is much more difficult than putting on a specialty show. The problems of suitable location, ring facilities, judges, scheduling, and all the various details associated with putting on a show or trial are more complicated for all-breed events and obedience trials than for specialty shows. For this reason, AKC routinely requires all-breed and obedience clubs to hold more Plan B matches over a longer period of time than specialty clubs or tracking clubs.

In order for a club to be considered for advancement to the holding of Plan A/OA matches the following must be submitted:

1. A separate copy of the club's most recent membership list with the letter designations, *B* for breeder (any member who has bred and registered a litter within the previous three years), *E* for exhibitor (any member who has exhibited at AKC licensed or member club shows within the previous two years), *DO* for a dog owner (any member who owns one or more AKC registered dogs but who is not a breeder or exhibitor).

2. Detailed breeding, exhibiting and dog owning records for each member. Breeding records should include litter numbers and whelping dates and should cover a period of approximately three years. Exhibiting records should include the names and dates of licensed or member club shows/trials at which the member has exhibited and should cover a period of about two years. Dog owning records should include the name and AKC registration number of each dog owned; in the case of an all-breed, obedience or tracking club, the breed of each pure-bred dog each member owns should be provided. If activity is extensive, it is only necessary to provide a random sampling of litters and shows/trials.

3. A brief update of the club's activities other than matches. This may be in outline or narrative form and should include mention of classes, demonstrations, educational programs, etc.

4. A copy of the bylaws under which the club is governed.

When reviewing a request for advancement to Plan A/OA matches, the committee considers, among other things, the continuity and development of membership; the quality of interest of the club's sustaining members; and the quality of activities and events, as well as its Plan B/OB matches.

Clubs are required to conduct two ''qualifying'' sanctioned A/OA matches, held at least six months apart, prior to entertaining representations requesting license status. The representations should include:

1. A separate copy of the most recent membership list with the letter designations, *B* (breeder), *E* (exhibitor) and *DO* (dog owner).
2. An update of the detailed breeding, exhibiting, and dog-owning records that were submitted when the club was approved for the holding of Plan A/OA matches.
3. Any revisions to the club's bylaws.
4. A list of activities other than matches, with locations and dates.

Michael Liosis

Women Delegates

Few sports have been as open to people from all walks of life as the sport of pure-bred dogs. When the Kennel Club in England was founded in 1873, by S. E. Shirley, it enjoyed the patronage of the royal family. E. W. Jaquet in *The Kennel Club: A History and Record of Its Work,* published in 1905, says:

> It is solely owing to the influence of the Club that today dog breeding and dog showing are pursuits that can be indulged in by gentlewomen, and dog shows held under Kennel Club Rules are patronised by every class of the community, including their Majesties the King and Queen— a wonderful testimony to the acumen and foresight of Mr. Shirley.

America followed England's lead in the sport but with its own variations. For example, when the American Kennel Club was formed, there was no provision for individual members. Its members were dog clubs, each of which was entitled to send a delegate to the club's meetings.

The constitution and bylaws as printed in Volume IV of the *Stud Book,* 1887, do not specify that the delegate be a male, although the pronouns *he* and *his* are used. When the AKC was incorporated in 1909, the bylaws stated ''The voting powers of each Member Club can and shall be exercised only by a male delegate selected by said club to represent it for that purpose.''

Women participated in the sport almost from the very beginning. The prestigious and influential Westminster Kennel Club ''encouraged'' the formation of the Ladies' Kennel Association of America. Westminster was the first club to have a female judge on its panel. At its 1888 show, a courageous Anna H. Whitney judged St. Bernards. For the next fifteen years she judged at Westminster and was always highly regarded by the press, by the dog world, and by the public. Indeed, at that period in time, a woman judge was a major attraction, a fact that did not escape Westminster's show committee.

As time went on, women assumed a greater role in dog shows but did not seem to be concerned that they were not part of the governing body. The feminist movement had not yet arrived.

In the late 1940s and early 1950s, the sport began to grow rapidly. As registrations grew, so did the number of dog clubs and dog shows. Women were even more active. Mrs. Geraldine Rockefeller Dodge presided over the spectacular Morris and Essex shows. Many of the best known kennels were run by women, who showed their own dogs with great success.

There is little documentation about any movement to seat women delegates before 1950. In December of that year, James M. Austin, delegate of the Ladies' Kennel Association of America and owner of the famous Fox Terrier, Nornay Saddler, proposed that the delegates go on record as being in favor of making women eligible to be elected as delegates. There was no second to the motion and no action was taken.

At the annual meeting in March 1951, Mr. Austin brought up the subject again. This time it was seconded and some discussion followed. A motion to table the proposal was made by John A. Brownell, delegate of the New England Dog Training Club. A debate about parliamentary procedure ensued and Mr. Austin eventually withdrew his motion. It was pointed out that in order to seat women, the bylaws would have to be changed and that there was a process available to do this. The ball was back in the Board's court.

At the June 1951 delegates' meeting, the president reported that the Board had decided to put the issue before the delegates at the annual meeting in March 1952. The provisions of the AKC By-Laws had been set in motion. Mr. Buckley further stated that any other method of bringing the issue before the delegates would infringe upon the rights of member clubs to instruct their delegates as to their wishes.

Apparently, there was no set voting procedure for amending the bylaws, and Mr. William Brainard, delegate for the Spaniel Breeders Society, proposed a secret written ballot. Mr. Austin spoke in favor of a roll-call vote but the opposition prevailed. The amendment was defeated. A request was made to reveal the count but was denied by a voice vote.

The issue lay dormant for twenty years. If there was sentiment to seat women, it was very low key. By 1970, the effects of feminism had filtered down to the sport of dogs. Equal opportunity litigation was rampant. Traditional male bastions fell one by one, and the American Kennel Club could no longer hold back the future.

In June 1972, AKC President John A. Lafore advised the delegates that the Board was considering the possibility of bringing before the delegates a proposal to amend the By-Laws to permit women to be seated as delegates. The decision had been reached after consulting with the club's attorney.

At the September 1973 meeting, Mr. Lafore announced that the proposal would be brought before the December meeting. The form of the amendment would be published in the *Gazette* as required.

At the December meeting, a motion was made to adopt the amendment. It was also decided to use a secret ballot. The motion was defeated by twenty-five votes.

However, at the Board meeting, a written notice had been submitted requesting that the proposed change be placed before the annual meeting in March. The issue was still alive.

The March 1974 annual meeting of the American Kennel Club was a historic event. The motion to decide about the amendment to delete the word *male* from Article VI, Section 1 was to be by roll call. There was no chance for a delegate to vote his own way secretly rather than follow his club's wishes. The amendment passed by a vote of 180 to 7.

The first female delegates' names were published in two issues of the *Gazette* as required. They were approved at the June 1974 delegates' meeting. They were: Mrs. Carol D. Duffy, Mid-Hudson Kennel Club; Mrs. Gertrude Freedman, Bulldog Club of New England; and Mrs. Julia Gasow, English Springer Spaniel Club of Michigan.

In March 1985, the delegates elected Dr. Jacklyn Hungerland, delegate of the Del Monte Kennel Club, as the first woman director of the American Kennel Club. Full equality had arrived.

Roberta Vesley

World Congresses

The first World Conference of Kennel Clubs was held in London on February 6-9, 1978.

The presiding officer was Mr. Leonard Pagliero. A member of the English Kennel Club's General Committee for some twenty-five years and its chairman from 1976 until 1981, it was Mr. Pagliero who, during his chairmanship, conceived the idea of a World Conference of Kennel Clubs and organized it with the backing of the English Kennel Club as host.

During his opening remarks at the first session, Mr. Pagliero said he believed the conference would mark "the dawn of a new era in the relationship between the kennel clubs of the world." Noting that is was not to be a conference of "great decisions," he said, "We are not intending to pass important or imposing resolutions but to use the conference as a forum in which we can exchange views, put forward ideas, come to a better understanding, and pave the way for future discussions. I hope that this will be the beginning of a series of conferences that may continue in the years to come."

The agenda for the business sessions, which were conducted at the Connaught Rooms in Great Queen Street, London, included the following subjects:

Unification of breed standards

International recognition of judges

Field trials

Working trials and obedience

Rare breeds

Canine abnormalities

Computerization of registration records

In addition, the delegates visited the Guide Dogs for the Blind Centre at Wokingham, the Animal Health Trust at Newmarket, and the Metropolitan Police Dog Training Centre at Keston. They also visited The Kennel Club at 1 Clarges Street, London. An official Kennel Club dinner for the delegates was held at the Connaught Rooms, and on the Friday and Saturday following the conference, the delegates were guests at The Kennel Club at the Crufts Dog Show at Olympia in London.

Delegates to the first World Conference were as follows:

AUSTRALIA
Australian National Kennel Council
Mr. J. G. W. Head
Mr. A Howie
Mr. H. Phillips
Dr. H. R. Spira
Mr. K. D. Turnbull

BARBADOS
Barbados Kennel Club
Mr. A. G. F. Seale

BELGIUM
Societe Royal Saint-Hubert
Mr. E. Vanherle

BERMUDA
Bermuda Kennel Club
Mrs. Mary E. Leighton
Mrs. Paula S. McAteer
Mrs. K. Trerice
Mrs. I. Voisey

BRAZIL
Brazil Kennel Club
Mr. Edmund Beim
Count Bonfrancesco Vinci

CANADA
Canadian Kennel Club
Mr. G. M. Ashcroft
Mrs. Hilda F. Pugh

CARIBBEAN
Caribbean Kennel Club
Mr. Charles Aqui
Mrs. Alma Hasler

DENMARK
Dansk Kennel Club
Mrs. E. Kopfod
Mr. O. Staunskjaer

ENGLAND
The Kennel Club
Mrs. Y. Bentinck
Mr. R. H. Oppenheimer
Mr. Leonard Pagliero
Mr. John S. Williams
Federation Cynologique Internationale
Mr. C. Schoor

FINLAND
Suomen Kennelliitto-Finska Kennelklubben r.y.
Mr. Paatsama

FRANCE
Societe Centrale Canine
Mr. G. Thorp
Mrs. Wibault

GERMANY
Verband fur das Deutsche Hundewesen e.V.
Dr. H. Wirtz

INDIA
Kennel Club of India
Mr. M. J. Krishnamoham
Mr. S. Pathy
Mr. S. Rangarajan
Maharaja Jaideep Singh of Baria

ITALY
Ente Nazionale Della Cinofilia Italiana
Avv. Giovanni Radice
Mr. Marco Valcarenghi

JAPAN
Japan Kennel Club
Mr. Kazumasa Igarashi
Mr. Junichiro Sawabe
Mr. Takashi Shimizu
Mr. Motokane Yukawa

JERSEY
Jersey Dog Club
Mr. M. I. R. Cook
Mrs. M. I. R. Cook

MALAYSIA
Malaysian Kennel Association
Mr. Lim Chong Keat

MONACO
Societe Canine de Monaco
H. S. H. The Princess Antoinette of Monaco

NETHERLANDS
Raad Van Beheer op Kynologisch Gebied in Nederland
Mr. C. Schoor
Mr. M. v. d. Weijer

NEW ZEALAND
New Zealand Kennel Club
Mr. H. Stewart Lusk
Mrs. H. Stewart Lusk
Dr. C. A. Tourelle
Mrs. C. A. Tourelle

NORWAY
Norsk Kennel Klub
Mr. T. Aasheim
Mr. P. Halmrast

PORTUGAL
Clube Portugues de Canicultura
Dr. Antonio Cabral
Ing. Luis Teixeira

SCOTLAND
Scottish Kennel Club
Mr. J. P. Butchart
Mr. I. M. Sim

SINGAPORE
Singapore Kennel Club
Mrs. Edith Cho
Mr. Francis Yeoh

SOUTHERN AFRICA
Kennel Union of Southern Africa
Mr. H. M. Bennett
Mr. R. M. Murchie

SPAIN
Real Sociedad Central de Fomento de las Razas Caninas
en Espana
Mr. Antonio Lozano
Marques de Perales
Mr. Andres del Rio Perez

SWEDEN
Svenska Kennelklubben
Mr. C. J. Adlercreutz
Mr. K. G. Fredricson
Mr. Bo Jonsson
Mrs. Ulla Magnusson
Dr. P. E. Sundgren

SWITZERLAND
Stammbuchsekretariat der SKG
Mr. Glattli
Mr. H. Muller

UNITED STATES OF AMERICA
American Kennel Club
Mr. William F. Stifel

WALES
Welsh Kennel Club
Mr. George Couzens
Mr. David Samuel
Mr. Leslie Thomas

Meeting on International Unification of Breed Standards

At the first world conference, it was unanimously agreed that efforts should be made to secure the unification of breed standards, and it was left to the English Kennel Club to convene a meeting with the American Kennel Club, the Australian Kennel Control, and the Federation Cynologique Internationale, to consider how this might be achieved. The meeting was held at The Kennel Club in London on November 13-14, 1980. Mr. Leonard Pagliero presided. The following delegates attended:

American Kennel Club

Mr. Haworth F. Hoch (chairman of the board)

Mr. William F. Stifel (president)

Federation Cynologique Internationale

Mr. Henri Lestienne (president)

Dr. H. Wirtz (Germany)

Dr. Tobjørn Aasheim (Norway)

Mr. Jean Catzenstein (general secretary)

The Kennel Club

Mr. Leonard Pagliero (chairman of the General Committee)

Brigadier A. P. Campbell (vice-chairman of the General Committee)

Mr. A. O. Grindey (chairman of the Breed Standards Sub-Committee)

Mr. G. F. Farrand (chairman of the Shows and Regulations Committee)

Mr. Michael J. R. Stockman, MRVCS

The Australian Kennel Control was invited but was unable to send representatives. However, they expressed great interest in the subject and asked to be kept fully informed of all developments.

The agenda for the meeting was limited largely to the discussion of breed standards. The group agreed unanimously that in order to achieve unification, all standards must be written in the same form and agreed to recommend the Guideline for Writing Breed Standards that was submitted by the American Kennel Club. The committee also reviewed individual breed standards, with particular reference to the discrepancies existing from country to country. In addition, the committee discussed the desirability of having a common nomenclature.

Two items that were not on the agenda or strictly within the purview of the committee were discussed briefly; namely, artificial insemination using fresh or frozen semen and the registration of offspring thus produced, and compulsory tattooing as a means of identification of dogs.

Second World Congress of Kennel Clubs

The second World Congress of Kennel Clubs was held in Edinburgh, Scotland, on May 18-21, 1981, in conjunction with the centenary celebration of the Scottish Kennel Club. It should be noted that while the meeting in London was called a world *conference* of kennel clubs, this meeting, as well as the subsequent meeting in the United States, was called a world *congress* of kennel clubs. The chairman was Mr. Ian Butchart, convener of the Scottish Kennel Club, and the agenda for the business sessions, which were conducted at the Gogar Park Curling Club, included the following:

Unification of breed standards

International recognition of judges
International communications
Canine show organization
Protection of affixes (kennel names)
Structure and movement of dogs
Dogs in the community

In addition, the delegates attended demonstrations of working dogs, sheep dogs, and police dogs; and delegates who were judges judged a match at the Royal Highland Showground in Ingliston near Edinburgh. They also attended a public meeting in the Assembly Rooms in Edinburgh on dog legislation and the place of the dog in the community.

At the final session of the congress, it was voted to appoint a steering committee to establish places and dates for subsequent world congresses, the committee to consist of one representative from each of the following groups of countries: a) the United Kingdom, Australia, and the United States; b) the Federation Cynologique Internationale countries; and c) other countries. Representatives of the various countries then met and elected the following committee: Mr. Leonard Pagliero of England; Dr. Karen Lindhe of Sweden; and Mr. Greg R. Eva of Southern Africa.

On Friday and Saturday following the congress, the delegates were guests of the Scottish Kennel Club at the Scottish Kennel Club's Centenary Championship Show at the Royal Highland Showground, and on Friday evening, the delegates were guests at a dinner honoring the congress and the centenary at the Prestonfield House Hotel in Edinburgh.

Delegates to the second World Congress were as follows:

AUSTRALIA
Australian National Kennel Council
Mr. W. Crowley
Mr. Robert L. Curtis
Dr. H. R. Spira

BERMUDA
Bermuda Kennel Club
Mr. John A. Ferguson
Mrs. John A. Ferguson
Mrs. Mary E. Leighton

CANADA
Canadian Kennel Club
Mr. W. Dawson
Mr. Ed Dixon
Mr. John C. Gough
Mrs. Hilda F. Pugh

ENGLAND
The Kennel Club
Mr. W. B. Edmond
Mr. A. O. Grindey
Mr. Leonard Pagliero

FINLAND
Suomen Kennelliitto-Finska Kennelklubben r.y.
Mr. R. Vuorinen

IRELAND
Irish Kennel Club
Mr. J. G. Plunkett

JAMAICA
Jamaican Kennel Club
Mrs. P. H. Tomlinson

KENYA
East Africa Kennel Club
Mr. J. L. Beecher
Mrs. A. S. Gray
Miss P. Strawhecker

MALAYSIA
Malaysian Kennel Association
Mr. Lim Chong Keat

MONACO
Societe Canine de Monaco
H. S. H. The Princess Antoinette of Monaco

NETHERLANDS
Raad Van Beheer op Kynologisch Gebied in Nederland
Mr. F. Heerens
Baronesse S. M. van Nagell

NEW ZEALAND
New Zealand Kennel Club
Mr. G. B. Catton
Dr. C. A. Tourelle

NORWAY
Norsk Kennel Klub
Mr. R. Campbell
Mr. P. Halmrast
Mrs. E. Mjerde

SCOTLAND
Scottish Kennel Club
Mr. W. R. Irving
Dr. Arthur E. T. Sneeden
Mrs. C. G. Sutton
Mrs. E. W. Whyte

SOUTHERN AFRICA
Kennel Union of Southern Africa
Mr. Greg R. Eva
Mr. R. M. Murchie

SWEDEN
Svenska Kennelklubben
Dr. Karen Lindhe

UNITED STATES OF AMERICA
American Kennel Club
Mr. William F. Stifel

WALES
Welsh Kennel Club
Mr. David Samuel
Mr. Leslie Thomas

Third World Congress of Kennel Clubs

The third World Congress of Kennel Clubs was held in Philadelphia, Pennsylvania, on November 12-14, 1984, in conjunction with the American Kennel Club's hundredth anniversary celebration.

The chairman was Mr. William F. Stifel, President of the American Kennel Club.

The agenda for the business sessions, which were conducted at the Bellevue Stratford Hotel in Philadelphia, included:

Future world congresses

Obedience, field trials, and junior showmanship

AKC's audio-visual presentations on breed standards

Genetic and infectious diseases of the dog

Restrictive canine legislation

American breeds

The quality of international judging

International breed standards

In addition, the delegates visited the University Museum at the University of Pennsylvania to see an exhibition on domesticated animals, put on by the School of Veterinary Medicine in connection with its centennial celebration, and an exhibition of canine art put on by the Dog Museum of America.

On Thursday, they were guests of the Dog Judges Association of America at an all-day program devoted to various breeds. On Friday, they attended an association of twenty-seven specialty shows at the Philadelphia Civic Center and were offered guided tours of the School of Veterinary Medicine. On Saturday and Sunday, they were guests at the AKC Centennial Dog Show and Obedience Trial at the Philadelphia Civic Center, and on Saturday night, were guests at the AKC Centennial Dinner at the Union League Club in Philadelphia.

The subject of future world congresses, which was the first item at the opening session, dealt with the question of formalizing the organization, with special emphasis on possible structure and financing, liaison committees, a permanent secretariat, and worldwide cooperation in dog affairs. At the final session on Wednesday afternoon, the following decisions were made: that world congresses should be convened at two-year intervals, with venues fixed two years ahead; that the next world congress should be held in New Zealand in 1986, and that the next congress should follow in Canada in 1988. The group then voted between two propositions: 1)that the New Zealand Kennel Club should have the responsibility for all the details of arranging the next conference and that, in the interim, AKC along with the New Zealand Kennel Club should form a committee for planning purposes; or 2) that a small committee should be formed to

Assembled Delegates to 3rd World Congress of Kennel Clubs—Philadelphia, PA—Bellevue Stratford Hotel, November, 1984.

Mrs. Beth Cooper of the Kennel Club of India, Mr. and Mrs. William F. Stifel, and Mrs. Leela Ratnam and Mrs. Dhyamala Murugesan, also representing the Kennel Club of India. (Meg Callea)

Chatting at the World Congress (left to right) Mrs. Ann Stevenson, Mr. Greg Eva—Kennel Club of South Africa, Mrs. Lynette Saltzman, Mrs. Patti Spears, and Mrs. Philip S. P. Fell. (Meg Callea)

Dr. Harry R. Spira, Delegate from the Australian National Kennel Council (right) listens intently to Contessa Lascelles de Premio Real of the Federacion Canofilia Mexicana, as Prof. Rafael de Santiago of the Federacion Canofilia de Puerto Rico, looks on. (Meg Callea)

act as a pivot and point of reference to assist with the arrangement of the agenda and the determination of what subjects and what papers should be presented. Following discussion, the delegates voted in favor of the first proposition.

Delegates to the third World Congress were as follows:

AUSTRALIA
Australian National Kennel Council
Mr. Robert L. Curtis
Mr. Laurence L. Grant
Mrs. Laurence L. Grant
Mr. W. C. Kinsman
Mrs. W. C. Kinsman
Dr. H. R. Spira

BARBADOS
Barbados Kennel Club
Mr. Christopher G. Leacock
Mrs. Christopher G. Leacock

BERMUDA
Bermuda Kennel Club
Mr. John A. Ferguson
Mrs. John A. Ferguson
Mrs. Mary E. Leighton
Mrs. Paula S. McAteer
Miss Natalie E. North

CANADA
Canadian Kennel Club
Mr. Ed Dixon
Mr. John C. Gough
Dr. Richard Meen
Mr. Robert W. Nutbeem
Mrs. Robert W. Nutbeem

ENGLAND
The Kennel Club
Mr. John A. MacDougall
Mrs. John A. MacDougall
Mr. Leonard Pagliero
Mr. Michael J. R. Stockman

INDIA
Kennel Club of India
Mrs. Leela Ratnam

ITALY
Ente Nazionale Della Cinofilia
   Italiana
Mr. Giuseppe Benelli

MEXICO
Federacion Canofila Mexicana A.C.
Ing. Robin F. Hernandez
Contessa Lascelles de Premio Real
Mrs. Thelma Von Thaden Warner

NETHERLANDS
Raad Van Beheer op Kynologisch Gebied
   in Nederland
Baronesse S. M. van Nagell

NEW ZEALAND
New Zealand Kennel Club
Mr. Malcolm P. Banks
Mrs. Malcolm P. Banks
Mr. J. Perfect
Dr. C. A. Tourelle

PANAMA
Club Canino de Panama
Mrs. Ingeborg Kincaid

PUERTO RICO
Federacion Canofila de Puerto Rico
Prof. Rafael de Santiago

SCOTLAND
Scottish Kennel Club
Major James G. Logan
Dr. Arthur E. T. Sneeden

SOUTHERN AFRICA
Kennel Union of Southern Africa
Mr. Greg R. Eva

SWEDEN
Svenska Kennelklubben
Mrs. Ulla Magnusson

VENEZUELA
Federacion Canina de Venezuela
Mr. Richard Guevara
Arq. Antonio Quiroga Novelli
Sra. Mary de Quiroga

UNITED STATES OF AMERICA
American Kennel Club
Mr. Charles A. T. O'Neill
Mr. William Rockefeller
Mr. William F. Stifel

WEST INDIES
Trinidad and Tobago Kennel Club
Mr. Richard Rezende

William F. Stifel

AKC Administration and Publications

The AKC Art Collection

Upon entering the reception area, visitors can view some of the outstanding works in the American Kennel Club's collection of fine art. Here is Richard Ansdell's painting *Highland Tod,* which depicts a group of men returning from the hunt with their dogs. On the opposite wall hang three Arthur Wardle paintings of Fox Terriers and Airedales. A large portrait of an English Setter by Percival Rosseau hangs in the stairwell. Nearby is Landseer's allegorical painting *Alexander and Diogenes*. Pictures by Maud Earl, George Earl, Percy Earl, John Emms, Philip Reinagle, and others are located in corridors and executive offices.

This collection has been amassed during the AKC's first hundred years through donations and purchases. It is cataloged and maintained by the library staff.

Most of the works have been acquired as gifts. The largest single assemblage of works of art was received in 1972 when the Shearer sisters, Judith and Fayetta-Julia, bequeathed their books, paintings, prints, and bronzes relating to Greyhounds and Whippets to the AKC. The works were first displayed in the library in 1973. The paintings and prints now grace the walls in one section of the twentieth floor. Some bronzes are in the library and others are in executive offices.

Two well-known dog artists were also directors of the American Kennel Club, Gustav Muss-Arnolt and S. Edwin Megargee. Paintings and drawings done by these two gentlemen make up a large portion of AKC's collection. Some items were given by the artists themselves. From 1895 through 1909, Muss-Arnolt provided pen-and-ink drawings as frontispieces for the *Gazette*. Prints of these, "suitable for framing," were available for ten cents. A few of the originals remain with AKC. Mr. Megargee's original drawing for the library bookplate is on display in the library, along with a set of twenty-six hand-colored photographs of paintings that once hung in the kennels of the S.S. *United States*. Only one of the original paintings is known to exist. The prolific output of these two men is well represented on the AKC's walls. The collection covers a wide range of dog art and has been admired throughout the years by the fancy and the general public alike.

The collection is divided into these categories:

Oil paintings	Decorative objects
Bronzes	Framed photographs
Works on paper	

In the list that follows, the items are arranged alphabetically by the artist, by title, or by subject. Measurements do not include frames and matting. Only height measurements are given for sculptures and figurines. An asterisk indicates the work is part of the Shearer Collection.

Roberta Vesley

Oil Paintings

Frederick Amistadt
Laddie, 1948 (Collie)
Oil on canvas, 42'' x 45''

Richard Ansdell, (English, 1815-1885)
Highland Tod, Fox Hunter, 1859
Oil on canvas, 29'' x 63½''

After George Armfield, (English, 19th century)
Three Terriers in a Landscape
Oil on canvas, 11½'' x 15½''

James W. Baldock, (English, 19th century)
Two Fox Terriers, 1881
Oil on canvas, 15'' x 23''

James W. Baldock, (English, 19th century)
Fox Terriers with Rabbit, 1881
Oil on canvas, 15'' x 23''

William Barraud, (English, 1810-1850)
Black Retriever with Pheasant, 1839
Oil on canvas, 42'' x 60''

Terri Bresnahan, (American, 20th century)
Ch. Heidi-Flottenberg, 1937 (Dachshund)
Oil on board, 22½'' x 29½''

Terri Bresnahan, (American, 20th century)
Ch. Laindon Lawds, 1929 (Scottish Terrier)
Oil on canvas, 12¾'' x 17¾''

Terri Bresnahan, (American, 20th century)
Fuh Sam, 1939 (Pekingese)
Oil on canvas, 19'' x 24½''

R. Burtis
Zepherine Black Night, 1979 (English Toy Spaniel)
Oil on canvas board, 12'' x 9''

Will Carlson
Ch. Elmcroft Coacher (Dalmatian)
Oil on canvas, 13'' x 10''

Lilian Cheviot, (English, 20th century)
Ch. Pinegrade Scotia Swell and Ch. Pinegrade's Perfection (Sealyham Terriers)
Oil on canvas, 24'' x 29''

F. C. Clifton, (American, 19th century)
Fire Chief, 1901 (Bull Terrier)
Oil on canvas, 26'' x 33½''

F. C. Clifton, (American, 19th century)
Ch. Yorkville Belle, 1901 (Bull Terrier)
Oil on canvas, 26'' x 33½''

Lois Contoit, (French, 20th century)
Ch. Feri-Flottenberg, (Dachshund)
Oil on canvas, 11½'' x 16''

Abraham Cooper R. A., (English, 1787-1868)
Crib and Rosa, 1817 (Bulldogs)
Oil on panel, 9½'' x 12''

Abraham Cooper R. A., (English, 1787-1868)
Three Terriers at the Base of a Tree
Oil on canvas, 11¾'' x 15½''

Cosma
Ch. Courmet's Sardar (Weimaraner)
Oil on board, 18½'' x 23½''

C. Cunaeus, (Dutch, 1828-1895)
Scottish Deerhounds in a Tudor Interior
Oil on panel, 15¾'' x 22½''

Kenneth Cushman
Platina (Miniature Poodle)
Oil on canvas, 25'' x 30''

F. T. Daws, (English, 19th century)
Ch. Badshah of Arisdart and Ch. West Mill Omar of Prides Hill, 1933 (Afghan Hounds)
Oil on canvas, 16'' x 21½''

F. T. Daws, (English, 19th century)
Ch. Queen of Lyons, 1923 (Airedale)
Oil on canvas, 12'' x 16''

T. Doran, (American)
Retriever with Woodcock
Oil on canvas, 21½'' x 17½''

N. Du Bois, (French, 19th century)
Pointer carrying a Woodcock
Oil on canvas, 27½'' x 21''

George Earl, (English, 19th century)
Prince, ca. 1870 (White English Terrier)
Oil on canvas, 14½'' x 16''

George Earl, (English, 19th century)
Warrior (Scottish Deerhound)
Oil on board, 20'' x 18½''

George Earl, (English, 19th century)
Judy (Dachshund with Rabbit))
Oil on canvas, 28'' x 36''

George Earl, (English, 19th century)
Barry (Mastiff)
Oil on canvas, 22'' x 22''

Maud Earl, (English, 20th century)
Yorkshire Terrier
Oil on canvas, 13½'' x 15½''

Maud Earl, (English, 20th century)
Ch. Lucknow Creme de la Creme, 1931 (Cocker Spaniel)
Oil on board, 20'' x 39''

Maud Earl, (English, 20th century)
Ti Ti, 1913 (Pekingese)
Oil on canvas, 30'' x 36''

Maud Earl, (English, 20th century)
Ch. Nunsoe Duc de La Terrace of Blakeen, 1935 (Standard Poodle)
Oil on board, 36'' x 60''

Maud Earl, (English, 20th century)
Silent Sorrow, 1910 (King Edward VII's favorite Wire Fox Terrier, Caesar)
Oil on canvas, 35½'' x 27½''

Maud Earl, (English, 20th century)
Two Pointers on Point in a Field, 1905
Oil on canvas, 25½'' x 45¾''

Percy Earl, (English)
Otter Hound
Oil on canvas, 19'' x 23''

Gladys Brown Edwards, (American, 20th century)
Five Lakeland Terriers, 1963
Oil on canvas, 21½'' x 27½''

John Emms, (English, 1843-1912)
Two Foxhounds and Fox Terriers on Kennel Bench
Oil on canvas, 19'' x 29¾''

John Emms, (English, 1843-1912)
Brown Ruby, 1882 (Smooth Fox Terrier)
Oil on canvas, 14'' x 17½''

John Emms, (English, 1843-1912)
Richmond Jock, 1881 (Smooth Fox Terrier)
Oil on canvas, 13¾'' x 16''

John Emms, (English, 1843-1912)
Ch. Briggs, 1883 (Wire Fox Terrier)
Oil on canvas, 11½'' x 15¾''

English School
Bloodhound
Oil on canvas, 23¹/₂'' x 19¹/₂''

English School (attributed to Reinagle)
Three Terriers around a Burrow
Oil on canvas, 7³/₄'' x 11³/₄''

Rene Maurice Fath, (French, 1850-1922)
La Chasse Aux Loups, After Oudrey (Great Pyrenees and Wolf)
Oil on canvas, 75'' x 100''

C. C. Fawcett, (20th century)
Ch. Bar Vom Weiherturchen, 1969 (German Shepherd Dog)
Oil on canvas, 19¹/₂'' x 15¹/₂''

George Fenn, (American, 19th century)
Two Greyhounds, 1855
Oil on canvas, 18¹/₂'' x 24''

W. M. Frazer, (English)
Sir Richard C. (Beagle)
Oil on canvas, 13¹/₂'' x 17¹/₂''

M. S. French
Ch. Tejano Texas Kid (Chihuahua)
Oil on board, 16'' x 20''

Marjorie Grossman, (American, 20th century)
Lakeland Terrier, 1971
Oil on board, 20'' x 24''

Dorothy Hardcastle, (20th century)
Ch. Dunbar's Democrat of Sandoone, 1978 (Scottish Terrier)
Oil on board, 18'' x 22''

Dorothy Hardcastle, (20th century)
Ch. Carmichael's Fanfare (Scottish Terrier)
Oil on canvas, 16'' x 20''

S. J. E. Jones, (English, Ex 1820-1845)
Two Sportsmen and Setters in the Field
Oil on canvas, 11'' x 17''

Jack Kalar
Ch. Aurora Mimi Reveille (Maltese)
Oil on canvas, 15'' x 12''

Dorothy Iola Keeler, (American, 20th century)
Ch. Far Land Thunderstorm, 1936 (Chow Chow)
Oil on canvas, 18¹/₂'' x 14³/₄''

Edward R. Klein, (20th century)
Ch. Atta's Gretchen, 1979 (Chihuahua)
Oil on board, 15'' x 13''

Edward R. Klein, (20th century)
Ch. Shroyer Rickee Robin, 1975 (Chihuahua)
Oil on board, 17'' x 14''

Edward R. Klein, (20th century)
Ch. Snowbunny D'Casa D'Cris, 1978 (Chihuahua)
Oil on board, 11'' x 13¹/₂''

James Lambert, (English, 1725-1788)
Lion, 1778 (Mastiff)
Oil on canvas, 15¹/₂'' x 19¹/₂''

Sir Edwin Henry Landseer R. A., (English, 1802-1873)
Alexander and Diogenes
Oil on canvas, 43¹/₂'' x 54''

Ivan L. Lotton, (American, 20th century)
Dual Ch. Saxon of Fredann, 1969 (Brittany)
Oil on board, 16'' x 22''

Gilman Low, (American, 19th century)
Ch. Barberryhill Bootlegger, 1924 (Sealyham Terrier)
Oil on canvas, 19³/₄'' x 25¹/₄''

W. Luckett
Ch. Williamsdale's Michael (Dalmatian)
Oil on canvas, 19'' x 17''

Phyllis Mackenzie, (American)
Li Lien Ying of Chasmu, Shadza of Chasmu, and Golden Tasmin of Chasmu (Shih Tzu)
Oil on canvas, 23³/₄'' x 19³/₄''

William Mangford, (American, after Sir Edwin Henry Landseer)
Odin (St. Bernard)
Oil on canvas, 19¹/₂'' x 24¹/₂''

Edwin Megargee, (American, 1883-1958)
Ch. Nornay Saddler, 1940 (Smooth Fox Terrier)
Oil on canvas, 17¹/₂'' x 23¹/₂''

Edwin Megargee, (American, 1883-1958)
Mr. Reynal's Monarch, 1937 (Harrier)
Oil on canvas, 23³/₄'' x 31³/₄''

Edwin Megargee, (American, 1883-1958)
Kerry Blue Terriers
Oil on canvas, 21'' x 27¹/₂''

Edwin Megargee, (American, 1883-1958)
Harrier
Oil on board, 12'' x 16''

Edwin Megargee, (American, 1883-1958)
Ch. Twin Ponds Belle (Welsh Terrier)
Oil on canvas, 19¹/₂'' x 23¹/₂''

Edwin Megargee, (American, 1883-1958)
Royaline White Foam, 1944 (Clumber Spaniel)
Oil on canvas, 24'' x 26''

Edwin Megargee, (American, 1883-1958)
The Pet Shop, (English Setter with Puppies)
Oil on board, 15'' x 18''

Mildred Megargee, (American, 20th century)
Ch. Flornell Spicy Bit of Halleston (Wire Fox Terrier)
Oil on board, 11¹/₂'' x 15¹/₂''

A. R. Mulder, (American, 20th century)
German Shepherd Dog, 1929
Oil on canvas, 24'' x 26''

G. Muss-Arnolt, (American, 1858-1927)
Ch. Arroyo Anarchist (Boston Terrier)
Oil on linen, 17³/₄'' x 27''

G. Muss-Arnolt, (American, 1858-1927)
Black, White and Tan English Setter, 1923
Oil on canvas, 9'' x 7''

G. Muss-Arnolt, (American, 1858-1927)
English Setter, Gordon Setter, and Pointer
Oil on canvas, 24'' x 26''

G. Muss-Arnolt, (American, 1858-1927)
Mark's Rush (Pointer)
Oil on canvas, 9'' x 7''

G. Muss-Arnolt, (American, 1858-1927)
The New King, 1906 (Airedale)
Oil on canvas, 22'' x 28''

George Earl, English, "Barry" (Mastiff), 1886, Oil on canvas.

G. Muss-Arnolt, (American, 1858-1927)
Rodney Druid (Welsh Terrier)
Oil on canvas, 10'' x 8''

G. Muss-Arnolt, (American, 1858-1927)
Two English Setters, 1886
Oil on canvas, 13½'' x 17½''

G. Muss-Arnolt, (American, 1858-1927)
Setter and Pointer on Point
Oil on canvas, 9¾'' x 15½''

G. Muss-Arnolt, (American, 1858-1927)
Blemton Vindex (Smooth Fox Terrier)
Oil on canvas, 10'' x 8''

G. Muss-Arnolt, (American, 1858-1927)
Real English (English Setter)
Oil on canvas, 10'' x 8''

G. Muss-Arnolt, (American, 1858-1927)
Beaufort (Pointer)
Oil on canvas, 7'' x 9¾''

G. Muss-Arnolt, (American, 1858-1927)
Wan Lung (Chow Chow)
Oil on canvas, 17'' x 14''

G. Muss-Arnolt, (American, 1858-1927)
English Setter
Oil on canvas, 10'' x 13''

G. Muss-Arnolt, (American, 1858-1927)
Beaumont (Gordon Setter)
Oil on canvas, 10'' x 8''

G. Muss-Arnolt, (American, 1858-1927)
Orange and White English Setter, 1887
Oil on canvas, 13¾'' x 11¾''

G. Muss-Arnolt, (American, 1858-1927)
White English Setter with Blue Ticking, Some Orange, 1923
Oil on canvas, 18'' x 8''

G. Muss-Arnolt, (American, 1858-1927)
Pointer
Oil on canvas, 10'' x 8''

G. Muss-Arnolt, (American, 1858-1927)
Ch. Windholme's Matchless, 1905 (Beagle)
Oil on canvas, 19'' x 26''

G. Muss-Arnolt, (American, 1858-1927)
Ch. Windholme's Robino III, 1909 (Beagle)
Oil on canvas, 18'' x 26''

John S. Noble, (English, 1848-1896)
Pug and Welsh Terrier, 1875
Oil on canvas, 35'' x 27''

*W. R. Noble, (19th century)
Transit, 1835 (Greyhound)
Oil on canvas, 21½'' x 17¼''

*W. R. Noble, (19th century)
Hector, 1835 (Greyhound)
Oil on canvas, 21¼'' x 17¼''

Marge Opitz, (American, 20th century)
Ch. Duke Sinatra (Beagle)
Oil on canvas, 22'' x 30''

Benedict A. Osnis, (American, 1872-1935)
Russell Johnson, 1937 (AKC President 1933-1940)
Oil on canvas, 55'' x 33''

Edmund Henry Osthaus, (German, 1858-1928)
Toledo Blade (English Setter)
Oil on canvas, 15³/4'' x 23¹/2''

Edmund Henry Osthaus, (German, 1858-1928)
Seven English Setters, 1911
Oil on canvas, 24'' x 36''

Frank Paton, (English, 1856-1909)
Salvo, 1892 (Bulldog)
Oil on canvas, 19¹/2'' x 23¹/2''

S. Raphael, (French, 19th century)
French Bulldog
Oil on canvas, 20¹/2'' x 23¹/2''

C. Reichert, (German, 19th century)
French Bulldog, 1874
Oil on canvas, 15'' x 12''

Philip Reinagle R. A., (English, 1749-1833)
Sportsmen with Setter and Pheasant
Oil on canvas, 13¹/2'' x 11¹/2''

Ramsey Richard Reinagle, (English, 1775-1862)
Pug
Oil on canvas, 25'' x 30''

Percival L. Rosseau, (French, 1828-1912)
Leda, 1906 (English Setter)
Oil on canvas, 57'' x 36¹/2''

William G. Schnelle, (American, 1897-1934)
Ch. Halleston Wyche Wondrous (Wire Fox Terrier)
Oil on canvas, 17'' x 23¹/2''

William G. Schnelle, (American, 1897-1934)
Ch. Barberryhill Bootlegger (Sealyham Terrier)
Oil on canvas, 17'' x 23''

Herman Simon, (German, b. 1750)
Sitting Pug
Oil on canvas, 15¹/2'' x 23¹/2''

Kole Sowerby, (English, 19th century)
Don Leon, 1894 (Bulldog)
Oil on canvas, 20¹/4'' x 25¹/4''

F. H. Stoll, (American, 19th century)
Ch. Kouwanna Fumi Konye (Japanese Spaniel)
Oil on canvas, 15'' x 19¹/2''

F. H. Stoll, (American, 19th century)
Styx, 1886 (Corded Poodle)
Oil on canvas, 11¹/2'' x 15¹/2''

P. Stretton, (American, 20th century)
Boxwood Barkentine and Boxwood Bashful (Airedales)
Oil on canvas, 38'' x 44''

George Stubbs, (attributed to; English, 1724-1806)
Mastiff
Oil on canvas, 11'' x 9¹/2''

Arthur Fitzwilliam Tait, (American, 1819-1905)
Two Spaniels
Oil on panel, 10'' x 13¹/2''

T. Tashiro, (Japanese, 20th century)
Ch. Bang Away of Sirrah Crest, 1957 (Boxer)
Oil on canvas mounted on board, 24¹/2'' x 20¹/2''

Stephen Taylor, (English, 19th century)
Orange and White English Setter, 1820
Oil on canvas, 18¹/2'' x 23''

John M. Tracy, (American, 1844-1893)
Petrel (English Setter)
Oil on board, 9'' x 13''

John M. Tracy, (American)
Bob (Gordon Setter)
Oil on canvas, 15'' x 21¹/2''

W. E. Turner, (English, 19th century)
Three Spaniels in Landscape with Rifle and Birds, 1868
Oil on canvas, 23'' x 29''

F. B. Voss, (German, 19th century)
Vernon Place Mischief, 1925 (Beagle)
Oil on canvas, 10'' x 11³/4''

Georges Vuilefroy, (French, 19th century)
Full Cry (Foxhounds)
Oil on canvas, 28³/4'' x 37¹/2''

Marvin Waite, (American, 20th century)
Terrier and Cat with a Dead Bird
Oil on canvas, 10'' x 12''

M. L. Waller, (English, 19th century)
Ch. Joe II, 1889 (Corded Poodle)
Oil on canvas, 26'' x 36''

School of James Ward, (English, 1769-1859)
Spaniels with Rabbit
Oil on board, 5³/4'' x 7³/4''

School of James Ward, (English, 1769-1859)
Spaniel with Duck
Oil on Board 5³/4'' x 7³/4''

Martin T. Ward, (English, 1799?-1874)
West Highland White Terrier and Welsh Terrier
Oil on canvas, 27'' x 35''

Arthur Wardle, (English, 1864-1949)
Ch. Mistress Royal and Ch. Master Royal (Airedales)
Oil on canvas, 21³/4'' x 29¹/2''

Arthur Wardle, (English, 1864-1949)
Two Dandie Dinmont Terrier Heads
Oil on canvas, 21³/4'' x 13³/4''

Arthur Wardle, (English, 1864-1949)
Three Spaniel Heads
Oil on canvas, 13¹/2'' x 21¹/2''

Arthur Wardle, (English, 1864-1949)
Totteridge XI, 1897 (Smooth Fox Terriers)
Oil on canvas, 28'' x 35¹/2''

Arthur Wardle, (English, 1864-1949)
Wait and See, 1936; Replica by the artist (Smooth Fox Terriers)
Oil on canvas, 15³/4'' x 21³/4''

Arthur Wardle, (English, 1864-1949)
Newfoundland
Oil on canvas, 32'' x 24''

*Dean Wolstenholme, (English)
Two Greyhounds Coursing
Oil on canvas, 16³/4'' x 13''

*Dean Wolstenholme, (English)
Greyhounds at Rest
Oil on canvas, 16³/4 x 13''

Artist Unknown

Greyhound Jumping Fence after Rabbit
Oil on board, 5¹/2'' x 8¹/2''

Spaniel Catching a Hare, ca. 1800
Oil on wood, 6'' x 8''

Water Spaniel with Mallard, ca. 1800
Oil on wood, 6'' x 8''

*Whippets and Rabbit
Oil on board, 13'' x 16''

Bronzes

*Antoine Louis Barye, (French, 1796-1875)
Lying Deer
Height: 1³/₄''

H. R. D.
Three Terriers Wrestling
Height: 7¹/₂''

Charles Di Goia, (20th century)
Two Basset Hounds, 1918
Height: 7''

F. Diller
German Shepherd Dog
Height: 7¹/₂''

Rene Maurice Fath, (French, 1850-1922)
Ch. Estat d'Argeles of Basquerie, 1935 (Great Pyrenees)
Height: 8''

*Christophe Fratin, (French, 1810-1864?)
Whippet and Rabbit
Height: 10¹/₂''

*Christophe Fratin, (French, 1810-1864?)
Whippets and Rabbits
Bas-relief, 8'' x 13''

*B. Froaman
Two Whippets Running, 1928
Height: 4¹/₂''

*Gorham, (American, 19th century)
Noble, 1895 (Whippet)
Height: 5¹/₂''

Pekka Ketoren, (Finnish, 20th century)
Finnish Spitz
Height: 4''

K. Lane, (American, 20th century)
Plaque celebrating 50th Year of Dachshund Club of America, 1945
14³/₄'' x 12¹/₂''

*Kathy Lyon, (American)
Whippet with Rabbit
Height: 8¹/₂''

Kathy Lyon, (American)
Miniature Schnauzer
Height: 3¹/₂''

Kathy Lyon, (American)
Yorkshire Terrier, 1973
Height: 2¹/₂''

Mackarness,(American,20th century)
American Spaniel Club Team Prize
Bas relief, 9'' x 13''

Mackarness,(American,20th century)
Ch. Baby Ruth (Cocker Spaniel)
Height: 7¹/₂''

Mackarness,(American,20th century)
Ch. Sabine Rarebit, 1919 (Smooth Fox Terrier)
Height: 7''

Mackarness,(American,20th century)
Ch. Sabine Result (Smooth Fox Terrier)
Height: 7''

Mackarness,(American,20th century)
Scottish Terrier
Height: 6¹/₂''

*Joe Mercer, (American, 20th century)
Mica of Meander, 1937, (Whippet)
Height: 9''

*Joe Mercer, (American, 20th century)
Whippet, 1947
Height: 6''

Kole Sowerby, (English,19th century)
Bulldog
Height: 7''

Gary Weisman, (American)
German Shepherd Dog, Head study
Height: 15''

*Whippet Head
Height: 4''

*Whippet Inkwell
Brass
Height: 7¹/₂''

Works on Paper

Henry Alken, (English, 1774-1850)
Sporting Dogs, 1822
Soft ground etchings, 7'' x 10''

*Samuel Alken
Piper, 1822 (Greyhound)
Colored engraving, 4³/₄'' x 7¹/₂''

*Samuel Alken
Coursing, 1823 (Greyhounds)
Colored engraving, 4³/₄'' x 7¹/₂''

Bauer, (German, 20th century)
Ch. Herman Rinkton (Dachshund)
Pastel, 20'' x 28¹/₂''

R.Ward Binks,(English,20th century)
Ch. Eli, 1934 (German Shepherd Dog)
Gouache, 10¹/₄'' x 12¹/₄''

R.Ward Binks,(English,20th century)
Ch. Cito Von Der Marktfeste, 1934 (German Shepherd Dog)
Gouache, 14¹/₂'' x 19''

R.Ward Binks,(English,20th century)
Ch. Nancolleth Markable, 1934 (Pointer)
Gouache, 14¹/₂'' x 19''

R. Ward Binks,(English,20th century)
Clumber Spaniels
Gouache, 18¹/₂'' x 23''

Thomas Blinks
Pick of the Pack, 1892 (Four Fox-hounds and Terrier)
Colored print, 23¹/₂'' x 19¹/₂''

*The Celebrated Master McGrath (Greyhound)
Colored engraving, 15'' x 19''

*Henry Bernard Chalon
Snowball (Greyhound)
Colored engraving, 20'' x 24''

Bert Cobb, (American, 20th century)
Ch. Giralda's Cito V.D. Marktfeste (German Shepherd Dog)
Pen and ink, 15'' x 17''

Louis Contoit
A Sabine Quartette (Smooth Fox Terriers)
Print, 12'' x 16''

*Abraham Cooper
Greyhound Head
Engraving, 11'' x 8¹/₂''

Leon Danchin, (French, 20th century)
Brittany Spaniels
Colored print, 13'' x 10''

Leon Danchin, (French, 20th century)
Irish Setter Heads, 1931
Photogravure, 18'' x 22''

Walt Disney,(American,20th century)
Donald Duck at AKC, 1964
Pen and ink, 5'' x 8''

George Earl, (English, 19th century)
The Field Trial Meet, ca. 1870
Artist Proof with Key to Figures
Print, 26'' x 34''

Maud Earl
Champion D'Orsay, 1892 (Smooth Fox Terrier)
Photogravure, 18½'' x 21½''

C.C.Fawcett,(American,20th century)
Ch. Hetherington Model Rhythm, 1953 (Wire Fox Terrier)
Pastel, 11'' x 12¾''

*Gentleman with Greyhounds and Foxhound
Watercolor, 7¾'' x 12''

William Giller (After G. W. Horlor)
A group of Favourites (Foxhounds)
Engraving, 22½'' x 25''

*Greyhound and Terrier 1820
Hand-colored steel engraving, 4''x 7''

*Greyhound by a Fence
Watercolor, 8'' x 12''

*Greyhound Chasing Rabbit
Watercolor, 7'' x 12''

*Greyhound
Watercolor and pen and ink,7¾''x12''

Harry Hall (ex. 1838-1886)
The Merry Beaglers
Aquatint, 30'' x 22½''

Elizabeth M. Harvey, (American 20th century)
Pomeranian, 1943
Pastel, 12'' x 13½''

*Howitt
Lurcher, 1798
Colored engraving, 5½'' x 7½''

*Howitt
Greyhounds, 1801 (2)
Colored engraving, 6½'' x 8½''

J.H.Hutchinson,(English,20thcentury)
Ch. Merlin (Bulldog)
Watercolor, 11½'' x 9''

Irish Setter Ch. St. Cloud's Fermanagh III
Head Studies (2)
Charcoal, 14½'' x 10¾''

*E. L. Jacobs
Whippet
Pen and ink, 8'' x 12''

Marguerite Kirmse
Scottish Terriers
Pen and ink, 8'' x 5½''

Marguerite Kirmse
Hemlock Hill Boy Scout, 1918 (Sealyham Terriers)
Pastel, 14'' x 20''

Marguerite Kirmse
Under Mistletoe, 1935 (Scottish Terrier and Welsh Terrier)
Pastel and oil, 26'' x 19½''

Marguerite Kirmse
King Orry (Bulldog)
White chalk and crayon, 6⅝'' x 8⅝''

*Marguerite Kirmse
The Fox, 1931 and *The Hound,* 1933
Prints, 19½'' x 15''

Ken Kopin
Bearded Collie, 1977
Woodcut (Artist's proof), 24½'' x 22½''

*H. Laporte and H. Pepperill
Coursing - In the Slips, 1860 (Greyhounds)
Engraving, 18¼'' x 27''

*H. Laporte and H. Pepperill
Coursing - The First Turn, 1860 (Greyhounds)
Engraving, 18¼'' x 27''

William Luckett
Ch. Emcroft Peggy (Dalmatian)
Watercolor, 11'' x 16''

*Michael Lyle
Dogs Chasing Rabbit, 1951
Watercolor, 13½'' x 20''

Map of Scotland
Colored print, 16'' x 12''

Johanna Mapes
Pekingese, 1948
Pastel, 17'' x 22''

*Newton Mayo
Whippet and Shadow
Watercolor, 17½'' x 19¾''

W. William McKim
Ch. Rollings Toowoomba, 1965 (Rhodesian Ridgeback)
Print, 19½'' x 13½''

Edwin Megargee
Head Study of Dog (26)
Hand-painted Photographs, 8'' x 10''

Edwin Megargee
Ex Libris The American Kennel Club, 1936
Pen-and-ink drawing for a Bookplate, 11'' x 14''

George Ford Morris, (American, 20th century)
Pointer, 1910
Lithograph, 21'' x 26''

G. Muss-Arnolt, (American, 1858-1927)
Gordon Setter
Pen and ink, 8¼'' x 11''

G. Muss-Arnolt, (American, 1858-1927)
Borzoi
Pen and ink, 9'' x 11''

G. Muss-Arnolt, (American, 1858-1927)
Borzoi
Pen and ink, 9'' x 11''

*J. W. Parratt
Two Greyhounds Coursing, 1825
Watercolor, 7'' x 11¼''

*F. Patan
Whippet
Pastel, 8'' x 11''

A. Pope, Jr.
Celebrated Dogs of America
Prints (19), 21'' x 17''

Thomas Quinn
Dual Ch. & Amat. Fld. Ch. Tiger's Cub e.d., 1975 (Chesapeake Bay Retriever)
Print, 27'' x 39''

Rabbit Beagles
Print, 8¼'' x 11''

*Phillip Reinagle, (English, 1749-1833)
Greyhound with Rabbit
Engraving, 7¼'' x 8¼''

*Phillip Reinagle, (English 1749-1833)
Italian Greyhounds
Engraving, 7¼'' x 8½''

B. Riab, (French)
Brittany Spaniels
Colored print, 13¼'' x 10¼''

B. Riab, (French)
Cocker Spaniel with Woodcock
Woodcut, 20½'' x 14½''

*Jill Rich
Two Whippets
Charcoal, 17¹/₂'' x 19¹/₂''

*Jill Rich
Smooth Fox Terrier, 1958
Pastel, 13¹/₄'' x 17¹/₂''

*Jill Rich
Whippet, 1963
Pastel, 25'' x 19''

*Jill Rich
Whippets, 1945
Pastel, 20¹/₂'' x 18''

*Jill Rich
Whippet, 1951
Pastel, 7³/₄'' x 9¹/₂''

*Jill Rich
Blunder (Whippet)
Pastel, 18¹/₂'' x 20¹/₂''

*Jill Rich
Whippet, 1951
Pastel, 11¹/₂'' x 13¹/₂''

Wallace Robinson
Busy Day in World's Court, 1916
Print, 13'' x 19''

Russian Dogs
Colored prints (8), 18¹/₄'' x 25''

Helen Wilson Sherman, (American, 20th century)
Three Wheaten Scottish Terriers, 1947
Pastel, 18¹/₂'' x 23¹/₂''

Helen Wilson Sherman, (American, 20th century)
Ch. Murray Rosenblunt, 1948 (Scottish Terrier)
Pastel, 14'' x 21''

Joseph P. Sims
Dog Map of the World, 1933
Print, 19¹/₂'' x 31''

Robert Gerard Sternloff, Sr.
Hare and the Hounds, 1943 (Beagles)
Tempera, 9'' x 14''

M. H. Stevens, (American)
Ch. Biggs Cover Charge (Cocker Spaniel)
Pastel, 23¹/₂'' x 30''

*Terry
Ch. Meander King Fisher (Whippet)
Pastel, 13¹/₂'' x 10''

J. M. Tracy, (American)
Rip Rap and Ch. King of Kent (Pointers)
Print, 9'' x 15''

Marjorie Walker, (American, 20th century)
Four Scottish Terriers, 1948
Pastel, 19'' x 26''

Marjorie Walker, (American, 20th century)
Bandy, 1949 (Miniature Schnauzer)
Pastel, 19'' x 25''

Marjorie Walker, (American, 20th century)
Ch. Rock Ridge Night Rocket, 1954 (Bedlington Terrier)
Pastel, 27'' x 32''

William Ward (After Henry Bernard Chalon, R. A.)
Wasp, Child and Billy, 1809 (Bulldogs and man)
Mezzotint, 17¹/₄'' x 23¹/₄''

Arthur Wardle, (English, 1864-1949)
Two Airedale Terriers, 1904
Photogravure, 17¹/₂'' x 22''

Arthur Wardle, (English, 1864-1949)
The Totteridge XI, 1897 (Smooth Fox Terriers)
Photogravure, 19¹/₄'' x 22¹/₂''

Arthur Wardle, (English, 1864-1949)
Ch. Blacket House Yet and Ch. Ancrum Fanny, 1897 (Dandie Dinmont Terriers)
Photogravure, 16¹/₂'' x 19''

Arthur Wardle, (English, 1864-1949)
Meersbrook Bristles, 1899 (Wire Fox Terrier)
Photogravure, 14'' x 16''

Arthur Wardle, (English, 1864-1949)
Smooth Fox Terrier, 1902
Photogravure, 13'' x 16¹/₂''

Arthur Wardle, (English, 1864-1949)
Smooth Fox Terrier, 1904
Photogravure, 13'' x 17''

Arthur Wardle, (English, 1864-1949)
Ch. D'Orsay's Donna and Ch. D'Orsay's Model, 1913 (Smooth Fox Terriers)
Photogravure, 13³/₄'' x 17¹/₂''

Arthur Wardle, (English, 1864-1949)
Ch. Coronation, 1905 (Pointer)
Photogravure, 21'' x 25¹/₂''

Arthur Wardle, (English, 1864-1949)
Ch. Donna Fortuna and Ch. Duchess of Durham, 1901 (Smooth Fox Terriers)
Photogravure, 15'' x 19''

*C. H. Weigall
Coursing
Engraving, 9'' x 11¹/₂''

Danny Westlake
Ch. Elmcroft Coacher, 1943 (Dalmatian)
Pastel, 14¹/₂'' x 13''

*Dean Wolstenholme
The Death
Engraving, 13¹/₄'' x 15³/₄''

*Dean Wolstenholme
The Hare's Last Effort
Engraving, 13¹/₄'' x 15³/₄''

Decorative Objects, Trophies, and Miscellaneous Items

Akita Statues (2)
Silver-painted metal, Height: 8¹/₄''

Hardie Albright
Bulldog
Semi-porcelain, Height 6³/₄''

American Kennel Club Centennial Tray, 1984
Gift of International Kennel Club of Chicago
Silver plate, Length: 21''

Atkinson
Dalmatian Heads, 1947
Sand molded silver-lume on wood, 11'' x 8''

Atkinson
German Shepherd Dog (head)
Sand molded silver-lume on wood
Height: 18''

Belgrave Joe (Fox Terrier)
Skeleton, Height: 18¹/₂''

Walter K. Ferguson Memorial Trophy, 1939
English Springer Spaniels
Sterling Silver Revere Bowl
Height: 6''

Walter K. Ferguson Memorial Trophy, 1940
English Springer Spaniels
Sterling Silver Revere Bowl, Height: 6''

Grand Trophy Bulldog Club of America
Sterling silver, Height: 12³/₄''

Stephanie Hedgepath
Needlepoint Rug, 125 AKC Breeds
Wool on canvas, 34'' x 41¹/₄''

Helene Whitehouse Walker Challenge Trophy
Poodle Jumping
Silverplate on bronze, Height: 12''

Inkwell with reclining Mastiff
Chamberlain Worcester porcelain
(English, 18th century)
Height: 8³/₄''

Japanese Chin
Painted metal, Height: 5''

Edwin Megargee
Dog Genealogy Chart, 1949, 14'' x 30''

After Pierre Jules Mene
Three Terriers at a Hole
Parian porcelain, Height: 7''

*Muller & Sons
White Metal Whippet
Height: 9¹/₂''

Pointer and Setter with Foliage
Painted lead alloy, Height: 7''

Pointer
Painted lead alloy, Height: 8''

Pointer
Painted metal, Height: 7''

Poodle
Royal Doulton Porcelain, Height: 9''

Sawyer Cup Bulldog Club of America
Sterling silver, Height: 6''

Setter
Painted lead alloy, Height: 8''

Sunninghill Brace Challenge Club, 1896
Black Field Spaniels
Sterling silver, Height: 4''

*Reclining Whippet Doorstop
Iron, Height: 6¹/₂''

Ndep (African dog bell)
Wood Height: 4''

Book Ends

Seated Collies
Brass on weighted silver base
Height: 6''

German Shepherd Dog Heads
Metal, Height: 4¹/₂''

*Reclining Greyhounds
Brass, Height: 4''

*Standing Greyhounds
Col. North's Fullerton and Farndoon Ferry
Brass, Height: 8''

Standing Setter
Brass, Height: 3³/₄''

*Reclining Whippets
Brass Height: 3¹/₂''

*Reclining Whippets
Brass, Height: 6''

*Seated Whippets
Copper on marble base
Height: 10¹/₂''

Framed Photographs

Arauco de lonko Lu (Dogo Argentino), 11'' x 8³/₄''

Dalmatians (5)
8'' x 10''

Havens
Pointer Puppies, 19'' x 38¹/₂''

Frasie
Ch. Dok of Fairway (Weimaraner), 15¹/₂'' x 19''

Edwin Levick
Ch. Lord Cholmondeley II (Chow Chow), 19'' x 23¹/₄''

G. Muss-Arnolt, (American, 1858-1927)
Ch. Tiny Lady Skylark (Pomeranian), 13'' x 16''

Pierce
Ch. Rebel Roc's Casanova von Kurt, 1962 (Miniature Pinscher), 19'' x 16''

Queen Elizabeth II with Dogs, 23'' x 29''

Ch. Rosemont Fortunatus (Greyhound), 24'' x 29''

St. Rohan's Ranger (Scottish Deerhound), 21'' x 24''

A. Wentworth Scott
Ch. Bistri of Perchina (Borzoi), 10'' x 14¹/₂''

Ch. Tioronda Kennels Ruinart (Greyhound), 14'' x 16¹/₄''

Trigger Hoord (Chesapeake Bay Retriever), 17'' x 15''

Ch. Williamsdale Michael (Dalmatian), 10'' x 13''

Rudolf Tauskey

Rudolf Tauskey
Drewston Barrage (Bulldog), 19'' x 15¹/₂''

Rudolf Tauskey
Ch. May Morn Weather (Old English Sheepdog), 15'' x 19''

Rudolf Tauskey
Yuban (Great Dane), 19'' x 15¹/₄''

Rudolf Tauskey
Ch. Victory Weather (Old English Sheepdog), 19'' x 15''

Rudolf Tauskey
Ch. Geelong Defiance (Airedale), 15¹/₂'' x 19''

AKC Personalities

August Belmont, Jr.
President, 1888-1916

Hildreth Bloodgood
Second Vice-President, 1909-1916

L. Loring Brooks
Boston

William H. Child
President, 1887-1888

Dr. John E. De Mund
President, 1923-1932

Hollis H. Hunnewell
President, 1916-1921

Dr. J. Frank Perry
President of Associate Members,
1889

W. C. Rodman, Jr.
Executive Committee, 1901-1903

Elliot Smith
President, 1885-1887

Major James M. Taylor
President, 1884-1885

Alfred Purdy Vredenburgh
Secretary-Treasurer, 1886-1920

Howard Willets
President, 1921-1923

A. Clinton Wilmerding
Director, 1910-1916

AKC Offices and Delegates Meetings

On September 17, 1884, the meeting that resulted in the organization of the American Kennel Club was held in the office of the Philadelphia Kennel Club, Thirteenth and Market Street, Philadelphia, Pennsylvania. During the next several years, the American Kennel Club did not have an official office. Meetings were even held in various cities: Baltimore, Maryland; Cincinnati, Ohio; Boston, Massachusetts; Newark, New Jersey; and New York, New York. In the absence of offices, the meetings were held in convenient hotels.

In New York City, several meetings were held at the Downtown Association on Pine Street. Another popular meeting place was the Hoffman House, located at Broadway and Twenty-fifth Street. Some meetings were even held in the old Madison Square Garden, on the site of which the New York Life Building, which is the present location of the American Kennel Club offices, was later erected.

The American Kennel Club's first office was in the Wall Street district of Manhattan, on the fourth floor of 44 Broadway. The office was one 15 foot by 20 foot room, modestly furnished with desk, chairs, and file cabinet. This served the needs of the club from 1887 until 1895.

Its second address was on the third floor of 55 Liberty Street in Manhattan. This was not much larger than the previous address, and just a few years later, another move was made to slightly larger quarters on the fourth floor of the same building.

By 1909, the American Kennel Club had again outgrown its offices and relocated to 1 Liberty Street for a ten-year stay. In 1919, having 116 member clubs and eight employees, the American Kennel Club moved again to what was to be its longest occupancy, a little over forty-four years, on the fifth floor of 221 Fourth Avenue, later renamed Park Avenue South. In 1923, it relocated to the twelfth floor of the same building.

During the early years of the American Kennel Club's history, delegates' meetings were held in convenient hotels. However, during the occupancy of offices at 221 Fourth Avenue, the quarterly delegates' meeting were held in the American Kennel Club offices. This practice continued until September 1946. After the September 1946 delegates' meeting, the quarterly delegates' meetings, which had grown considerably in size, were relocated to hotel accommodations.

On January 27, 1964, with over three hundred employees and a library grown from a ''shelf of books'' to the largest canine library in the world, the American Kennel Club moved to its

Reception area at 221 4th Avenue, New York City. The designation 4th Avenue was later changed to 221 Park Avenue South.

Delegates Meeting Room at 221 4th Avenue.

present address, the New York Life Building at 51 Madison Avenue, New York City, New York.

Starting with the December 1946 delegates' meeting, the Hotel Commodore at Lexington Avenue and Forty-second Street, New York City, was the site of the delegates' quarterly meetings until March 9, 1954.

The June 1954 delegates' meeting found the American Kennel Club at the Roosevelt Hotel at Forty-fifth and Madison Avenue, where the quarterly delegates' meetings remained until December 1956.

The March 12, 1957, American Kennel Club delegates' meeting moved to the Hotel Biltmore, Madison Avenue at Forty-third Street, where the quarterly meetings remained until the June 9, 1981, delegates' meeting. Thereafter, from September 15, 1981, until present, the American Kennel Club quarterly delegates' meetings have returned to the Roosevelt Hotel.

Charles A. T. O'Neill

Audio-Visual Education Activities

The American Kennel Club, under the direction of Executive Vice-President John Neff, produced a film for the first time in 1953. This was the beginning of what has developed into an ongoing effort to produce audio-visual materials for the fancy. AKC's first film was titled *221*—the street address of AKC headquarters on Fourth Avenue in New York City. AKC Librarian Beatrice Peterson Agazzi won an employee contest to name the film.

As the film's title suggests, *221* was an office-operations film. The sixteen-millimeter color film was an account of what happens inside the American Kennel Club—and why. The film was intended for dog clubs, and it was to be both instructive and entertaining. *221* was an overwhelming success, so much so that, in 1954, AKC produced its second film, *The Dog Show and You*. This film featured a bench-show hearing, with the message that the sport of dogs is built on mutual respect and sportsmanshiplike conduct. By the time they were retired from circulation in the 1960s, *221* and *The Dog Show and You* had been seen by hundreds of clubs in every section of the country.

In 1973, the American Kennel Club began another series of films. Eleven films were produced between 1973 and 1980 by Dan Wise, under the direction of AKC staff member John Mandeville. The first film in this series was an office operations film titled *Inside AKC*. Like its predecessor *221*, *Inside AKC* was intended to give the fancy a tour of the American Kennel Club. *Inside AKC* was an instant hit with dog clubs.

By the mid-1970s, the sport of dogs in the United States was in the midst of a gigantic growth spurt. The number of dog clubs had climbed into the thousands, all of which had program chairmen eagerly seeking informative materials for their meetings. AKC's films were snapped up by dog clubs.

The most successful film produced by AKC was *Gait: Observing Dogs in Motion,* which premiered at the "Day with AKC" symposium in Chicago, Illinois, on November 9, 1974. The subject of how dogs move is of critical interest to fanciers, and, of course, the ideal subject matter for a film. The *Gait* film employs all the special techniques so useful in fully analyzing movement, most notably superslow-motion and stop-action photography.

Rachel Page Elliott, the noted authority on canine movement, served as a special consultant of *Gait*. *Gait* won numerous awards, including the Silver Screen Award of the United States Industrial Film Festival. *Gait* was viewed by thousands of dog clubs, purchased for use by more than forty other kennel clubs around the world, and in mid-1985, nearly eleven years after its release, is as useful as when it first appeared. In fact, with the advent of home videotape players, *Gait* is enjoying an ever greater circulation.

Two of AKC's films are concerned with dog shows. These are *In the Ring with Mr. Wrong* and *The Quest for a Quality Dog Show*. *In the Ring* is a humorous look at what can go wrong in the judging process. "Mr. Wrong" was played by the late AKC Vice-President of show operations, William M. Schmick. *The Quest* is a visual checklist of what goes into staging a successful dog show.

Two of AKC's films are devoted to obedience. *200?*, which is the score possible for a perfect performance in obedience competition, is a look at what goes into a truly outstanding performance in obedience. *Exercise Finished. A Day with an Obedience Judge* is a judge's eye view of obedience competition with emphasis on ring procedure and the judge's responsibilities.

Two films are devoted to field trial activities. *Carrying the Line* is all about Beagle field trials, and *With Courage and Style: The Field Trial Retriever* is a comprehensive look at the world of retriever trials.

AKC and the Sport of Dogs was the one film intended for nondog, general audiences. The film opens with a two-minute history of pure-bred dogs and follows with a look at field trials, obedience, and dog shows. Each year, four thousand different schools and other groups request this film, distributed for AKC by Modern Talking Pictures.

Three films were produced in cooperation with breed parent clubs. These films were *The Irish Setter, The Doberman Pinscher,* and *The Shetland Sheepdog*. They were precursors to the American Kennel Club's joint parent club breed sound/slide show program. The sound/slide program began in the early 1980s with *The Dalmatian* and *The Basset Hound,* under the driving force of Alfred Treen and Barbara Wicklund, respectively. The sound/slide show program has expanded into a comprehensive effort to provide judges, and everyone else seriously interested in a breed, with a quality audio-visual educational aid.

In August 1982, all parent clubs were contacted and invited to participate in the sound/slide show program. The response was overwhelming. By mid-1985, twenty-seven breeds were completed and sixty more were in some stage of development. The rapid growth of the home videotape industry means breed audio-visuals can be produced as video cassettes for convenient home study.

One unique educational activity of the American Kennel Club should be noted. Between December 1, 1973, and May 24, 1975, the American Kennel Club hosted four all-day symposiums all about AKC. Called "A Day With AKC," these symposiums were held on December 1, 1973, in Atlantic City, New Jersey; on March 23, 1974, in San Mateo, California; on November 9, 1974, in Chicago, Illinois; and on May 24, 1975, in Fort Worth, Texas. In all, more than five thousand fanciers attended these symposiums, which were intended to bring the American Kennel Club to dog people throughout the country.

Throughout its hundred years of existence, the American Kennel Club has been committed to educational activities about dogs. Few subjects are as appealing on film as the dog. AKC has been and will continue to be committed to providing the fancy with quality audio-visual projects about pure-bred dogs.

John J. Mandeville

Sound/Slide Shows Completed as of June 1985

Brittany	Whippet	West Highland White Terrier
Cocker Spaniel	Bernese Mountain Dog	Italian Greyhound
Golden Retriever	Boxer	Bulldog
Afghan Hound	Great Dane	Dalmatian
Basenji	Mastiff	Belgian Tervuren
Basset Hound	Saint Bernard	German Shepherd Dog
Borzoi	Standard Schnauzer	Old English Sheepdog
Dachshund	Border Terrier	Pembroke Welsh Corgi
Rhodesian Ridgeback	Kerry Blue Terrier	

Canine Health, Research and Education

The title of this section of the *Source Book* coincidently is the name of one of the standing committees of the Board. The Canine Health Research and Education Committee has existed longer than all the other board committees.

Early on, the Board of Directors of the American Kennel Club recognized the need to assist with the solution of canine health problems by supporting worthy research projects. In the early years, financial support was limited. Even today, the American Kennel Club would like to encourage more research on canine health problems. Our funding today is large compared to the early years, but the need for our support is still larger and growing.

On December 29, 1952, the American Kennel Club's Board of Directors made the first formal appropriation of funds to an account known as "Reserve for Educational Purposes and Research on Dog Health." The initial appropriation was in the amount of $15,000. It was stipulated to be used for the calendar year 1953. In prior years, gifts from the American Kennel Club for canine health and research were sporadic, and specific to a particular problem, as well considerably lower in dollar value. December 29, 1952, was really a landmark date because, for the first time the American Kennel Club used the term "Reserve for Educational Purposes and Research on Dog Health."

The $15,000 appropriated for 1953 was awarded to fund a project titled "Research on Canine Diseases." Cornell University, College of Veterinary Medicine, Utica, New York, was the recipient of this landmark grant for canine health research.

Canine health research was always a top-priority subject with the American Kennel Club Board of Directors. One must remember that the American Kennel Club went through a dynamic growth explosion following World War II. Funds for canine health grants were not then as readily available. However, in each of the succeeding years since the first grant in 1953, right up to and including 1985, the American Kennel Club has funded canine health research grants at the Cornell University College of Veterinary Medicine, the University of Missouri College of Veterinary Medicine, and the University of Pennsylvania College of Veterinary Medicine.

The first fellowship sponsored by the American Kennel Club was recorded in 1961. The fellowship went to the Animal Medical Center for a study of comparative radiology. This first fellowship with specific focus was for $5,000, covering the year 1961.

The second American Kennel Club fellowship followed in 1963. It was also awarded to the Animal Medical Center for a study in canine cardiology. This fellowship was for the amount of $5,000, covering the year 1963. The year 1963 also saw the American Kennel Club funding the American Veterinary Medical Association's symposium on hip dysplasia. This project of the AVMA was awarded a grant of $4,000 to help defray the costs of the symposium.

In 1983, the Board of Directors of the American Kennel Club decided to set up two postdoctoral fellowships for research in specific fields of canine health. The two fellowships were to be awarded to outstanding postgraduate students who wished to pursue a canine research project, eventually writing their theses for a postdoctoral degree on the subject of their residency. The two original American Kennel Club postdoctoral fellowships were awarded to the following outstanding researchers for the year 1984:

Mary C. Walter, D.V.M., University of California School of Veterinary Medicine at Davis, California; residency in Canine Orthopedic Surgery at the University of Pennsylvania Veterinary Hospital—$15,000

Collin R. Parrish, B.S.C., Ph.D., University of New Zealand; residency in Virology at Cornell University, Baker Institute, College of Veterinary Medicine, Ithaca, New York—$15,000

Appropriations by the Board of Directors of the American Kennel Club for Canine Health, Research, and Education since December 29, 1952, to December 11, 1984, total $2,313,161.08. This figure includes all research grants, fellowships, postdoctoral fellowships, educational films, slide projects, American Kennel Club symposiums, and related legal and public affairs budgets.

The principal beneficiaries of the American Kennel Club's funding are listed here in total. The individual funding of projects varied from year to year. Sixteen small grants, which have ranged from $100 to $2,000 in size have been grouped together under the heading *All Other Projects*.

Canine Health Research Grants, Fellowships and Postdoctoral Fellowships

Cornell University Baker Institute	$570,000.00
University of Missouri	207,364.00
Frozen Canine Semen (various research projects)	187,777.00
Morris Animal Foundation	186,148.28
University of Pennsylvania Veterinary School and Veterinary Hospital	151,200.00
Postdoctoral Fellowships, 1984	30,000.00
Health Research, Inc., at Albany, New York	29,735.00
American Veterinary Medical Association	25,758.61
Orthopedic Foundation for Animals	17,000.00
Dr. Priscilla Stockner, Project Monitor	16,146.15
University of South Carolina	15,000.00
Animal Medical Center	10,000.00
All Other Projects	24,714.33

Educational Projects

"Dog Buyers" Advertising; "Buy From a Breeder" National Coverage	$165,262.18
American Kennel Club Educational Breed Films	52,819.76
American Kennel Club Symposiums	103,746.05
American Kennel Club Breed Slide Programs	112,539.23
American Kennel Club Foundation, Inc.	20,000.00
Canine Legislation, Reporting Services, Public Affairs Information	143,932.34

The efforts of the American Kennel Club to work with the field of canine research and the research units in the United States is well documented. On occasion, we have had to choose between two or three equally deserving proposals, for our funds are limited, as our needs are growing. A point that should be noted is the fact that the dog is an excellent model for the study of human disease. Oncology research done on malignant mammary tumors by Dr. Ann Jeglum at the University of Pennsylvania Veterinary School is a perfect example. The parallels between canine and human disease benefited the humans in this particular field of canine research.

The statement "The Dog Is Man's Best Friend" has been proven to be true repeatedly. We hope that the American Kennel Club's Canine Health, Research, and Education Committee's efforts will repay, in some small way, the friendship and devotion of our canine friends.

Charles A. T. O'Neill

Commemorative Stamp Issue

United States Postal Services Ceremony, honoring the first day of issue of the "Dog Stamps and the Sport of Pure-Bred Dogs in the U.S.A.," was held on September 7, 1984, at 51 Madison Avenue, New York, in the thirteenth floor auditorium of the New York Life Insurance Company.

The first day of issue ceremony for the U.S. Postal Services commemorative block of four stamps, honoring a hundred years of pure-bred dogs in the United States was hosted by the American Kennel Club.

The effort originated on October 6, 1982, when the U.S. Postal Service advised the American Kennel Club of their plans to do a block of four dog stamps. Mr. Dennis J. Holm called from Washington, D.C., to say that Mr. Roy H. Andersen would be the designer of this commemorative issue. Mr. Holm also stated that the stamps would be ready for distribution in October, 1984.

As it later developed, the commemorative block of canine stamps was ready for September 1984 issue. In fact, for a few days, there was a strong possibility that they could be released on September 17, 1984. This would have been a marvelous coincidence; September 17 was the date of the American Kennel Club's founding. However, given the many conflicting release dates, the official release date was set for September 7, 1984. The American Kennel Club was chosen to host the first day of issue ceremony for the block of four twenty-cent stamps; and New York

(left to right) Rev. Thomas V. O'Connor; William F. Stifel, President American Kennel Club; William Rockefeller, Chairman of Board, American Kennel Club; James C. Gildea, Assistant Postmaster General USA; Colorguard U.S. Military Academy West Point, New York; George F. Shuman, Postmaster, New York City; Charles A. T. O'Neill, Executive Vice-President American Kennel Club; Mrs. Nan R. Ayling, Vice-President American Kennel Club; Roy H. Andersen, Designer of the Centennial Stamps; and Miss Jeanine Thames, Soprano, Graduate Student, The Julliard School. (Grace Satriale)

First Day of Issue Cover showing the block of four centennial Stamps honoring the sport of pure-bred dogs issued by the United States Postal Service. This Cover bears two cancellations—September 7, 1984 the First Day of Issue for the stamps and November 17, 1984 bearing the special cancellation for the 100th Anniversary Centennial Show in Philadelphia.

Life; the AKC's landlord at 51 Madison Avenue very graciously offered the use of its newly redecorated auditorium for this function. Approximately 250 guests attended the first day of issue ceremony. Immediately following the ceremony, the speakers, the U.S. Military Academy Color Guard, the soloist, and musicians from the Juilliard School, and honored guests adjourned to the 200 Club, 200 Fifth Avenue, New York, for a social hour and luncheon.

The program for the first day of issue ceremony is reproduced here:

Presiding	**George F. Shuman** District Manager/Postmaster New York, New York
Presentation of Colors	**U.S. Military Academy Color Guard** West Point, New York
National Anthem	**Jeanine Thames** Soprano, Graduate Student, The Juilliard School Accompanied by The Eroica Brass Quintet of The Juilliard School, New York City
Invocation	**Rev. Thomas V. O'Connor** St. Peter's Preparatory School Jersey City, New Jersey
Welcome	**William Rockefeller** Chairman of the Board American Kennel Club
Introduction of Distinguished Guests	**Charles A. T. O'Neill** Executive Vice President American Kennel Club
Remarks	**William F. Stifel** President American Kennel Club
Musical Interlude	**Eroica Brass Quintet** The Juilliard School
Address and Presentation of Albums	**James C. Gildea** Assistant Postmaster General
Benediction	**Rev. Thomas V. O'Connor**
Honored Guests:	**Roy H. Andersen** Designer of Stamps **Mrs. Nan Ayling** Vice President American Kennel Club

Charles A. T. O'Neill

The Commemorative Stamp Block and Text designed by Roy H. Andersen

Reproduction of first day of issue American Kennel Club Centennial cover, showing cancellation. Also, special Centennial Dog Show cancellation. U.S. Postal Services set up a field post office at the Philadelphia Civic Center to honor our centennial dog show with the special American Kennel Club cancellation.

The Complete Dog Book and AKC Publications

The American Kennel Club is the publisher of the all-time most successful book on dogs. In print continuously since 1929, AKC's *Complete Dog Book* has sold well over 1,250,000 copies. The seventeenth edition of the book appeared in spring 1985.

The first edition of the book was titled *Pure-Bred Dogs: The Breeds and Standards as Recognized by the American Kennel Club*. The main purpose of the book was to offer the public a single source containing all official standards of the breeds. Accordingly, of the book's 315 pages, all but the final 15 pages of glossary were devoted to the standards of the eighty-nine breeds then recognized. Each standard was introduced by a single paragraph that summarized the breed's personality. A photograph of a typical representative of the breed accompanied the standard. The majority of these photographs were taken by the celebrated dog photographer Rudolf W. Tauskey.

Through the years, *The Complete Dog Book* has grown, but its essential purpose has remained the same. The 1929 total of eighty-nine breeds would be eighty-five by today's count. Two breeds today, Collies and Poodles, were four breeds then. Collies, Smooth, and Collies, Rough, and Poodles, Toy and Non-Sporting—which today are recognized as varieties— were in 1929 treated as separate breeds. Two breeds recognized in 1929 are no longer with us today: the Eskimo and the Mexican Hairless.

The seventeenth edition of *The Complete Dog Book* contains the standards of the 129 breeds currently recognized—50 percent more breeds than when the book was first published. 1929's eighty-odd breeds were divided into six groups: Sporting, Hound, Working, Terrier, Toy, and Non-Sporting. The 1985 edition of the book is the first to incorporate the seventh category, Herding Group, which came into being in January 1983. The Herding Group breeds were formerly in the Working Group.

The first two editions of the book (1929 and 1935) were handled for the American Kennel Club by G. H. Watt Publishers. Subsequent editions were handled by Halcyon House (1938, 1941, and 1942); Garden City Publishing (1945, 1947, and 1949); and Garden City Books (1951, 1954, 1956, 1961, and 1964). In 1968 Doubleday's name appears on the edition. Since the fourteenth edition of the book in 1972, the Howell Book House has handled the book for AKC. At Howell, senior editor Ab Sidewater, for many years associated with the Foley Dog Show organization's renowned magazine *Popular Dogs,* shared editorial work on the book for the fourteenth, fifteenth, sixteenth, and seventeenth editions, with AKC's John Mandeville.

The Complete Dog Book acquired its name when the third edition of the book appeared in 1938, which was also the first time the book contained a section on care. While vastly expanded since 1938, the book's basic contents are similar. The official standard of all recognized breeds appears together with a brief history of the breed and a high-quality black-and-white photograph of a typical example of the breed. There is an extensive section on care, now titled, "Healthy Dog: Keeping Your Dog Healthy, Happy, and Well-Behaved"; as well as a glossary, pointers on selecting a breed; an explanation of how AKC registration services work; and a description of the sporting activities—field trials, obedience trials, dog shows, and junior showmanship— that take place under AKC rules. There are also anatomical drawings of the dog and sixty-four pages of color plates, 115 full-color pictures of pure-bred dogs in all their diversity—one of the finest collection of dog photographs ever assembled. The color sections were added to the golden anniversary edition of the book, which appeared in 1979.

The 1985 edition of *The Complete Dog Book* contains 768 pages, a whopping 453 more pages (an increase of 144 percent) than the first edition. More than ever, *The Complete Dog Book* is dogdom's complete, essential source for everyone entering the world of pure-bred dogs.

The Complete Dog Book has long been AKC's most visible publishing endeavor, apart from the *Gazette*, AKC's monthly magazine. Each year, however, the American Kennel Club also publishes tens of thousands of pamphlets, booklets, rule books, and other specialty publications associated with the administration of the sport of pure-bred dogs in the United States.

The accompanying table lists these publications and their annual printings. Topping the list is the *Obedience Regulations,* with well over sixty thousand printed each year. The *Obedience Regulations* are followed by the *General Information* booklet and the *Rules* with forty-three thousand and thirty-two thousand printed, respectively.

One of the American Kennel Club's charter responsibilities involves the issuing of a monthly publication titled *The Stud Book Register.* One of the principal responsibilities of all agencies involved with the improvement of animals through selective breeding is the maintenance of pedigree information or a stud book. Until 1925, AKC stud book registrations were published as part of the *Gazette.* From 1925 to 1952, all stud book registrations were published in a separate publication. Since 1952, only dogs or bitches producing a litter for the first time have been published in the *Stud Book Register.* A dog's *Stud Book Register* publication date becomes part of that dog's vital registration records at AKC.

The *Stud Book Register* publication date is always indicated in parenthesis after the dog's name. A publication date indicates the month and year in which the dog appears. A publication date of *7-65* means that the dog was published in the July 1965 issue of the *Register.* The *Register* is arranged in Group order. Breeds are listed alphabetically, and the name of the dogs are printed alphabetically under their breed. For every entry the name of that dog's sire and dam and their *Stud Book Register* publications date appear. Thus, the dog's entire pedigree can be traced by referring to the issues of the *Register* in which preceding generations of sires and dams appeared.

Even though any dog or bitch will appear only once in the *Register,* following the registration of the first litter produced by that dog, the *Register* annually contains the names of approximately 200,000 new sires and dams.

The *Register* is, then, a highly specialized but vital dimension of AKC's role in the promotion and protection of pure-bred dogs. Publication of the *Register* has been greatly facilitated by computerization. Today the entire *Register,* which appears monthly, is generated by computer. The principal users of the *Register* are serious students of pedigrees. This includes breeders, specialty clubs, and certified pedigree services, who will research a dog's ancestry for a fee. The monthly print order for the *Stud Book Register* is 650.

As part of its celebration of its hundredth anniversary in 1984, the American Kennel Club prepared and published a very special commemorative book titled *The AKC's World of the Pure-Bred Dog: A Celebration of the Pure-Bred Dog in America.* This book was a deluxe, oversize, handsome pictorial that touched on all facets of the sport of dogs, from AKC's office operations to the dog in art and literature. The book is a delight to leaf through. Its 344 pages contain more than 350 illustrations, and there is an additional 16-page full color insert of the dog in art from the collections of the AKC and the Dog Museum of America. A. Hamilton Rowan, AKC's director of field trials, was principally responsible for steering this unique publishing effort to conclusion. The book was a Nick Lyons Book distributed by the Howell Book House.

The American Kennel Club has had a long history of publishing a myriad of materials intended to aid people interested in dogs. These activities are certain to continue in the ongoing effort to provide people with the best, most useful, and up-to-date information on pure-bred dogs.

AKC Publications and Annual Usage

Obedience Regulations	63,000
General Information Books	43,000
Rules & Regulations	32,000
The A. K. C. Pamphlet	20,000
Regular-Size Record Books	18,000
Field Trial Rules	15,000
Are You a Responsible Dog Owner?	15,000
Large-Size Record Books	12,000
A.K.C. Policies and Guidelines for Registration Matters	10,000
Guide for Bench Show and Obedience Trial Committees	10,000
Beagle Field Trial Rules	7,000
Judges Directory	6,000
Match Regulations	5,000
Guidelines for Obedience Judges	4,000
Junior Showmanship	4,000
Guidelines for Dog Shows	4,000
Standing Recommendations of The Retriever Advisory Committee	3,000
Dog Show Stewards	1,500
The Formation of Dog Clubs	1,500
Dealer Record Books	500
Working Group	500
Non-Sporting Group	300
Basset Field Trial Rules	300
Hound Group	250
Terrier Group	250
Sporting Dog Group	200
Toy Group	200
Charter, Constitution, and Bylaws	100
First Information for Clubs Seeking to Hold Field Trials under A.K.C. Rules, Regulations, and Procedures	100

John J. Mandeville

Data Processing

The American Kennel Club realized in the early 1960s that it would have to take steps to modernize its office operations to keep up with the steadily increasing workflow. As the number of dogs registered and show and trial activity increased, the office staff and floor space also had to be increased. Faced with these rising costs and a desire to maintain a high degree of quality of service, the American Kennel Club entered the computer age.

A Honeywell computer was installed in 1967, and its top priority was the computerization of the registration system. The American Kennel Club's first attempt at computerization was not a startling success. Not only were unrealistic deadlines set for implementation of the system, but the manual registration system had never been properly documented. This early system was put on hold in 1969 for a period of three years, while AKC documented the manual registration systems.

By 1971, registrations, show, and trial activity of the American Kennel Club had reached an all-time high. In this same year, Mr. David Wachsman was hired to head the data-processing department and to spearhead the American Kennel Club's second effort at computerization. A new IBM computer was selected and a programming staff was put in place. The final registration system that emerged took several years to complete.

By 1974, litter applications were processed under the new system. There was a period of six months during which all applications were processed both manually and using the computer, to ensure that the system was functioning properly. By 1977, all individual dog and litter registration applications were being handled by the computer. However, the storage capacity of the early computer was not sufficient to accommodate all groups at the same time. Therefore, the records for some groups could be accessed each morning, with the remaining groups being available in the afternoon. This problem was eliminated in 1981, with the installation of an IBM 4341 computer. At the same time, a storage capacity of 6.864 billion bytes was established.

The computer system that was put in place eliminated much of the manual checking that had previously been necessary. Now, the computer checked such things as whether the owners and breeders were in good standing with the American Kennel Club, if a name choice was unique and did not infringe upon a registered kennel name prefix, if the age of the sire and dam were within acceptable limits, if there was a proper gestation period, and so forth. The computer system also generated registration certificates, litter kits, and three-generation pedigrees. By the start of 1985, the records of approximately 13 million dogs and 6 million litters were contained in the computer storage system.

While all registration certificates were generated by the computer in 1984, there were still a number of manual operations in the registration system; for example, the initial screening of applications, the checking of signatures, the numbering of applications, and the processing of application fees. These areas were being monitored in 1985, with the idea of eventually increasing their efficiency through further computerization.

Mr. Frederick G. Sheppard, who was hired in June 1981, as director of data processing, was given the assignment of computerizing the show-operations area at the American Kennel Club. This was the next logical area at the American Kennel Club where the computer could improve on a major manual operation. Mr. Sheppard was uniquely suited to this task, as he had an extensive background as a breeder, an exhibitor, and a dog club official, as well as a strong background in computers. The initial systems documentation and programming work for the show plans department was completed by February 1982. The approval of show and obedience trial dates and the maintenance of judges' files were the first systems implemented. This was followed in fall 1982 with the system that enabled the show plans department to process judges panels utilizing the computer. In December 1984, the recording of show and obedience trial awards was computerized. The show-and-trial-awards section of the *Gazette* was generated by the computer for the first time in March 1985.

Computerization will continue to be an ongoing project at the American Kennel Club. As the organization moves into its second hundred years, the computer will be an integral part of the dog-recordkeeping process.

Frederick G. Sheppard

Dog Museum of America

Virtually every culture has cherished the special relationship between man and dog. Cave paintings are alive with dogs and doglike creatures, and that tradition has continued throughout the history of art in depictions of the canine in its many roles: as an ally to the hunter, to the farmer, and to the sportsman; and, in more recent centuries, as a companion and honored pet.

Major museums around the world have collected works of art that depict the dog, but these artifacts are scattered among heterogeneous collections, with many works hidden from view in storage vaults. Others are in private collections, not available to the general public. Indeed, the dispersion of one major art collection related to the dog dramatically illustrated the need for a museum dedicated to the dog and the dog in art.

In June 1980, the American Kennel Club responded to that need, creating the American Kennel Club Foundation, the primary goal of which was to set up a national repository for works of art, books, and artifacts on the dog. The foundation moved quickly toward the establishment of the Dog Museum of America, the first repository for the display and study of canine art. The museum formally opened in September 1982 in space provided for it on the main floor of the AKC headquarters at 51 Madison Avenue in New York City. The museum is open Tuesday through Saturday, from 10 a.m. to 5 p.m., and on Wednesday until 7 p.m.

From its inception, the museum's exhibitions, publications, and educational programs have been designed to illuminate the extraordinary part the dog has played in our lives. The premier exhibit, "Best of Friends: The Dog in Art," revealed this rich heritage. The show featured art works and artifacts spanning twenty-seven centuries, from the dog's earliest appearance in prehistoric cave drawings to twentieth-century artworks, including Alberto Giacometti's attenuated sculpture, *Dog*. In photographs, paintings, sculptures, lithographs, and watercolors, humankind's high regard and love for the dog were profusely illustrated.

Other shows have been more of a documentary nature: "Show Dog!," a visual history of showing dogs in England and America, and "The Dog World"—How the Dog Made Man More Human, a sweeping survey of organizations and institutions that have nurtured, studied, and honored our canine companions.

And, of course, the dog has been featured as pet. Two very different exhibitions have highlighted the unique bond that exists between people and dogs. "Pampered Pets" traced the care and attention lavished on the dog from 350 B.C., represented by an Egyptian mummified

Best of Friends: The Dog in Art—September—December 1982

Show Dog! February—May 1984

Fidos and Heroes in Bronze   February—June 1983

dog, to the twentieth century represented by clothing, collars, and furnishings. A media extravaganza was staged during this show, "Canine Couture" a fashion showing of over twenty-five contemporary and vintage outfits. The press came in droves to film and record this stunning event.

"Era of the Pet: Four Centuries of People and Their Dogs" at the University Museum in Philadelphia honored the centennial of the American Kennel Club. Paintings, drawings, etchings, and sculptures recorded the evolution of today's concept of the pet from its earliest stages under the reign of Louis XIV in the seventeenth century. This show will also travel, as the museum continues to reach out to people across the country—educating, enthralling, and exciting the enormous public who love the dog.

Special exhibitions for children have been presented annually. Designed to develop an understanding between youngsters and pets, programs have been given on the care of animals, and numerous films with canine stars have been shown. Over ten thousand New York City schoolchildren have visited in the past three years, enjoying the imagery of "Color Me Dog," "D, Is for Dog" and, in 1984, "Presidential Pets: Finny, Furry, and Feathered Friends in the White House." Coloring books, posters, and games accompanied these educational and entertaining shows.

In-depth art historical shows have also been curated. "Fidos and Heroes in Bronze," a landmark exhibition, depicted dogs in bronze sculpture from prehistoric Greece to the present day. Images ranged from faithful companion, guardian, hunter, and shepherd to religious symbol, mythological beast, and fantastical creature, reflecting the changing attitudes of civilization.

Fidos and Heroes in Bronze   February—June 1983

In 1983, the museum mounted, "The Dog Observed: Photographs 1843-1983." The exhibition, which was extremely well received by the press, including *Newsweek,* the *New York Times,* and *Smithsonian* magazine, in 1985-1986 traveled under the auspices of the Smithsonian Institution Traveling Exhibition Service to thirteen cultural institutions in the United States and Canada. A lavishly illustrated book published by Alfred A. Knopf accompanied the show. Works in the exhibition are drawn from the museum's expanding collections and from major private and public collections around the world, bringing into public view treasures that have often been hidden for years.

Upcoming exhibitions are equally diverse, designed to attract people of all ages, with a wide variety of interests, highlighting the importance of the dog in history, art, and contemporary life.

Geraldine Rockefeller Dodge—art collector, philanthropist, and a woman whom many call the greatest dog aficionado ever—will be the subject of a major exhibition and a book. Her extensive art collection, including thousands of works depicting animals, which was dispersed by auction in the late 1970s, will be the basis for this exhibition, along with family photos, scrapbooks, and memorabilia. This, too, will be an exhibition that will appeal to dog, art, and history lovers alike.

Through these exhibitions, publications, and educational programs, along with the developing research library, oral-history program, film archive, and lectures on the dog and the dog in art, the museum will continue to expand its ever-widening national audience.

William Secord

The Gazette: A Magazine for All Reasons

A period of four years elapsed between the founding of the American Kennel Club and the acknowledgment of the real need for this new "club of clubs" to have a voice that would carry its word and work throughout the sporting world. What better way to communicate the decisions of this fledgling organization, its rules and regulations relating to such sporting events as dog shows and trials, and the importance of its newly acquired canine registry than a journal, or, as it was known then and even today, almost a hundred years later, the *Gazette*.

By 1889, AKC had as its president one of the most innovative guiding spirits in the dog world, August Belmont, Jr. A gentleman of great vision and even greater wealth, Belmont put the wheels in motion to produce a "gazette" by guaranteeing against any losses for five years with his own personal security of $5,000 per year. In January 1889, the *Gazette* made its first appearance and survived not only those first five years without any blemish on its financial record but has been published without interruption for almost a century, thus making it the oldest dog magazine in existence and possibly one of the oldest continuously published magazines anywhere.

August Belmont was one of the foremost American breeders and exhibitors of Smooth Fox Terriers and a prominent, if somewhat colorful, judge. One remark preserved for posterity in an early *Gazette* reads: "The champion bitches were old matrons whose quondam charms have mostly fled." Would that current issues embellished their pages with such succinctness today!

The first issue of the *Gazette* was truly a collector's item. The cover, by today's standards, was an artist's nightmare and an advertiser's dream. It featured a lengthy advertisement for "Spratt's Patent Meat Fibrine Vegetable Dog Cakes with Beefroot and Cod Liver Oil." Visually, it left a lot to be desired.

The inside front cover of the premiere issue announced the thirteenth annual Westminster event; and the masthead listed AKC officers, thirty-six active member clubs, applications for five new member clubs, and the resignation of the Western Pennsylvania Poultry Society of Pittsburgh!

Wasting no time with editorial frivolities, Page 2 plunged into "Champions of Record"— ninety-four dogs in fifteen breeds—and a show date section, called "Fixtures," listed eleven upcoming venues. A "Greeting" from the American Kennel Club stated its editorial policy, and from its tone was more likely to reassure the competition than to garner subscriptions:

> The American Kennel Club. . .will endeavor, as much as lies in their power, to meet what they feel the Kennel World requires in the shape of an official organ; taking as their guide the expressions of opinion on the subject from breeders and exhibitors, both in the past and since the adoption of the plan of publishing this *Gazette*.

> It is proposed to afford the Kennel Club and its individual members an official medium for the publication of all proceedings and announcements bearing upon any subject embraced by the interests of the Kennel World, and to keep and publish a complete and official record of all that transpires during the year, either in connection with shows, field trials or matters affecting the breeding, kennel, or field management of any known breed of dog.

> It will be the policy of the *Gazette* to infringe in no way upon the province or enter into the field of the regular sporting journals. Having received the most flattering assurances of friendly feeling and professional co-operation from such sound and powerful sporting authorities as the *American Field*, the *Turf, Field and Farm*, and other journalistic friends, any fears respecting the advisability of the movement may be dismissed.

THE AMERICAN
KENNEL GAZETTE

AN OFFICIAL JOURNAL, PUBLISHED MONTHLY BY THE
AMERICAN KENNEL CLUB.

VOL. I.—No. I. JANUARY, 1889. PRICE {$2.00 per annum. 20c single number.

CONTRACTORS TO THE LEADING AMERICAN AND EUROPEAN KENNEL CLUBS.

BY SPECIAL APPOINTMENT. TRADE MARK BY SPECIAL APPOINTMENT

Spratts Patent (America), Limited.
PATENT MEAT FIBRINE VEGETABLE
DOG CAKES (with Beetroot).

Ms. H. R. T. COFFIN, GlensFalls, N. Y., writes 7th July, 1887:
"The continual use of your dog cakes has proved very satisfactory to me in feeding all my kennel dogs, both large and small, old and young, and they are thriving on the use of it to the *exclusion of all other food.* I shall and do take pleasure in recommending Spratts Patent Dog Cakes."

MR. JAMES MORTIMER says of our PATENT
COD LIVER OIL MEAT FIBRINE DOG CAKES, WITH BEETROOT.

WESTMINSTER KENNEL CLUB, BABYLOS, L. I., October 6, 1887.

SPRATTS PATENT (AMERICA), LIMITED.

GENTLEMEN—I think it proper to state that I attribute the excellent condition of our pointers, and particularly of Bang-Bang (always a most difficult dog to get right), to the fact that six weeks prior to the Waverly, N. J., show I fed them almost entirely on your Cod Liver Oil Cakes.

I have also found the cakes invaluable for puppies recovering from distemper and other complaints of a debilitating nature. Send 500 pounds some time next week.

JAMES MORTIMER, Superintendent.

Especially valuable for preparing BAD FEEDERS for EXHIBITION.

In cases of DISTEMPER, ECZEMA and other diseases, they are especially valuable, and are a most successful food for DELICATE and DAINTY FEEDING DOGS.

The abundance of natural phosphates they contain insures their being a perfect food for young, growing puppies, particularly of a larger breed, such as St. Bernards.

Celebrated **MANGE CURE** Sold in Bottles, Gallon and Half Gallon Jars.

"**THE COMMON SENSE OF DOG DOCTORING.**" Price 25c., or post free, 28c.

Spratts Patent Limited DOG MEDICINES. Small pamphlet on Canine Diseases, post free.

DOG SOAP. Is entirely **Free from Poison**, and most effective in the destruction of Lice, Fleas and Ticks, and in keeping the skin free from scurf.

239-245 EAST FIFTY-SIXTH STREET,
DOWNTOWN DEPOT, 18 SOUTH WILLIAM STREET, NEW YORK.

Covers convey trends of the time and in the GAZETTE's 96-year history, they have spoken eloquently about the things that interest the dog fancy. The first cover was an ad for Spratts Dog Cakes and if it failed in eye-appeal, it certainly succeeded in longevity; it appeared monthly for 25 years.

Almost a hundred years later, these concepts still guide the magazine's editorial policy. The monthly "Secretary's Pages" and quarterly delegates' meeting minutes keep the fancy informed of the business of the American Kennel Club and is a true record of all that transpires during the year. Feature articles on individual breeds, breeding and related subjects bring the most up-to-date information available to subscribers. It still continues to enjoy friendly relations with those sporting authorities still publishing.

That first issue was a brisk twenty pages and contained one particularly intriguing entry: Under "Stud Visits," the Messrs. W. Atlee Burpee, of flower-and-vegetable-farm fame, kept two stud dogs busy in December with nuptial visits from seven collie bitches. This little item

The first cover featuring a pure-bred dog made its appearance in 1924 with famous illustrator Carl Anderson's Boston Terrier, titled "An American Gentleman" (left, below); this change heralded a new approach appealing to the subscriber's aesthetic senses. Covers tended to be quite straightforward, with photographs by both amateur and professional photographers covering almost all recognized breeds over the next six decades. From time to time, particularly during World War II, there was an attempt to be "newsworthy" with dogs in situations relevant to the war effort. A number of handsome paintings have also been featured but in the main, the covers have depicted the breed at its best.

One of the few "special covers" created for the GAZETTE was the birthday party featuring one representative from each group for the celebration of the AKC Centennial Issue (November, 1984, below, right). Although the picture took many days to set up in terms of concept, decoration and lighting, the actual shoot took only 17 minutes. Photographers Ann and Jim Monteith commented that the "magnificent seven" were better behaved than many of their two-legged clients. The breeds (from left to right) are Boxer (Working), Golden Retriever (Sporting), West Highland White Terrier (Terrier), Borzoi (Hound), Dalmatian (Non-Sporting), Shetland Sheepdog (Herding) and representing the Toy Group, the Yorkshire Terrier who occupies a daily perch on, or next to, a GAZETTE editorial desk. (Photograph Jim and Ann Monteith)

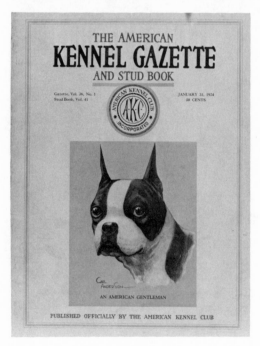

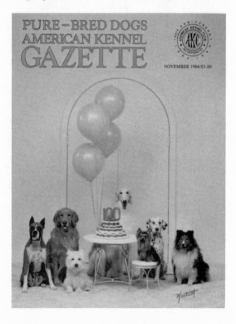

was a forerunner, no doubt, of the breed club departments' publications, coyly titled "Literally Speaking," or "From the Litter Box."

No death notices of mere mortal judges or others subject to such human frailties appeared, but a discreet obit column of canines was found on the last page. Rosecroft English Setters fared badly, losing one dog to distemper and two to "inflammation of the bowel." Could this have been a warning sign of the parvo epidemic of the 1980s?

Advertising was accepted, and the rates would make present advertisers wild: The cover sold in inches, at $2 per inch, and inside the book, on a descending scale, a twelve-time, one-inch insertion cost seventy-five cents.

By June of that momentous first year, official breed standards were published, and show reports detailed the judges' findings with finely honed criticism.

For many years, the *Gazette* was published without identifying the current editorial staff, a policy that can be beneficial when coping with an outraged exhibitor who discovers superdog's third-place-win in American-Bred identified as a fourth in the Show Awards.

In its embryonic years, these weighty matters rested on the shoulders of James Watson, an AKC founder, delegate from the Collie Club of America and a newspaper man of some renown. He was officially appointed editor in 1898; in 1900, he founded *Field and Fancy,* which, in 1928, became the great and now greatly lamented *Popular Dogs,* a truly unique dog magazine in its time.

After Watson's resignation, it is unclear who assumed the daily editorial duties, but no doubt A. P. Vredenburgh, secretary-treasurer of AKC, who dominated the offices for over thirty-five years, had a hand in things. Finally, in 1924, Louis de Casanova was identified as editor-in-chief, ably assisted by a young man whose presence would have a profound effect on the magazine for over forty years.

Arthur Frederick Jones was an editor with unerring good taste and longevity, to say nothing of tenacity. His continuing series, "Great Kennels of the Past," written in conjunction with Freeman Lloyd—no slouch himself as a fine writer—provoked the acerbic reporter for *The New Yorker* to comment in his two-part dissection of the AKC: "[Jones' series is] the work of a single appallingly persevering author." The "Great Kennels" series may well have set the world's record for articles on a single theme; Jones wrote 365 and Lloyd 220, and they appeared in the *Gazette* for over seventeen years. Some even made two trips into print.

Jones became editor-in-chief in 1942, a position he held until his retirement in 1968. His was a distinguished career indeed. He drew many top dog writers to the doors of the *Gazette* and wrote volumes himself under the monthly deadline. His account of the sesquicentennial show bears a careful reading to capture the true flavor of an exciting dog event.

No mention of the *Gazette's* editorial pages would be complete without singling out Freeman Lloyd, one of the most knowledgeable dog writers of his day. John Marvin, another long-time contributor to the *Gazette,* wrote of Lloyd: "[His] knowledge of dogs, art pertaining to dogs, and general activities involving them has never been equalled. . .he was truly 'one of a kind.'"

Following Jones's retirement in 1968, Henry Bernacki took the helm for the major part of the next decade. In 1978, Bernacki retired, and Robert Sherretta became editor-in-chief. His was a brief tenure, but distinguished by the innovative new graphic design and format initiated under his supervision. Pat Beresford, a veteran breeder and exhibitor who had worked for over twenty years in the book-publishing field, succeeded Sherretta in February 1979 and, at this writing, still continues to guide the magazine.

Covers continued to be ads until 1924 and Spratt's Dog Cakes hung in there to the bitter end. Finally, photographs and fine artwork made their appearance on the covers. The January

The great Arthur Frederick Jones, GAZETTE Editor-in-Chief for 26 years. His continuing series of articles on ''Great Kennels of the Past'' set a tone of affluence among breeders during the prosperity years. (Right), Present Editor-in-Chief, Pat Beresford, joined the GAZETTE in 1979 after twenty years in the book publishing field and an equal number as a breeder and exhibitor of Dachshunds and English Cocker Spaniels. (Photographs Grace Satriale)

1924 cover featured a pen-and-ink drawing of a Boston Terrier titled ''An American Gentleman,'' by famous illustrator Carl Anderson. The inside pages featured drawings by Muss-Arnolt and Edwin Megargee that today are museum collectibles.

For those who thrive on statistics, the dimensions of the *Gazette* resemble those of Pandora's box: In 1889, it was a trim and tidy 7^1/$_2$ by 10^1/$_2$ inches. By 1924, it had gained weight and girth, becoming 9 by 12 inches. World War II economies reduced it to 6 by 9 inches and following a complete redecoration in the years after the war, it finally measured in at 8^1/$_4$ by 10^3/$_4$ inches, with roughly 192 pages each month. For many years, of course, the girth was explained by the burgeoning Show Awards section that in January 1981 became a separate publication called *The American Kennel Club Show, Obedience, and Field Trial Awards.*

Inflation has taken its toll. From twenty cents per copy and $2 per year in 1889, it is currently $3 per copy and $18 per year for a subscription. Measured against other long-running publications, it is probably still the best buy for the money among specialized publications.

The *Gazette,* as it became known, has gone through as many name changes as a much-married matron. It started out as a maiden publication called *The American Kennel Gazette.* In 1918, when it annexed the *Stud Book,* it was known as *The American Kennel Gazette And Stud Book.* When the *Stud Book* went off on its own, it went back to its original name. In March 1943, it burst forth as *Pure-Bred Dogs* (with the emphasis on the masthead on the *Dogs) American Kennel Gazette.* An announcement of this on the editor's page called attention to ''our new spring bonnet'' and got so carried away with its own whimsy, it never managed to say exactly what the new title was.

For those still keeping score, today it is officially known as *Pure-Bred Dogs/American Kennel Gazette*.

What is the *Gazette* today? In some ways, at least in physical characteristics, it has changed a lot and stands with feet planted firmly in a media-oriented society. In philosophy, it has changed very little. It is still the official publication of the American Kennel Club and, as such, tries to meet what AKC required in the role of an official voice.

In addition to the "Secretary's Pages" and reports of the quarterly delegates' meetings, it publishes show dates and judging panels as they are approved by the show plans department; a multitude of statistics relating to all aspects of registration, all-breed and specialty shows, obedience trials, and field trials; and geographical lists of clubs. There are bimonthly breed columns, written by a designated member of the parent club, which cover almost all breeds registered by AKC. There is a healthy crop of departments relating to individual dog interests: veterinary news, grooming, nutrition and health, dog legislation, and junior showmanship. There is a general news column, "On All Fronts"; occasional book reviews; "Mailbag"; and an editorial from the editor-in-chief. One of the most popular monthly columns is "Dog Trainer's Diary," by Carol Benjamin, which is leavened with humor and written with great skill and understanding of the individual dog owner's needs. There is a resident cartoon dog, "K.C." created by talented Bryan Hendrix, who passes judgment on a variety of subjects each month. The diverse material published is a cornucopia of professional information for the experienced dog fancier right down to the new pet owner.

The fun part, of course, is the wide variety of features published each month. The *Gazette* has had interviews with Snoopy of *Peanuts* fame, the man from the *New York Times,* Walter Fletcher, it has published hundreds of articles by veterinarians discussing the latest techniques in veterinary medicine, research, and clinical methods of disease control. It has had studies of herd-guarding dogs and the philosophy of the art of walking the dog. It has contained articles about rescue organizations, about terminology relating to the anatomy of the dog, and about society's concern with the role of the canine in our lives today. It has covered all aspects of the human-animal bond, including articles on seeing-eye dogs, hearing-aid dogs, dogs for all manner of handicapped people, dogs for the aged and for therapy work in hospitals and nursing homes. The *Gazette* has an ongoing love affair in its "Breeding Better Dogs" series and its fascination with puppies. On a scale of one to ten, puppies get an unqualified ten for audience appeal, particularly when pictured in full color.

The past years have added extensive coverage of national specialties and a number of issues with a "theme," such as an all-Irish breeds issue, the Mastiff/Bullmastiff issue, and 1984's "When Is a Collie Not a Collie . . ." Most important, the *Gazette* attempts to bring to the dog fancy in general, as well as aspiring judges, in-depth articles on interpretation and understanding the breed standards through education.

And, finally, the *Gazette* sponsors a highly successful photography contest, initiated in 1980, with entries running well over a thousand from both amateur and professional photographers.

The *Gazette* has effected editorial changes in the 1980s that reflect positive changes in the world of pure-bred dogs. It has resisted pressures to indulge in media hype and flights of fancy contrary to its historical roots and the concepts of the organization that it represents. With traditional values securely in place, the *Gazette* looks forward to the challenge of the next hundred years, unintimidated by the innovations of this fast-moving world in which we live with our dogs.

Pat Beresford

The Library

At its April 10, 1934, meeting, the Board of Directors of the American Kennel Club appointed a committee to oversee the establishment of a library in its new headquarters at 221 Fourth Avenue in New York City. The committee was chaired by Hubert H. Brown, AKC director and delegate of the Irish Terrier Club of America, a publisher by profession. The other members were Louis de Casanova, editor of the *Gazette;* William Cary Duncan, AKC director and delegate of the Irish Setter Club of America; S. Edwin Megargee, AKC director, delegate of the Los Angeles Kennel Club and later of the Louisiana Kennel Club, a professional artist; James W. Spring, counsel for the American Kennel Club. Mr. Megargee became chairman of the committee when Mr. Brown died in 1936 and held the position until his own death in 1958.

The first library was situated at one end of what was called the Club Room. It was a cozy, comfortable area with three sections of bookshelves built into one wall. The books that were placed there had originally been in bookcases in the *Gazette* offices.

In November 1934, a report from Mr. Brown was published in the *Gazette,* informing readers that the American Kennel Club Library was a reality. He stated, ''It is the aim of the American Kennel Club to compile a great reference library of books treating all recognized breeds, and everything in which the dog is concerned.'' The report included a letter that was sent to all member clubs asking them to submit lists of desirable books. The letter also announced that donations would be most welcome.

In 1936, Mr. Megargee designed a special library letterhead and a bookplate that was placed in the 1,125 books then in the collection. The design featured three breeds native to North America: the American Foxhound, the Newfoundland, and the Chesapeake Bay Retriever. The Statue of Liberty appears in the background. The original drawing still hangs in the library. A special bookplate was used in commemorative gifts and featured the name of the donor and the date of the gift.

In 1937, Miss Beatrice Peterson was appointed librarian. She held the job until her retirement in 1975. During Miss Peterson's long tenure, the collection grew from three bookshelves to more than ten thousand volumes, plus works of art and memorabilia.

When Miss Peterson retired, the library and its staff were supervised for a time by John Mandeville, assistant to the then-AKC President, John A. Lafore. It was during this period that the entire collection was recataloged according to the Dewey decimal system, with special modifications.

In September 1979, Roberta Vesley became library director. Mrs. Vesley received a master of library science degree in 1975 from Long Island University's Palmer Graduate Library School. She was employed by the American Kennel Club in July of that year and worked in the show plans department and later in show records. Before coming to AKC, Mrs. Vesley raised and showed Soft-Coated Wheaten Terriers. She was a founding member of the local breed club and served on the board of the parent club.

The other members of the staff have all been employed by AKC for a long time. Marie Fabrizi began working in the library in 1962. She is a graduate of the Kathleen Dell Secretarial School in Boston and has studied at the Art Students League in New York. For a time she also studied dance with Madame Fokine.

Aida Ferrer was born in the Philippines and emigrated to the United States in 1970. She began working for AKC in 1971, first in show records and later in show plans, while attending

Queens College School of Library Science. After receiving her MLS degree, she was assigned to the library.

One of the most familiar faces at AKC is that of Ann Sergi, AKC receptionist. Miss Sergi has been with AKC since 1956. She has worked in registration and show plans. When all registration work was done manually, she supervised the section that worked on Poodles. As computerization came in, she was transferred to the library where she spent about five years before taking her present job. Miss Sergi was born and raised in Brooklyn and still resides there.

The heart of any library is its collection. In 1984, the collection was estimated to be about fifteen thousand volumes. These include bound periodicals and foreign and domestic stud books. The areas covered include individual breeds, art, literature, history, nutrition, breeding, training, disease, care, kennel management, showing and judging, and sports. Other peripheral subjects, such as works on wolves and on animal behavior, also have their place on the shelves.

The library maintains files and records for AKC's extensive art collection, much of which is on display in the halls and offices. There is a large clipping file. Tear sheets of *Gazette* articles are filed along with historical and archival matters, for example, materials dealing with breed standards and recognition. There is a large photographic archive, a bookplate collection, a medal collection, and a stamp collection, all housed in ever-decreasing space.

The book collection is one of the largest and best collections of canine literature in the world. It is unique in that it is available to the public for research. The library owns many of the major rare books about dogs. Among these treasures is *De Canibus Britannicis* (1570), the first book devoted to dogs. It was written in Latin by Johannes Caius, physician to Queen Elizabeth I and founder of Caius College, Cambridge. A translation into English was done in 1576 by Abraham Fleming and the library has the 1881 reprint, itself a rare work, which it acquired in 1983. The significance of the book lies in the system of classification of dogs set down by Dr. Caius.

Another important work is *The Master of Game*, written between 1406 and 1413 by Edward of Norwich, second Duke of York, although it was not published until 1904. The library's copy is one of the first six hundred issued and has a foreword by Theodore Roosevelt.

Space does not permit more than a brief mention of the library's outstanding books. There is the 1881 facsimile of Dame Juliana Berner's *The Boke of St. Albans,* written about 1480, which was the first book in the English language to discuss dogs. The author describes the British dogs as she knew them. Sydenham Edwards's fascinating book, *Cynographia Britanica* was the first illustrated dog book and was published in 1800. The library obtained a copy with most of the pictures in 1983. In 1803, William Taplin wrote a two-volume work called *The Sportsman's Cabinet,* which discussed the various dogs used in sports. The oldest breed book in the collection is *A Treatise on Greyhounds,* written in 1819 by Sir William Clayton.

There are books in foreign languages including French, German, Italian, Spanish, and Russian. Special collections of prominent dog people such as John Cross, the Shearer sisters, Alva Rosenberg, Robert Wiel, Dorothy Howe, and Major and Beatrice Godsol are shelved separately.

Each year the library receives and files almost four hundred periodicals and newspapers from all over the world. Among these are forty foreign magazines, thirty-five sporting, thirty-five hound, sixty working and herding, twenty terrier, fourteen toy, and seventeen non-sporting publications. Also, there are veterinary journals, rare-breed publications, and those relating to humane societies and pet owners. A complete set of bound copies of the *Gazette* from 1889 to date and all AKC *Stud Books* are available for researchers.

The library staff handles AKC's popular film-rental program. There are eleven films available to clubs and individuals. The subjects covered are: breeds, judging, structure and movement, field trials, and obedience. Some films are being transferred to video-cassette format but are only available for purchase.

In 1980, the stamp collection was started. There are nearly a thousand stamps depicting dogs either as primary subjects or as part of a larger scene. The stamps come from all over the world. The oldest is a U.S. stamp from 1898 on which a small dog is seated on the seat of a plow in a wheatfield. The official presentation block of the 1984 dog stamp issued by the postal service was added to the collection in September 1984. Many people have contributed stamps, among them: Princess Antoinette of Monaco, the Briard Club of America, Dr. Wolfgang Casper, Marie Fabrizi, Charles Kubiak, F. Mashel of Belgium, Mrs. Herbert Miller, Mrs. Rose Radel, Patricia R. Robertson, Ms. Lorna Spangenberg, and Valerie Wilson. The collection can be seen with special permission from a staff member.

A primary activity of the library is answering requests for information that cannot be handled by other departments at AKC. These inquiries are made by telephone, by letter, or in person. Over a thousand visitors come into the library each year, in addition to AKC personnel who are its major users. People want to find out what kind of dog to get, what to feed the dog they have, and how to train it. Some come to trace pedigrees. Many of the well-known dog writers have done much of their research here on the twentieth floor.

The library is service-oriented. To this end, indexes to magazines are being prepared. Bibliographies are compiled for distribution. AKC does not recommend or endorse foods, products, trainers, breeders, etc., but the staff makes every effort to provide its patrons with sufficient information to make an intelligent choice in these matters.

During its fifty-one years, the AKC library has grown and changed and these processes will go on. Technology will surely become important if the library is to continue to provide high-quality service to an ever-growing public. As "man's best friend," the dog deserves to be better cared for, better understood, better trained, and more appreciated. The resources of AKC's superb library can provide the means to this end.

Roberta Vesley

Organizational Structure

The American Kennel Club has functioned as a "club of clubs" from its inception. While there was a provision for individual associate members, later called associate subscribers, during the early years of the American Kennel Club's existence, this practice was stopped in 1924, and ever since only dog clubs may become members. It is the delegates of each member club who elect the Board of Directors from their ranks and vote on any amendments to the AKC By-Laws or rules.

The organizational structure of the American Kennel Club has been adjusted over the years as the interest in pure-bred dogs has grown. Before the establishment of the Board of Directors in 1906, an advisory committee, and then an executive board, consisting of delegates, handled the affairs of the club between quarterly delegates' meetings. The actual guardianship of the AKC office was in the hands of the secretary, who operated with a very small staff. After 1906, it was stipulated in the By-Laws that the secretary could not serve as a delegate. In 1906, when AKC began to pursue incorporation actively, the American Kennel Club created the Board of Directors, consisting of thirty members (five classes of six members each). The size of the Board was reduced in 1931, so that it subsequently consisted of twelve members (four classes with three members each). Throughout most of the history of the American Kennel Club, the Board was chaired by the President of The American Kennel Club, who was an amateur sportsman. In 1913, Dr. John E. DeMund was briefly designated as chairman of the board. However, it was specified that the chairman of the board was only to preside at the board meetings in the absence of the president or vice-presidents, who were also members of the Board. The actual running of the AKC on a day-to-day basis was variously in the hands of the secretary, the executive vice-president, or the executive secretary, who were full-time employees.

In 1968, Mr. Alfred M. Dick was named the first President, who was to function as the chief operating officer on a full-time basis. Simultaneously, a provision was added to the bylaws that enabled the Board to appoint one or more vice-presidents, who also were to devote their full-time efforts to the affairs of the AKC. The bylaws in effect prior to 1968 only provided for a president, an executive vice-president, an executive secretary, a treasurer, and a secretary.

In 1972, Mr. John A. Lafore, Jr., then AKC President, proposed an amendment to the by-laws; "In order to blend the advantages of a professional President, and at the same time, have an amateur officer in the top position in the same tradition as our policy for more than 80 years. . ." would create the position of chairman of the board.

Many of the changes that came about in the organization of the American Kennel Club resulted from the increasing volume of work associated with the sport of pure-bred dogs. Over the years, both registrations and dog-show activities steadily increased. This necessitated a larger office force and a more complicated management structure to supervise that staff.

The greatest growth at AKC took place in the years following World War II. In 1946, there were 204,957 dogs registered, and a total of 806 AKC approved dog events. There were 179,967 dogs in competition, and a staff of 149 employees at the AKC handled this volume. In 1984, the American Kennel Club registered 1,071,299 dogs and 9,926 dog events were held. There were 1,351,379 dogs in competition, and 409 employees handled this volume. The employees on the staff of the American Kennel Club reached a peak in 1971 with a total of 724. The reduction in employees from 1971 to 1984 was made possible with the advent of system design and comput-erization. To illustrate the growth of the American Kennel Club since World War II, registra-tions, dog events, dogs in competition, and number of employees are given below:

Year	Registrations	Dog Events	Dogs in Competition	Number of Employees
1946	204,957	806	179,967	149
1950	251,812	2,878	190,188	188
1960	442,875	5,264	322,390	242
1970	1,056,225	7,063	751,518	636
1980	1,011,799	8,885	1,151,347	422
1984	1,071,299	9,926	1,351,379	409

Robert G. Maxwell

Charter, Constitution and By-Laws

Adopted January 5, 1909

Amended to September 8, 1976

CHARTER

SECTION 1. William G. Rockefeller, Dwight Moore, Howard Willets, B. S. Smith, Marcel A. Viti, Frederick H. Osgood, John E. De Mund, Clair Foster, Laurence M. D. McGuire, Henry Jarrett, August Belmont, William B. Emery, Edward Brooks, Charles W. Keyes, James W. Appleton, George B. Post, Jr., Thomas Cadwalader, Winthrop Rutherfurd, James Mortimer, George Lauder, Jr., William Rauch, Samuel R. Cutler, John G. Bates, J. H. Brookfield, Chetwood Smith, Hildreth K. Bloodgood, Singleton Van Schaick, Hollis H. Hunnewell, J. Sergeant Price and William C. Codman, and all other persons, corporations, associations and organizations as shall hereafter become associated with them as members, as may be provided for by the constitution or by-laws, under and for the purposes of this charter and act of incorporation, are hereby organized and constituted a body corporate and are a corporation under and by name of The American Kennel Club.

SECTION 2. The objects of the corporation shall be to adopt and enforce uniform rules regulating and governing dog shows and field trials, to regulate the conduct of persons interested in exhibiting, running, breeding, registering, purchasing and selling dogs, to detect, prevent and punish frauds in connection therewith, to protect the interests of its members, to maintain and publish an official stud book and an official kennel gazette, and generally to do everything to advance the study, breeding, exhibiting, running and maintenance of the purity of thoroughbred dogs. And for these purposes it shall have power to adopt a constitution, by-laws, rules and regulations, and enforce the same by fines and penalties, which it shall have the right to collect and enforce by suit, or by suspension or expulsion from membership, or by a suspension or denial of any or all of the privileges of said corporation. It may,

from time to time, alter, modify or change such constitution, by-laws, rules or regulations.

SECTION 3. Said William G. Rockefeller shall call a meeting of said incorporators hereinbefore named by giving written notice of the time and place of said meeting by mail to each of them at least fifteen days before the time of said meeting, and in event of his failure so to do within thirty days after this act shall take effect, any one of said incorporators may so call said meeting. At said meeting a majority of said incorporators shall form a quorum. Said incorporators at said meeting or any adjournments thereof shall adopt a constitution, by-laws, rules and regulations hereinbefore authorized, and shall elect all the present members and delegates and associate subscribers of The American Kennel Club members, delegates and associate subscribers, of the corporation.

SECTION 4. Such corporation shall, subject to the provisions of this act, have all the powers and be subject to all the liabilities of a membership corporation organized under the membership corporations law.

SECTION 5. The directors of The American Kennel Club, a corporation heretofore incorporated under the membership corporations law by certificate filed in the office of the Secretary of State and the Clerk of New York county, upon obtaining the consent of the members of such corporation as provided by this section, are hereby authorized to transfer, without consideration, all the property of such corporation to the corporation created by this act. The board of directors of such corporation shall appoint a time for holding a special meeting of the members of the corporation. At least thirty days before such meeting, the secretary of the corporation shall mail to every member thereof a notice of the time and place of such meeting and stating that there will be submitted to the members at such meeting a proposition to transfer all of its property, without consideration, to The American Kennel Club incorporated by Chapter 280 of the laws of nineteen hundred and eight. At any time prior to such meeting any member of the corporation may vote on such proposition by mailing to the secretary of the corporation his assent or dissent in substantially the following form: I hereby assent to (dissent from) the proposition to transfer the property of The American Kennel Club to The American Kennel Club as incorporated by Chapter 280 of the laws of nineteen hundred and eight. Such proposition shall be submitted to the members present at the special meeting. If all such members voting thereon shall vote in the affirmative and no dissent has been filed with the secretary as authorized by this section, the proposition shall be deemed adopted, and thereupon the directors of the corporation shall transfer to The American Kennel Club incorporated by this act all the property of such corporation subject to any outstanding debts or liabilities of such corporation existing at the time of such transfer, which debts and liabilities the corporation incorporated hereby must assume as a condition of such transfer and shall be liable for the same in the same manner and to the same extent as such corporation. Upon completing such transfer the directors of the corporation or a majority of them shall execute in duplicate a certificate to the effect that a special meeting was held by the members of the corporation pursuant to this act, that the members thereof assented to the transfer of its property to The American Kennel Club as required by this section, and that such transfer has been made accordingly, and upon the filing of such certificate in the offices in which the original certificate of incorporation is filed, such corporation shall be deemed dissolved.

SECTION 6. This act shall take effect immediately. May 18, 1908

CONSTITUTION and BY-LAWS

ARTICLE I

NAME

The name of this Club shall be "THE AMERICAN KENNEL CLUB."

ARTICLE II

SEAL

The Seal of The American Kennel Club shall be circular in shape, having on the outer rim thereof the words "American Kennel Club Incorporated" and in an inner circle the capital letters "A.K.C."

ARTICLE III

OBJECTS OF THE CLUB

The objects of the Club shall be to adopt and enforce uniform rules regulating and governing dog shows, obedience trials and field trials, to regulate the conduct of persons interested in breeding, registering, selling, purchasing, exhibiting and running pure-bred dogs, to prevent, detect, and punish frauds in connection therewith, to protect the interests of its members, to maintain and publish an official stud book and an official kennel gazette, and generally to do everything to advance the study, breeding, exhibiting, running and maintenance of pure-bred dogs.

ARTICLE IV

MEMBERSHIP

SECTION 1. All Clubs or Associations which have held at least three Dog Shows, Obedience Trials or Field Trials in consecutive years under rules of The American Kennel Club and all Specialty Clubs which have been or shall be formed for the improvement of any breed of pure-bred dogs shall be eligible to become members of The American Kennel Club.

SECTION 2. Candidates for membership must apply in writing to The American Kennel Club on forms the terms of which shall be approved by the Board of Directors of The American Kennel Club which forms will be supplied by the Secretary of The American Kennel Club upon request. Each application must be accompanied by a copy of the Constitution and By-Laws of the applicant and a list of the names of its officers and members. Each candidate also must send with its application a check or cash for the amount of its admission fees and dues for the current year which will be returned to the candidate if and when it shall fail to be elected.

SECTION 3. No Club or Association shall be eligible to be admitted to membership in The American Kennel Club unless its Constitution and By-Laws shall provide that among the objects for which said Club or Association has been formed are the holding of annual dog shows, annual obedience trials or annual field trials or that said Club or Association was formed for the protection or benefit of dogs.

SECTION 4. If one or more Specialty Clubs formed for the improvement of any given breed of pure-bred dogs already are members in good standing of The American Kennel Club, no other Specialty Club formed for the improvement of the same breed of pure-bred dogs shall be admitted to membership unless and until the candidate for membership first has obtained in writing the permission of the member Specialty Club which first was admitted to be a member, known as the Parent Club, allowing the non-member Specialty Club to apply.

If a Parent Club shall fail to give another Specialty Club permission in writing to apply for admission to membership in The American Kennel Club, said non-member Specialty Club may appeal to the Board of Directors of The American Kennel Club at any time after two but not later than three months from the time when said permission was requested. The Board shall hear the parties, who may present their respective contentions either orally or in writing, and in its discretion, which must be by three-fourths affirmative vote of the members of the Board, may permit said non-member Specialty Club to apply for membership in The American Kennel Club.

SECTION 5. It shall be the duty and privilege of each parent member Specialty Club to define precisely the true type of the breed of pure-bred dogs which it was organized to promote and improve and its definition when approved by the Board of Directors of The American Kennel Club shall and will be recognized by The American Kennel Club as the sole standard of excellence for which such breed of pure-bred dogs shall be bred and by which specimens of such breed must be judged in the awarding of prizes of merit.

The standards of excellence of all breeds of pure-bred dogs now adopted by parent member Specialty Clubs and approved by the Board of Directors of The American

Kennel Club shall not be changed in any respect until the wording of any proposed change or changes first has been submitted to the Board of Directors of The American Kennel Club and its approval of the same has been obtained.

It shall be the duty of the Board of Directors of The American Kennel Club to and it shall define precisely the true type of each breed of pure-bred dogs recognized by The American Kennel Club as eligible for registration in its Stud Book for which no standard of excellence has been adopted by any member Specialty Club and submitted to and approved by said Board of Directors in the manner set forth in the preceding paragraphs of this section.

Any member Specialty Club shall have the right at any time except as hereinafter provided to propose to the parent member Specialty Club of its breed changes in the standard of excellence of its breed. In the event of the failure of such parent club to act upon such proposals within a reasonable time, or in the event that any such parent club in acting upon such proposals, shall make a decision which is wholly or partly unsatisfactory to any member specialty club or clubs of that breed, including the member Specialty Club making the proposals, such aggrieved member Specialty Club or clubs shall have as a matter of right an appeal to the Board of Directors of The American Kennel Club. When such appeal is taken, the Board of Directors of The American Kennel Club shall hold a hearing after notice has been given to all member specialty clubs of the breed affected and such other persons as the Board of Directors of The American Kennel Club shall in its discretion decide to summon. After such hearing the Board of Directors shall make a decision respecting the matter fully and thereafter for a period of two years no proposal to that parent member Specialty Club for changes in the affected portion or portions of the standard or standards of that breed shall be made to or entertained by that parent member Specialty Club without permission of the Board of Directors of The American Kennel Club.

SECTION 6. The name of each candidate and the fact that it has applied for membership must be published in the first issue of the AMERICAN KENNEL GAZETTE which shall be published after the receipt by the Secretary of The American Kennel Club of such application and again in the next succeeding issue of said GAZETTE and such application then shall be referred to the Board of Directors of The American Kennel Club for its approval or disapproval.

SECTION 7. Any person, Club or Association which may desire to object to the admission of a candidate for membership may do so by sending a letter to the Board of Directors of The American Kennel Club stating the reasons for such objection and such letter will be considered a privileged communication the contents of which must not be disclosed.

SECTION 8. The Board of Directors of The American Kennel Club shall report to The American Kennel Club at the next regular meeting of the Club its findings as to the eligibility of all candidates for membership the names of which duly have been published as provided in Section 6 of this Article, indicating the approval or disapproval of the Board by using the word "approved" or the word "disapproved" as the case may be, and said Board or any member of it in no instance shall be required to give any reason for the findings of said Board.

SECTION 9. The election of all candidates for membership which have been reported "approved" or which have not been reported "disapproved" by the Board of Directors of The American Kennel Club in accordance with the provisions of Section 8 of this Article shall be by ballot at any regular meeting of The American Kennel Club and it shall require the affirmative vote of four-fifths in number of all the delegates present and voting at such meeting to elect.

SECTION 10. Any club or association elected to membership shall notify the Secretary of The American Kennel Club of all changes in its officers as they occur, and no change in its Constitution and/or By-Laws shall go into effect until the proposed change be duly approved by the Board of Directors of The American Kennel Club.

SECTION 11. No candidate for membership which shall be disapproved by the Board of Directors of The American Kennel Club or which shall fail to be elected may again become a candidate until after one year from the date of such failure.

ARTICLE V

ADMISSION FEE AND DUES

SECTION 1. The amount of the admission fee for all new members of The American Kennel Club which may be elected after January 1, 1933, shall be two hundred and fifty ($250) dollars. The amount of the admission fee for all former members which may be re-elected after January 1, 1933, shall be determined in each instance by the Board of Directors of The American Kennel Club.

SECTION 2. The amount of the annual dues of the members of The American Kennel Club shall be determined by the Board of Directors of The American Kennel Club subject to approval by the delegates to The American Kennel Club, and shall be payable January 1 in each year, in advance. Any member which shall have failed to pay its annual dues on or before February 1, in any year, shall stand suspended from all privileges of The American Kennel Club. Any member which shall have failed to pay its annual dues on or before the day of the annual meeting of The American Kennel Club, may have its right to membership terminated at the election of the Board of Directors of The American Kennel Club which may take such action in each instance as it shall deem wise or may impose such fines or penalties as it may deem just and proper under the particular circumstances. This section of Article V shall be printed on each bill for dues so that no member may be in ignorance thereof.

ARTICLE VI

DELEGATES

SECTION 1. The voting powers of each Member Club or Association can and shall be exercised only by a delegate selected by said club to represent it for that purpose.

SECTION 2. Any member Club or Association which desires to be represented by a delegate must apply in writing to The American Kennel Club on a form of credentials the terms of which shall be approved by the Board of Directors of The American Kennel Club and which will be supplied by the Secretary of The American Kennel Club upon request. Each such application must be signed by the President or the Vice-President or the Secretary of the Member Club or Association making the application.

SECTION 3. The name and address of each candidate for the position of delegate and the fact that application has been made for his appointment must be published in the first issue of the AMERICAN KENNEL GAZETTE which shall be published after the receipt by the Secretary of The American Kennel Club of his credentials and again in the next succeeding issue of said GAZETTE and his credentials then shall be referred to the Board of Directors of The American Kennel Club for its approval or disapproval.

SECTION 4. Any person, Club or Association desiring to object to the appointment of any person named to be a delegate may do so by sending a letter to the Board of Directors of The American Kennel Club stating the reasons for such objection and such letter will be considered a privileged communication the contents of which must not be disclosed.

SECTION 5. Each candidate for the position of Delegate must personally be known by at least one member of the Board of Directors of The American Kennel Club or if not so known must be vouched for by some one person in good standing with The American Kennel Club who is known by at least one member of said Board or if the candidate can comply with neither of these conditions, the candidate must personally appear before the Board of Directors of The American Kennel Club at such time as it shall request him to appear.

SECTION 6. Professional judges of dog shows, obedience trials or field trials, professional reporters of dog activities, professional handlers or trainers of dogs, professional superintendents of shows or trials, employees of kennels, persons who are solicitors for or sell kennel advertising, persons who are actively engaged in directly selling dog foods, remedies, or supplies, or who in any way trade or traffic in dogs for the distinct purpose of deriving gains therefrom, are not eligible to become or remain delegates. For the purpose of this section, traveling salesmen who sell a limited amount of dog foods, remedies or supplies as part of a comprehensive merchandise line, or retail merchants or their salesmen who do not promote the sale of dog foods, remedies or supplies, but handle limited quantities of these commodities as part of their general stock of merchandise shall not be considered as being "actively engaged in directly selling dog foods, remedies, or supplies"; "trade and traffic in dogs" does not refer to the normal activities of a breeder who sells surplus dogs of his own breeding, or resells dogs bought for breeding purposes.

SECTION 7. The Board of Directors of The American Kennel Club shall report to The American Kennel Club at the next regular meeting of the Club its findings as to the eligibility of all candidates for the position of Delegate the names and addresses of whom duly have been published as provided in Section 3 of this Article indicating the approval or disapproval of the Board by using the word "approved" or the word "disapproved" as the case may be, and said Board or any member of it in no instance shall be required to give any reason for the findings of said Board.

SECTION 8. The election of all candidates for the position of Delegate who have been reported "approved" or who have not been reported "disapproved" by the Board of Directors of The American Kennel Club in accordance with the provisions of Section 7 of this Article shall be by ballot at any regular meeting of The American Kennel Club and it shall require the affirmative vote of two-thirds in number of all the Delegates present and voting at such meeting to elect.

SECTION 9. No candidate for the position of Delegate who shall be disapproved by the Board of Directors of The American Kennel Club or who shall fail to be elected may again become a candidate as Delegate from any Club or Association until after one year from the date of such failure.

SECTION 10. No Delegate can represent more than one member club or association. No delegate who duly has been elected shall continue to exercise the voting powers of the member club or association which appointed him after he has resigned or his appointment has been withdrawn or if his appointment has not been withdrawn after the credentials of the person named to succeed him have been acted upon with approval by the Board of Directors of The American Kennel Club.

ARTICLE VII

BOARD OF DIRECTORS

ELECTION, MEETINGS AND QUORUM

SECTION 1. The Club shall be governed by a Board of Directors consisting of twelve (12) members. Such Board shall be elected as follows:

At each annual meeting the Delegates shall elect three (3) Directors from the list of candidates nominated in the manner hereinafter provided in Article VIII of these By-Laws to hold office for four (4) years or until their successors are elected and such other director or directors from the list of candidates nominated in the manner hereinafter provided in Article VIII of these By-Laws as shall be required to fill the place or places of any director or directors who has or have died, resigned or been removed before the expiration of the term or terms for which he or they were elected.

In the event that at any such annual meeting following that in the year 1933 no Directors shall be elected, the Directors then in office, whose terms except for the provisions hereof would have expired at the time of said annual meeting, shall continue in office until their successors shall have been elected.

SECTION 2. Any vacancy in the Board shall be filled by the Directors by a majority vote of those present at any meeting; such Directors shall hold office until the next annual meeting of the Club.

SECTION 3. When a Delegate who also is a Director of The American Kennel Club shall resign his position as Delegate or shall be removed therefrom and shall not offer his resignation as Director of The American Kennel Club, he nonetheless may continue to hold the office of Director until the next annual meeting unless at the first regular meeting of the Board of Directors which shall be held subsequent to the date of his resignation or removal as a delegate which meeting he must not attend, the majority of the Board of Directors present shall vote to drop him from said Board, in which case he shall at once cease to be a Director of The American Kennel Club.

SECTION 4. There shall be a regular meeting of the Board each month, the date of which meeting shall be determined by the Board and seven (7) days' notice of said date must be given to each Director by mail.

SECTION 5. Special meetings of the Board shall be called by the Secretary at the direction of the President, or upon the written request of three (3) Directors. Five (5) days' notice of the date of such special meeting must be given to each Director by mail unless a waiver of notice of such meeting shall have been signed by every Director

SECTION 6. Seven (7) members shall constitute a quorum of the Board for the transaction of business at all meetings.

SECTION 7. The unexplained and by the directors unexcused absence of a Director from three consecutive regular meetings of the Board of Directors shall operate as the accepted resignation of that Director from the Board of Directors.

SECTION 8. Each member of the Board of Directors who attends a regular or special meeting of the Board may be paid a nominal director's fee for attending each such meeting and shall be reimbursed for the actual cash outlay made by him for travel from his home to the offices of The American Kennel Club and return and for food and lodging while engaged in the business of The American Kennel Club.

ARTICLE VIII

BOARD OF DIRECTORS

NOMINATING COMMITTEE

The Board of Directors on or before the first day of January in each year shall designate five delegates no one of whom shall be an officer of the club or a member of its Board of Directors to be a nominating committee whose duty it shall be to nominate candidates for such vacancies on the Board of Directors as are to be filled at the next annual meeting of the Club. The Nominating Committee shall make its selection and report its nominations in writing to the Secretary of the Club on or before the thirty-first day of said January and it shall be the duty of and said Secretary forthwith shall notify in writing each delegate and each member club or association which shall not be represented by a delegate of the names of the candidates so selected.

If, after such nomination, the name of any candidate so nominated is withdrawn, the Nominating Committee shall nominate a new candidate in his place, and the Secretary of said Club, upon receipt of the news of such action, shall give such notice thereof to the delegates and the member clubs or associations not represented by delegates as may be reasonable under the circumstances.

Any delegate whose name does not appear upon said list so selected by said Committee shall be eligible for election to the position of director if and only if his name, endorsed by at least twenty other delegates in writing, shall be sent by registered mail or delivered to said Secretary on or before the twentieth day of February following said January thirty-first, in which event it shall be the duty of said Secretary and said Secretary forthwith shall notify in writing each delegate and each member club which shall not be represented by a delegate of the name or names of the additional candidate or candidates so nominated. The names of all candidates for election as directors shall be published in the March issue of the AMERICAN KENNEL GAZETTE of the year in which they come before the annual meeting to be voted upon. No nominations may be made from the floor at the annual meeting of the Club.

ARTICLE IX

BOARD OF DIRECTORS

GENERAL POWERS

The Board of Directors shall have the general management of the business and affairs of the Club and generally perform all duties appertaining to the office of director provided, however, that all the powers conferred by this Article of the By-Laws shall be exercised subject to all other provisions of these By-Laws and to the statutes of the State of New York and all amendments thereof and additions thereto.

ARTICLE X

BOARD OF DIRECTORS

SPECIFIC POWERS

Without detracting from any general powers of the Board of Directors but by way of explanation it shall be understood that:

SECTION 1. The Board shall have supervision of the funds, assets and property of the Club and shall determine how much thereof shall be left in the hands or under direct control of the Treasurer for current needs, and how the balance thereof shall be deposited or invested, and shall have power to withdraw or transfer said deposits or dispose of or change said investments for the benefit of the Club.

SECTION 2. The Board may appoint from time to time and at will discharge committees with such powers and authority as in the judgment of said Board may be necessary to facilitate and carry out the objects and business of the Club; and in order to facilitate business may appoint one (1) or more persons who shall represent The American Kennel Club in such territory of the United States and with such jurisdiction as may be designated by said Board.

SECTION 3. The Board shall examine all proposed amendments or alterations to the Constitution, By-Laws, Rules or Regulations of The American Kennel Club and report thereon to the Club for action.

SECTION 4. All matters in dispute as to interpretation of the Rules or Regulations of The American Kennel Club shall be submitted to the Board for its construction, which shall be decisive.

SECTION 5. The Board shall have supervision and control of the Stud Book, the registration of dogs, kennel names and the transfers thereof, and determine the manner in which such records shall be preserved.

SECTION 6. The Board shall determine all matters which may arise affecting pedigrees of pure-bred dogs.

SECTION 7. The Board shall have supervision and control of the official kennel gazette now called the AMERICAN KENNEL GAZETTE and shall determine the manner and form in which it shall be published.

SECTION 8. The Board shall have power to approve or disapprove any or all applications for show, obedience trial or field trial dates.

SECTION 9. The Board shall have power to issue and

revoke licenses to Judges, Superintendents of Dog Shows, Obedience Trials and Field Trials and Handlers of Dogs.

SECTION 10. The Board also shall have the power to determine and fix the rating of each breed of dog to qualify for Championship and may from time to time change such rating.

SECTION 11. The Board shall have the power to sanction or disapprove applications for informal shows.

SECTION 12. The Board shall have power to issue such regulations as it may deem necessary for the governing or holding of dog shows, obedience trials and field trials.

SECTION 13. The Board shall have power to consider charges preferred by Bench Show Committees, Obedience Trial Committees, Field Trial Committees, Clubs, Associations, or persons, and to determine whether the charges alleged have been sustained, and if sustained what penalty shall be imposed.

The powers of the Board of Directors in this connection are more fully set forth in Article XII of these By-Laws entitled "Discipline."

SECTION 14. The Board shall have power to appoint and at will remove Trial Boards of not less than three (3) members each, whose duty it shall be to hear such charges in the first instance as may be referred by the Board of Directors to such Trial Boards. The powers and duties of Trial Boards are more fully set forth in Article XIII of these By-Laws entitled "Trial Boards."

SECTION 15. The Board shall have power to determine and fix and from time to time change the amount of all fees to be charged by The American Kennel Club, whether for registration, listing and change of ownership of dogs, the granting of kennel names and the transfer thereof, the issuing of certificates or otherwise.

SECTION 16. The Board shall have power without previous hearing to fix and determine the amount or extent of the penalty and to impose a penalty for all uncontested violations of the Rules and Regulations of The American Kennel Club.

ARTICLE XI

OFFICERS

SECTION 1. The Officers of the Club shall be a President, Chairman of the Board, an Executive Vice-President, one or more Vice-Presidents, an Executive Secretary, a Secretary and a Treasurer, who shall be elected annually by the Board of Directors at a meeting which shall be held immediately following the annual meeting of the Club.

The President, Chairman of the Board and Treasurer must be directors.

The Executive Vice-President, the Vice-Presidents, the Executive Secretary and the Secretary need not be directors.

Vacancies in any of the above offices may be filled for the unexpired term by the Directors by a majority vote of those present at any meeting.

The Directors, by a majority vote of those present at any meeting, may determine, for such period or periods as they deem appropriate, that one or more of the above offices may remain vacant or that the same person may hold one or more of the above offices.

PRESIDENT

SECTION 2. The President shall perform the usual duties of a chief executive officer, shall preside at all meetings of the Club and shall perform such other duties as may be assigned to him by the Board of Directors. All contracts on behalf of the Club shall be executed by him or by such other officer or officers as he may designate. In the absence or disability of the President, the Executive Vice-President, and in the absence or disability of both the President and Executive Vice-President, the Executive Secretary shall perform the duties of the President. The President shall devote his whole time to the affairs of the Club. The salary of the President shall be fixed by the Board of Directors.

CHAIRMAN OF THE BOARD

SECTION 3. The Chairman of the Board shall preside at all meetings of the Board of Directors. In his absence an Acting Chairman shall be elected by a majority vote of those present at any meeting. The Chairman of the Board shall perform such additional duties as may be assigned to him by the Board of Directors. The Chairman of the Board may be paid a nominal salary if the Board of Directors so determines, the amount of which shall be fixed by the said Board.

EXECUTIVE VICE-PRESIDENT

SECTION 4. The Executive Vice-President shall perform such duties as may be assigned to him by the President or the Board of Directors and shall devote his whole time to the affairs of the Club. The salary of the Executive Vice-President shall be fixed by the Board of Directors.

VICE-PRESIDENTS

SECTION 5. If the Board of Directors elects one or more Vice-Presidents, the Board may designate one Vice-President as the Senior Vice-President.

The Vice-Presidents shall exercise the usual functions of executive officers in the management of the Club's affairs under the direction of the President. They shall perform such other duties as may be assigned to them by the Board of Directors.

The Vice-Presidents shall devote their whole time to the affairs of the Club. Their salaries shall be fixed by the Board of Directors.

EXECUTIVE SECRETARY

SECTION 6. The Executive Secretary shall perform such duties as are assigned to him by the President or by the Board of Directors, devoting his whole time to the affairs of the Club. The salary of the Executive Secretary shall be fixed by the Board of Directors.

SECRETARY

SECTION 7. The Secretary shall keep the records of all the meetings of the Club and Board of Directors and shall issue calls for the same. He shall keep a roll of members and delegates, and shall have charge of all records and papers of the Club. He shall have custody of the seal of the Club. He shall perform such other duties as may be assigned to him by the President or by the Board of Directors, devoting his whole time to the affairs of the Club. The salary of the Secretary shall be fixed by the Board of Directors.

TREASURER

SECTION 8. The Treasurer shall keep the financial records of the Club in such manner as may be directed by the Board of Directors; shall be responsible for the collection, custody and control of the funds of the Club, subject to the supervision of the Board of Directors; and shall perform such other duties as may be assigned to him by the Board of Directors.

The Treasurer, under the direction of the Board of Directors and with the approval of the President, may delegate the performance of any or all of the duties of the Treasurer to the member of the Club's administrative staff who shall be designated as Controller; but the responsibility for the performance of such duties shall be that of the Treasurer under the direction of the Board of Directors.

A bond of indemnity shall be executed in favor of the Club in an amount satisfactory to the Board of Directors to insure the Club against loss incurred by the handling of the Club's funds by any officer or employee of the Club, the premium on such bond to be paid out of the funds of the Club.

The Treasurer may be paid a salary, if the Board of Directors shall so determine, the amount of which salary shall be fixed by said Board.

ARTICLE XII

DISCIPLINE

SECTION 1. Any club or association or person or persons interested in pure-bred dogs may prefer charges against any other club or association or person or persons for conduct alleged to have been prejudicial to the best interests of pure-bred dogs, dog shows, obedience trials or field trials, or prejudicial to the best interests of The American Kennel Club, which charges shall be made in writing in duplicate setting forth in detail the nature thereof, shall be signed and sworn to by an officer of the Club or Association or by the person or persons making the same before some person qualified to administer oaths and shall be sent to The American Kennel Club, together with a deposit of ten ($10) dollars, which sum shall become the property of The American Kennel Club if said charges shall not be sustained, or shall be returned if said charges are sustained, or if The American Kennel Club shall refuse to entertain jurisdiction thereof.

SECTION 2. The bench show, obedience trial or field trial committee of a club or association shall have the right to suspend any person from the privileges of The American Kennel Club for conduct prejudicial to the best interests of pure-bred dogs, dog shows, obedience trials, field trials or The American Kennel Club, alleged to have occurred in connection with or during the progress of its show, obedience trial or field trial, after the alleged offender has been given an opportunity to be heard.

Notice in writing must be sent promptly by *registered mail* by the bench show, obedience trial or field trial committee to the person suspended and a duplicate notice giving the name and address of the person suspended and full details as to the reasons for the suspension must be forwarded to The American Kennel Club within seven days.

An appeal may be taken from a decision of a bench show, obedience trial or field trial committee. Notice in writing claiming such appeal together with a deposit of five ($5) dollars must be sent to The American Kennel

Club within thirty days after the date of suspension. The Board of Directors may itself hear said appeal or may refer it to a committee of the Board, or to a Trial Board to be heard. The deposit shall become the property of The American Kennel Club if the decision is confirmed, or shall be returned to the appellant if the decision is not confirmed.

SECTION 3. Upon receipt of duly preferred charges the Board of Directors of The American Kennel Club at its election either may itself consider the same or send the same to a Trial Board for hearing.

In either case a notice which shall state that said charges have been filed and shall set forth a copy of the same shall be sent to the club or association, or person or persons against which or whom said charges have been preferred which club or association, or person or persons herein shall be known as and called the defendant. The club or association or person or persons which or who shall have preferred said charges herein shall be known as and called the complainant.

Said notice also shall set forth a time and place at which the defendant may attend and present any defense or answer which the defendant may wish to make.

If the complainant shall fail or refuse to appear and prosecute said charges or if the defendant shall fail or refuse to appear and present a defense at the time and place designated for the hearing of said charges, without giving a reasonable excuse for such failure or refusal, the Board of Directors or the Trial Board to which said charges have been referred may suspend whichever party shall be so in default from the privileges of The American Kennel Club for a period of six months or until such time as the party so in default shall be prepared to appear ready and willing to prosecute or defend said charges, as the case may be.

SECTION 4. The Board of Directors shall have the power to investigate any matters which may be brought to its attention in connection with the objects for which this Club was founded, or it may appoint a committee or trial board to investigate, in which event the same procedure shall be followed and the same rules shall apply as in a trial before a Trial Board.

If after such investigation the Board of Directors believes that sufficient evidence exists to warrant the filing of charges, it may file or direct the filing of such charges. The Board of Directors acting in accordance with the provisions of this Article may prefer charges for conduct prejudicial to the best interests of The American Kennel Club against persons who shall bring to its attention any matter which upon investigation shall be found to have been reported to it from malicious or untruthful motives or to have been based upon suspicion without foundation of fact or knowledge.

SECTION 5. The Board of Directors of the American Kennel Club shall have power to prefer charges against any association, or other club, or person or persons, for conduct alleged to be prejudicial to pure-bred dogs, dog shows, obedience trials or field trials or to the best interests of The American Kennel Club, and pending the final determination of any such charges, may withhold the privileges of The American Kennel Club from any such other person or body against whom charges are pending.

SECTION 6. The Board of Directors shall have the power to suspend from the privileges of The American

Kennel Club any member or delegate pending final action by the delegates in accordance with the provisions of this section, for conduct alleged to have been prejudicial to the best interests of The American Kennel Club or for violation of its constitution, by-laws or rules.

The Board of Directors shall then file charges and promptly set a date for a hearing and send to such suspended member or delegate by registered mail at least ten days prior to the date so fixed, notice of the time when and the place where the suspended member or delegate may be heard in its or his defense. Said notice shall also set forth a copy of the charges.

The Board of Directors may itself hear the evidence of the suspended member or delegate and any witnesses or may refer the charges to a committee of the Board or to a Trial Board to take the testimony and to report its findings or recommendations to the Board of Directors.

The Board of Directors, after hearing or reviewing the evidence, shall report its findings to The American Kennel Club at the next regular meeting of the Club, whereupon the delegates shall take action upon said findings and by a majority vote of the delegates present may reinstate, continue the suspension for a stated time or expel such member or delegate from The American Kennel Club.

SECTION 7. The American Kennel Club shall have the power by a two-thirds vote of the Delegates present and voting at any regular meeting to suspend from the privileges of The American Kennel Club any member or delegate for conduct alleged to have been prejudicial to the best interests of The American Kennel Club or for violation of its constitution, by-laws or rules.

The order of suspension thus made shall then be referred to the Board of Directors for hearing and report under the procedure as set forth in Paragraphs 2, 3 and 4 of Section 6 of this Article.

SECTION 8. The Board of Directors of The American Kennel Club shall have power to hear as an original matter any charges preferred and to review and finally determine any appeal which may be made to the Board of Directors from the decision of a Trial Board, Bench Show, Obedience Trial or Field Trial Committee, and in each instance in which it shall find the charges to have been sustained, it shall impose such penalty as said Board of Directors may decide to be just and proper.

SECTION 9. The Board of Directors of The American Kennel Club and any Trial Board of The American Kennel Club with the permission of the Board of Directors of The American Kennel Club first obtained in writing, may in the discretion of said Board of Directors, and if necessary at the Club's expense, summon witnesses or a member of any Trial Board, Bench Show Committee, Obedience Trial Committee or Field Trial Committee to attend any and all hearings held under the provisions of Articles XII and XIII of the Constitution and By-Laws of The American Kennel Club. Said Board of Directors may suspend from the privileges of The American Kennel Club for a period of six months or until such time as he or she shall appear and be prepared and willing to testify, any person so summoned who without reasonable excuse shall fail to appear and testify.

SECTION 10. The Board of Directors of The American Kennel Club shall, at the next meeting of the Board after an appeal is made from the decision of a Trial Board, Bench Show, Obedience Trial or Field Trial Committee, name a date for the hearing of such appeal and shall cause notice of the time when and the place where said hearing is to be held to be sent to all parties in interest by registered mail at least fourteen (14) days prior to the date named.

SECTION 11. Penalties may range from a reprimand or fine to suspension for life from all privileges of The American Kennel Club.

SECTION 12. The Treasurer of The American Kennel Club shall enforce all monetary penalties.

SECTION 13. The suspension or disqualification of a person shall date from the day of the perpetration of the act or from any date subsequent thereto which shall be fixed after hearing by a Trial Board or by the Board of Directors of The American Kennel Club and shall apply to all dogs owned or subsequently acquired by the person so suspended or disqualified.

SECTION 14. All privileges of The American Kennel Club shall be withheld from any person suspended or disqualified.

SECTION 15. Any club, association or organization which shall hold a dog show, obedience trial, field trial or dog exhibition of any kind not in accordance with the rules of The American Kennel Club which apply to such show, obedience trial, field trial or exhibition may be disciplined even to the extent of being deprived of all privileges of The American Kennel Club for a stated period of time or indefinitely, and if such club, association or organization shall be a member of The American Kennel Club, it may be expelled from membership therein.

SECTION 16. No club or association licensed by The American Kennel Club to give a show, obedience trial, hold a field trial or give a dog exhibition of any kind shall employ in any capacity, accept the donation of a prize or money from, or permit to be within the walls or boundaries of its building or grounds, if a dog show or obedience trial, or its grounds, if a field trial, save only as a spectator, any person known to be under suspension or disqualification from the privileges of The American Kennel Club, or any employee or member of a corporation which shall be under suspension or disqualification from the privileges of The American Kennel Club. And any contract for floor space at a show, or contract for advertising space in a catalogue, premium list or other printed matter, in connection with the giving of said show, shall bear upon it the following condition: "This space is sold with the understanding that should the privileges of The American Kennel Club be withdrawn from the purchaser of this space prior to the carrying out of this contract, this contract is thereby automatically cancelled, and any money paid by the purchaser for such space shall be refunded."

SECTION 17. No member club or association under suspension shall be represented by its delegate and no delegate under suspension shall act for a member or in any official capacity for The American Kennel Club during the period of suspension.

SECTION 18. Any association, club, person or persons suspended or disqualified by The American Kennel Club or from whom the privileges of The American Kennel Club have been withheld, may apply for reinstatement or restoration of privileges upon paying a fee, the amount of which may be fixed and determined by the Board of Directors of The American Kennel Club. Until said fee has been paid the application shall not be acted upon.

SECTION 19. As much of Article XII of these By-Laws as the Board of Directors of The American Kennel Club shall indicate shall be printed in any book or pamphlet which The American Kennel Club shall cause to be published containing the Rules of said Club.

ARTICLE XIII

TRIAL BOARDS

SECTION 1. Trial Boards shall be appointed from time to time by the Board of Directors of The American Kennel Club and shall consist of three members for each Board, one of whom, if practicable, should be an attorney-at-law, and no one of whom shall be a director of The American Kennel Club. In case one or more members of a Trial Board shall be unable to sit in any given case, the President, or in his absence, the Executive Vice-President of The American Kennel Club may appoint a substitute or substitutes for such case. In case of the absence of one or more members of said Board the remaining member or members may hear and determine a case if the parties being heard shall consent thereto.

SECTION 2. Trial Boards shall hear and decide by a majority vote matters submitted to them by the Board of Directors and shall have power to impose a fine not to exceed twenty-five ($25) dollars and/or withhold the privileges of the Club for a period of not more than six months, or may recommend to said Board of Directors the withholding of privileges for a longer period or may recommend disqualification or the imposition of fines exceeding twenty-five ($25) dollars.

If a Trial Board recommends the withholding of privileges or disqualification to the Board of Directors, the privileges of the Club shall be automatically withheld until the Board of Directors has adopted or refused to adopt such recommendation.

SECTION 3. Trial Boards shall have power to disqualify any person or withhold from any person all the privileges of The American Kennel Club for a period of not more than six months or to recommend to said Board of Directors the penalty of disqualification or the withholding of privileges for a longer period for improper or disorderly conduct during a hearing or a trial.

SECTION 4. Trial Boards shall keep minutes of their sittings.

SECTION 5. The decisions of Trial Boards shall be in writing signed by all members attending, and have annexed thereto all exhibits and papers offered before them. Each decision, together with complete copies of the minutes and testimony taken, shall be filed with the Secretary of The American Kennel Club within ten days of the date of the rendering of the decision. It shall be the duty of the Secretary of The American Kennel Club when received, at once to notify in writing all parties in interest of the decision of a Trial Board.

SECTION 6. An appeal may be taken to the Board of Directors from any decision of a Trial Board, whether it be a decision in which the Trial Board itself imposes a certain penalty and/or fine, or one in which the Trial Board recommends that the Board of Directors shall impose a certain penalty and/or fine. Notice in writing claiming such appeal together with a deposit of twenty-five ($25) dollars must be sent to The American Kennel Club within thirty days after the receipt of the notice of the decision or recommendation of the Trial Board. The Board of Directors may itself hear said appeal or may

refer it to a committee of the Board to be heard. The deposit of twenty-five ($25) dollars shall become the property of The American Kennel Club if the decision or recommendation of the Trial Board shall be confirmed, or shall be returned to the appellant if it shall not be confirmed. If the aggrieved party shall fail to take such appeal to the Board of Directors, there shall be no further right of appeal of any kind.

SECTION 7. Article XIII of these By-Laws shall be printed in any book or pamphlet which The American Kennel Club shall cause to be published containing the Rules of said Club.

ARTICLE XIV

FISCAL YEAR

The fiscal year of the Club shall end with the thirty-first day of December of each year.

ARTICLE XV

AUDIT

The Board of Directors shall have the books and accounts of the Treasurer audited at least once a year, either by a professional auditor approved by said Board or by an auditing committee appointed by said Board. A comprehensive summary of the auditor's report shall be published in the AMERICAN KENNEL GAZETTE and a copy of said summary of said report shall be sent to each member club or association and to each delegate as soon as the same can be prepared and printed.

ARTICLE XVI

MEETINGS AND QUORUM

SECTION 1. The annual meeting of The American Kennel Club shall be held in March of each year. There shall also be regular meetings of the Club in June, September and December. The exact hours and dates of all of such meetings shall be determined by the Board of Directors.

SECTION 2. Special meetings of the Club shall be called by the Secretary upon the written request of any twenty or more Delegates. No other business shall be transacted at any special meeting other than that specified in the call.

SECTION 3. Notice of the hour and date of the annual meeting and of each regular meeting shall be printed in that issue of the AMERICAN KENNEL GAZETTE which shall be published next before the date fixed for each said meeting and also mailed to each member club or association and each delegate at least fifteen days before the date of each said meeting.

SECTION 4. Notice of the hour and date of each special meeting and the business to be transacted thereat shall be sent to each member club or association and each delegate within seven days of the receipt of the written request for said meeting and at least ten days before the date of said meeting.

SECTION 5. All meetings of The American Kennel Club shall be held in the city in which the principal offices of said Club are located.

SECTION 6. One-tenth of the total number of Delegates shall constitute a quorum of the Club for the transaction of business at all meetings.

ARTICLE XVII

CONDUCT OF BUSINESS

SECTION 1. The Robert's Rules of Order shall govern all meetings of the Club and its Directors as far as they are applicable and not inconsistent with these By-Laws.

SECTION 2. No person not a Delegate or Officer of the Club, except employees, shall be present at a meeting thereof without the consent of the majority present.

SECTION 3. All elections shall be by ballot.

ARTICLE XVIII

ORDER OF BUSINESS FOR DELEGATES

Roll Call
Reading of Minutes
Report of Secretary
Election of Members, Delegates and Directors in order named
Report of Treasurer (at annual meeting)
Report of Special Committees
General Business

ARTICLE XIX

ORDER OF BUSINESS FOR DIRECTORS

Reading of Minutes
Report of Secretary
Election of Officers
Report of Treasurer
Report of Special Committees
General Business

ARTICLE XX

RULES

The Delegates to The American Kennel Club shall have sole power to make the Rules governing dog shows and field trials and the clubs or associations formed to conduct them.

ARTICLE XXI

AMENDMENTS
TO
CONSTITUTION, BY-LAWS AND RULES

SECTION 1. The Constitution and or By-Laws of The American Kennel Club may be amended only at the annual meeting of the Club.

Notice of any proposed amendment to the Constitution and or By-Laws must be filed in writing at least sixty (60) days before the date of said annual meeting.

As soon as any such proposed amendment shall be filed it shall at once be referred to the Board of Directors which Board shall examine the same and report its conclusions thereon by way of approval or otherwise to the Secretary of said Club giving its reasons for whatever action it shall have taken if said Board shall so choose.

If the Board of Directors shall report to the Secretary of said Club that it disapproves any such proposed amendment, it shall be the duty of said Secretary forthwith to notify the delegate who proposed the amendment which has been disapproved of the action of the Board, and said delegate must then elect whether to withdraw the amendment which has been disapproved or to insist upon its being presented at the annual meeting of the Club for adoption.

Any such proposed amendment to the Constitution and or By-Laws which has been approved or not disapproved by said Board, or, if disapproved, is one which its proposer, after being notified, has insisted be presented at the annual meeting of the Club for adoption, together with the report of the Board of Directors theron shall be printed in at least one issue of the AMERICAN KENNEL GAZETTE published before the date of the annual meeting.

SECTION 2. The Rules of The American Kennel Club may be amended at any regular or special meeting of the Club. Notice of any proposed amendment to the Rules of The American Kennel Club must be filed in writing and shall at once be referred to the Board of Directors which Board shall examine the same and report its conclusions thereon by way of approval or otherwise to the Secretary of said Club giving its reasons for whatever action it shall have taken if said Board shall so choose.

If the Board of Directors shall report to the Secretary of said Club that it disapproves any such proposed amendment it shall be the duty of said Secretary forthwith to notify the delegate who proposed the amendment which has been disapproved of the action of the Board, and said delegate must then elect whether to withdraw the amendment which has been disapproved or to insist upon its being presented at a meeting of the Club for adoption.

Any such proposed amendment to the Rules which has been approved or not disapproved by said Board, or, if disapproved, is one which its proposer, after being notified, has insisted be presented to the delegates for action, together with the report of the Board of Directors thereon shall be printed in two consecutive issues of the AMERICAN KENNEL GAZETTE, which shall be published following the making of the report thereon by said Board of Directors and shall be presented to the delegates for action thereon at the first regular or special meeting of the Club which shall be held following the second publication of said report of the Board of Directors.

SECTION 3. The Board of Directors may propose amendments to the Constitution and/or By-Laws and/or the Rules of The American Kennel Club at the Annual or any Regular Meeting of the Club. Such proposed amendments shall be printed, prior to such meeting, in PURE-BRED DOGS—AMERICAN KENNEL GAZETTE in at least one (1) issue, in the case of proposed amendments to the Constitution and/or By-Laws and in at least two (2) consecutive issues, in the case of proposed amendments to the Rules of The American Kennel Club.

SECTION 4. No new rule or amendment of any old rule shall take effect until the expiration of ninety (90) days after its adoption, unless the Delegates when voting to adopt said new rule or amendment also shall unanimously vote that it shall become effective at some earlier date or when adopted.

SECTION 5. It shall require the affirmative vote of three-quarters in number of the Delegates present and voting at a meeting to adopt any amendment to the Constitution and/or By-Laws and/or Rules of The American Kennel Club.

Registered Breeds

The following list includes the first dog of each breed entered into the AKC Stud Book. The number in parentheses represents the number of dogs of that breed registered in the first year. If a breed was dropped from the Stud Book, the year that this occurred is also indicated.

BREED	DATE REG.		PEDIGREE
Affenpinscher	November 1936	(4)	Nolli v. Anwander, (B) #A107711. By Prinz v.d. Franziskusklause ex Mira v. Anwander by Strubi v.d. Franziskusklause ex Paula v.d. Franziskusklause by Terzl v.d. Aumuhle ex Gertraud Munchner Kindl; Strubi v.d. Franziskusklause by Funkerle v.d. Franziskusklause ex Gertraud Munchner Kindl. Prinz v.d. Franziskusklause by Mohrle ex Gertraud Munchner Kindl by Kuckuck Munchner Kindl ex Gerda Munchner Kindl; Mohrle by Gift v. Adelsheim ex Susi v. Anwander. Owner: Mrs. Bessie Mally. Breeder: Sixtus Anwander, Germany. Whelped 3/11/1934. Black.
Afghan Hound	October 1926	(3)	Tezin, #544928. By Bhaloo ex Oolu, by Ooty ex Pushum, by Sher ex Ghoree. Ooty by Zordwar ex Dil. Bhaloo by Ba-

luch ex Ranee, by Rajah ex Be-
gum. Baluch by Taiza ex
Nurm. Owner: Dunwalk Ken-
nels. Breeder: J.C. Manson,
Scottland. Whelped 8/25/1925.
Brindle.

Airedale Terrier	1888	(2)	Pin, #9087. Breeder, date of birth, and pedigree are un-known. Owner: Prescott Law-rence. Groton, MA. Black and tan. Won first in NY in 1886 and 1887.
Akita	1972	(255)	Akita Tani's Teruhoshi, (D) #WC292650. By Akita Tani's Makoto ex Akita Tani's Waka Bata Tama. Owner: E. and K. Greisen. Breeder: G. and S. Rasmussen. Whelped 11/7/1968. Fawn and brown, black and white mask, white markings.
Alaskan Malamute	July 1935	(3)	Rowdy of Nome, #998426. No pedigree given. Owners: Mr. and Mrs. Milton J. Seeley. Whelped 1928. Grey.
American Staffordshire Ter-rier (Registered as Staf-fordshire Terrier until 1972)	August 1936	(12)	Wheeler's Black Dinah, #A86066. By Garm D. ex Topsy W., by Paxtons Black Phantom ex Kennetts Black Mary. by Tudors King ex Rum-pus Beauty. Paxtons Black Phantom by Black Smuggler ex Bakers Tiffy. Garm D. by Tu-dor King ex Rumpus Beauty, by Gallants Rumpus ex Gal-lants Patsy. Tudors King by Tu-dors Jack II ex Tudors Texas Tess. Owner: J. Maurice Wheeler. Breeder: Mrs. Edna Fleckinger, Ann Arbor, MI. Whelped 5/30/1931. Black.
Australian Cattle Dog	1980	(1685)	Glen Iris Boomerang, CDX, (D) #WE507650. By Park Ridge Simple Simon ex Glen Iris Belle. Foundation Stock. Owner: Mrs. I. Heale. Breeder: C. Mork. Whelped 4/30/1964. Blue, black, and tan.

Australian Terrier	1960	(323)	Canberra Kookaburra (England), (B) R-258126. By Tawny Boy of Billaboug ex Victory of Zellah. Owner: I.M. Cecily Brush. Breeder: Mrs. Calburn Hart, England. Whelped 12/1/1948. Sandy.
Basenji	June 1944	(39)	Phemister's Bois, (D) #A738970. No pedigree or breeder given. Foundation Stock. Owners: Mr. and Mrs. Alexander Phemister. Whelped 1936. Fawn and white.
Basset Hound	1885	(2)	Bouncer, #3234. By Major ex Venus. Owner: Mr. Colin Cameron, Brickerville, PA. Breeder: Mr. Pottinger Dorsey, New Market, MD. Whelped 3/1881. Black, white, and tan.
Beagle	1885	(35)	Blunder, #3188. By Oscar ex Melody, by Lee ex Lil. Oscar by Dutch ex Lil. Owner: Prof. W. W. Legore, Walhalla, SC. Breeder: Dr. L. H. Twaddell, Phila., PA. Whelped 3/15/1880. Black, white, and tan.
Bearded Collie	1976	(998)	Cannamoor Cartinka, (UK), (B) #WD439250. Foundation Stock. By Bravo of Bothkennar ex Cannamoor Brighde. Owner: L. M. Levy. Breeder: Mrs. G. A. Wheeler. Whelped 5/9/1962. Black and white.
Bedlington Terrier	1886	(9)	Ananian, #4475. By Quayside Lad ex Jean. Owner: W. S. Jackson, Upper Canada College, Toronto, Canada. Breeder: J. Hall, England. Whelped 5/13/1884. Dark blue. Won first at Crystal Palace in 1885.
Belgian Malinois (Registered as Belgian Sheepdog until 1959)			
Belgian Sheepdog	1912	(2)	Rumford Dax, #160405. By Gyp ex Miss, by Neron ex O'Roseand, by Franz de

Wohne ex Madge. Neron by Duc de Gronendael ex Margot de Tournai. Gyp by MacKinley ex Sappho, by Max ex Louve. MacKinley by Dax ex Diane de Forest. Owner: Rumford Kennels, Strathglass Farm, Port Chester, NY. Breeder: B. H. Manus, Amsterdam, Holland. Whelped 3/7/1910. Black and white.

Belgian Tervuren (Registered as Belgian Sheepdog until 1959)			
Bernese Mountain Dog	June 1937	(2)	Quell v. Tiergarten, (D) #A156752. By Galant v. Tiergarten ex Sylvia v.d. Rothohe, by Olaf v.d. Rothohe ex Lora v.d. Rothohe by Bello v.d. Rothifluh ex Afra v.d. Rothohe; Olaf v.d. Rothohe by Lord v.d. Rothohe ex Belline v.d. Rothohe. Galant v. Tiergarten by Lord v.d. Rothohe ex Carola v.d. Rothohe by Max (Pulfer)-ex Bella-Sonne; Lord v.d. Rothohe by Bello v.d. Rothifluh ex Afra v.d. Rothohe. Owner: Glen L. Shadow. Breeder: A. Schoch, Switzerland. Whelped: 6/14/1935. Black, tan and white markings.
Bichon Frise	1972	(430)	Sha-Bob's Nice Girl Missy, (B) #NS077900. Foundation Stock. By Rank's Ronnie ex Sha-Bob's Sugar Girl. Owner: Gertrude E. Fournier. Breeder: Mrs. George E. Roberts. Whelped 12/27/1969. White.
Black and Tan Coonhound (Registered as Coonhound (Black and Tan) until 1972)	December 1945	(107)	Grand Mere Big Rock Molly, (B) #A898800. By Jocassee Valley Pilot ex Ohio Black Molly by Tailbys Black Diamond ex Tailbys Black Mack Princess by Black Mack ex Black River Queen; Tailbys

			Black Diamond by Owahgena Midnight Trailer ex Tailbys Nellie. Jocassee Valley Pilot by Tailbys Black Storm ex Tailbys Black Belle by Tailbys Black Diamond ex Owahgena Model Maid; Tailbys Black Storm by Locust Knoll Drum ex Locust Knoll Queen. Owner: John C. Ellsworth. Breeder: John F. Evans, Big Rock. Illinois. Whelped 3/12/1936. Black and tan.
Bloodhound	1885	(2)	Carodoc, #3237. By Forester ex Maythorn. Forester by Rufus ex Empress. Owner: Prof. H. B. Roney, East Saginaw, Michigan. Whelped 6/1877. Black and tan. Won first at Toronto, 1880.
Border Terrier	February 1930	(6)	Netherbyers Ricky, #719372. By Redheugh Rick ex Rogie, by Twink ex Nessel, by Riccarton Jock ex Riccarton Meg. Twink by Teri ex Vixen. Redheugh Rick by Catcleugh Flint ex Riccarten Betty by Riccarten Billy ex Bess. Catcleugh Flint by Gyp ex Bess. Owner: Don E. Hewat. Breeder: Miss E. Hardy, Scotland. Whelped: 12/5/1927. Grizzled.
Borzoi (Registered as Wolfhound (Russian) until 1936)	1891	(2)	Princess Irma, #20716. By Krilutt ex Elsie, by Prince ex Lady Krilutt, by Dorogi ex Nagla, by Kosir ex Schelma. Dorogi by Krilutt ex Iskra. Owner and breeder: Hornell-Harmony Kennels, Covert, NY. Whelped 2/18/1890. White and lemon. Won first open, first puppy at National Greyhound Club show; first and spec., NY; first, Chicago; second, Cleveland, in 1891.
Boston Terrier	1893	(7)	Hector, #28814. By Bixby's Toney ex Dimple, by Pippo ex

Betsy, by Watterman's Tatters
ex Colburn's Madge. Pippo by
Townsend's Sprig ex Goode's
Lilly. Toney by Tommy ex
Wrinkles, by Townsend's Sprig
ex Goode's Lilly. Tommy by
Barnard's Mike ex Simpson's
Topsy. Owner: Joseph A.
Locke, Chicago. Breeder:
George H. Huse, Boston, MA.
Whelped: 7/19/1891. Brindle
and white.

Breed	Date		Description
Bouvier des Flandres	May 1931	(2)	Hardix, #780160. By Lutin de Mouscron ex Zette du Roy d'Espagne, by Azur ex Blondine, by Duc ex Diane. Azur by Goliath de la Lys ex Durca de la Lys. Lutin de Mouscron by Dragon de la Lys ex Sarah de Sottegem, by Piston ex Coralie. Dragon de la Lys by Nic ex Draga. Owner: George MacCullough Miller. Breeders: Tabellion and Gand, France. Whelped 11/20/1926. Grizzled.
Boxer	1904	(1)	Arnulf Grandenz #78043. By Prinz Mark of Grandenz ex Rose of Grandenz, by Bosko-Immergrun ex Flora Fuhr, by Flock St. Salvator ex Molly St. Salvator. Bosko-Immergrun by Moreau ex Meta. Prinz Mark of Grandenz by Wotan Frey ex Meta Frey, by Piccolovum Augerthor ex Blankavom Augerthor. Wotan Frey by Nero Aschenbrenner ex Weber's Ella. Owner: James E. Welch, Harvey, Illinois. Breeder: Max Schachner, Downers Grove, Illinois. whelped 4/2/1903. Brindle, black, and dark gray.
Briard	June 1928	(9)	Dauphine de Montjoye, #635613. By Aymon III de Montjoye ex Moina III de Montjoye, by Mais I ex Osera

de Montjoye, by Marco de Montjoye ex Armelle de Montjoye. Mais I by Pastour ex Charmante. Aymon III de Montjoye by Stellio de Montjoye ex Vega de Montjoye, by Milan de Montjoye ex Star de Montjoye. Stellio de Montjoye by Aimery de Montjoye ex Nera de Montjoye. Owner: Frances Hoppin. Breeder: E. Raoul Duval, France. Whelped 9/10/1925. Tan and black.

Brittany (Registered as Spaniel (Brittany) until 1982)	October 1934	(3)	Edir Du Mesnil, #949896. By Billy du Mesnil ex Drolette du Mesnil, by Braco du Mesnil ex Dandine du Cosquerou, by Paber dun Cosquerou ex Stris du Cosquerou. Braco du Mesnil by Whiskey ex Zad du Mesnil. Billy du Mesnil by Azur de Picardie ex Zita du Mesnil, by Xipo du Mesnil ex Vivette du Mesnil. Azur de Picardie by Yoko de la Marphie ex Yrabelle du Mesnil. Owner: Louis A. Thebaud. Breeder: G. Metayer, France. Whelped 2/12/1930. White and orange.
Brussels Griffon (Registered as Griffon (Brussels) until 1972)	1910	(4)	Dolley's Biddy, #137219. By Witchampton Triton ex Witchampton Belle, by Copthorne ex Copthorne Chyrsanthemum, by Copthorne ex Lobster. Copthorne by Tom ex Mirza. Witchampton Triton by Monkey ex Red Rag, by Mousquetaire Rouge ex Scrap. Monkey by Marquis ex Bellá. Owner: Mrs. Williams Caster, Manor Farm, Kingston, New York. Breeder: Mrs. Cochran, England. Whelped 9/18/1908. Red.
Bulldog	1886	(1)	Bob, #4982. By Taurus ex Milly, by Sultan ex Kate. Taurus by Guillermo ex Lillie Langtry. Owner: Thomas Patten, Jr., Appleton, Wisconsin.

Breeder: Associate Fanciers, Philadelphia, Pennsylvania. Whelped 2/26/1886. Brindle and white.

Bullmastiff (Registered as Bull Mastiff until 1960; became one word in 1960)	March 1934	(3)	Fascination of Felons Fear, #914895. By Farcroft Felons Frayeur ex Farcroft Fortitude, by Farcroft Finality ex Farcroft Silvo, by Hamil Grip ex Farcroft Belltong. Farcroft Finality by Farcroft Fidelity's Filius ex Farcroft Fealty. Farcroft Felons Frayeur by Farcroft Faction ex Farcroft Fend, by Farcroft Formidable ex Farcroft Crystal. Farcroft Faction by Hamil Halberd ex Farcroft Ferox. Owner: John W. Cross, Jr. Breeder: S. E. Moseley, England. Whelped 3/18/1933. Fawn.
Bull Terrier (Registered as Bullterrier until 1937; became two words in 1937)	1885	(2)	Nellie II, #3308. No sire or dam given. Owner: Mr. H. C. Tellman, Leesburg, Virginia. Breeder: Mr. J. P. Barnard, Boston, Massachusetts. Whelped 8/12/1878. Brindle.
Cairn Terrier	1913	(1)	Sandy Peter out of the West, #173555. By Sandy ex Fort Ellen out of West, by Ossian ex Nonian McCleod, by Cuillean Bhan ex Calla Mohr. Ossian by Man of Sligachan ex Gateside Fanny. Sandy by Tony ex Crudy by Crudles ex Fanny. Tony by Gobbs ex Gran. Owner: Mrs. H. F. Price, Noroton Heights, Connecticut. Breeder: Mrs. N. Fleming, England. Whelped 4/1913. Sandy, black points.
Chihuahua	1904	(5)	Midget, #82291. By Pluto ex Blanca, by Napoleon ex Beauty, by Rex ex Maria. Napoleon by Rags ex Molly. Pluto by Chihuahua ex Portia, by Don Juan ex Kitty I. Chihuahua by Diaz ex Juanita. Owner and

			Breeder: H. Rayner, El Paso, Texas. Whelped 7/18/1903. Red.
Chow Chow	1903	(2)	Yen How, #74111. Breeder, date of birth, and pedigree not given. Owner: Mrs. H. Jarrett, Philadelphia, Pennsylvania. Red. Won 1st in New York and Philadelphia, in 1903.
Collie	1885	(22)	Black Shep, #3249. By Bruce ex Highland Collie. Owner: Mr. R. F. Henry, Columbus, Mississippi. Breeder: Mr. J. A. Armstrong, Owosso, Michigan. Whelped 4/7/1882. Black and tan.
Dachshund (Longhaired) (Separate until 1937)	February 1931	(16)	Beauty (Ger.), #767927. By Jupp v. Habichtshof ex Vossa v. Habichtshof. (752759, volume 47). Jupp v. Habichtshof by Schalk v. Bergwald ex Mausle v. Habichtshof, by Schlupp v. Bergwald ex Traudel v. Habichtshof. Schalk v. Bergwald by Wacker ex Walda. Owner: Mrs. Clara Miller. Breeder: C. Wissman, St. Louis, Missouri. Whelped 4/17/1927. Red.
Dachshund (Smooth) (Registered as Dachshund)	1885	(11)	Dash, #3223. By Waldman ex Gretchen. Owner: Dr. G. D. Stewart, Detroit, Michigan. Breeder: Mr. W. H. Todd, Vermillion, Ohio. Whelped 1/1879. Black and tan. Won 1st at Ann Arbor, 1880.
Dachshund (Wirehaired) (Separate until 1937)	February, 1931	(22)	Raubautz v. Laudecker, #767783. By Rio v.d. Buschkante ex Heidi v. Laudecker, by Klausner's Mentor, ex Mausi Besigheim, by Lausbub Besigheim ex Gretel Dirndel. Klausner's Mentor by Klausner's Bautz ex Fiffi v. Alsen. Rio v.d. Buschkante by Luning v. Eichwald ex Liesel v. Forststeig by Klausner's Bautz ex Lore v. Forststeig. Luning v. Eichwald by Strampel v.

Waldrevier ex Hexe v.d. Hass-furt. Owner: Frida Vovegel. Breeder: P. Muller, Germany. Whelped 7/15/1929. Pepper and salt.

Dalmatian	1888	(1)	Bessie, #10519. Breeder and pedigree unknown. Owner: Mrs. N. L. Havey, San Francisco, California. Whelped 10/1887. White, black, and tan. Won 2nd at San Francisco, 1888.
Dandie Dinmont Terrier	1886	(3)	Bonnie Britton, #4472. By Border Minstrel ex Wee Miss, by Pool's Dirk ex Patterson's Old Miss, by Pepper ex Pyne. Border Minstrel by Milnes Old Jock ex Charlton's Bitch. Dirk by E. Bradshaw Smith's Incomparable Dirk ex Gyp. Owner: Mrs. John H. Naylor, Chicago, Illinois. Breeder: A. Steele, Scotland. Whelped 2/1884. Won 2nd at Cincinnati, 1885; 1st at Chicago in 1885; 2nd and spec. with Pansy for best pair of Dandies at Milwaukee, 1885.
Doberman Pinscher	1908	(1)	Doberman Intelectus, #122650. By Doberman Bertel ex Doberman Hertha, by Schill von Deutz ex Blanka von der Kieler Fohrde, by Troll Apolda ex Wanda von Thuringen. Schill von Deutz by Junker Slenz ex Kunigunde II. Doberman Bertel by Greif von Gronland ex Helmtrude von Hohenstein, by Busso von Michelhorst ex Bella von Hohenstein. Greif von Gronland by Linx ex Tilly von Gronland. Owner: Carl Schulyheiss, New Haven, Connecticut. Breeder: Doberman Kennels, Pittsford, New York. Whelped 6/20/1908. Black and tan.
English Toy Spaniel (Blenheim)	1886	(3)	Bowsie, Jr. (formerly Carlo), #4458. By Ch. Bowsie

(12093E), by Prince Charley ex Sis, by Frisk ex Rosa. Prince Charley by Napoleon ex Lillian. Owner: Sans Souci Kennels, Philadelphia, and Greenville, South Carolina. Breeder: Mrs. L. E. Jenkins, England. Whelped 8/1884. Red and white.

English Toy Spaniel (King Charles)	1886	(2)	Mildmay Park Beauty, #4456. By Bevan's Victor ex Mrs. Benton's Pet (sister to Alexander the Great), by Sambo ex Tottie. Owner: Mrs. B. F. Wilson, Pittsburgh, Pennsylvania. Breeder: Mrs. Benton, England. Whelped 6/1883. Black and tan. Won 2nd Brighton, England; 2nd and spec. Pittsburgh, 1886.
English Toy Spaniel (Prince Charles)	1888	(2)	Prince Rupert, #9238. By Rex ex Flora. Owner: John E. Diehl, Beverly, New Jersey. Breeder: A. C. Lucy, New York. Whelped 1/17/1886. Black and white, tan markings.
English Toy Spaniel (Ruby)	1890	(1)	Marguerite, #18159. By Duke (9227, vol. V) ex Clifton Belle (9233, vol. V). (Both parents are King Charles Spaniels). Owner and Breeder: Mrs. A. W. Lucy, New York. Whelped 5/10/1890. Ruby.
Eskimo (until 1959; no longer eligible for registration)	1888	(3)	Bruno S., #10773. By Alexis ex Sieru. Alexis by Kapetah ex Anak. Owner: Miss J. R. Shafter, San Francisco, California. Breeder: Pat Ryan, New York City. Whelped 1884. Brownish black. Won 2nd at San Francisco, 1888.
Foxhound (American)	1886	(1)	Lady Stewart, #4320. By Stormer ex Topsy, by Watchman ex Starlight. Owner: John H. Naylor, Chicago, Illinois. Breeder: F. T. Stewart, Hoosick Falls, New York. Whelped 4/14/1885. Black,

			white, and tan. Won 1st and spec. at Chicago and Milwaukee, 1885.
Foxhound (English)	1909	(80)	Auditor, #129533. By Bondsman ex Alice, by Senator ex Dainty, by Cardinal ex Stylish. Senator by Wiseman ex Gladsome. Bondsman by Paradox ex Beeswing, by Bruiser ex Garland. Paradox by Rambler ex Virtue. Owner: Clarence Moore, Hibbs Buidling, Washington, D.C. Breeder: Mrs. O. Pryce-Rice, Lianwrda, South Wales. Whelped 1907. Black, tan, and white.
Fox Terrier (Registered as Foxterrier); became two words in 1937)	1885	(17)	Cricket, #3289. By Vandad ex Mettle, by Rebel ex Mettle. Vandad by Torment ex Venus. Owner: Mr. J. P. Stinson, Leavenworth, Kansas. Breeder: Mr. Charles Walton, New York. No whelping date. Black, white, and tan.
Fox Terrier (Wire) (Registered separately until 1966 as Fox Terrier and Fox Terrier (Wire))	1887	(4)	Broxton Virago, #5479. By Pincher ex Squish, by Pincher ex Venom (E. 9005), by Old Venture ex Vice. Pincher by Cleveland Crab ex Colling's Vic. Cleveland Crab by Kendall's Old Tip. Owner: R. W. Dean, Oakville, Ontario. Breeder: G. Whitaker, Shady Bay, Ontario. Whelped 4/1885. Badger pie head, black patch on left side, white body.
French Bulldog	1898	(1)	Guguss II, #49705. By Sidi ex Finette, by Rabot de Beaubourg ex Blidab, by Billy ex Dora. Rabot de Beaubourg by Loupie ex Souris. (Sire and dam have the same pedigree). Owner: C. C. Hardwick, New York. Breeder: M. Gallas, Paris, France. Whelped 1/8/1898. Brindle and white.
German Shepherd Dog	1908	(1)	Queen of Switzerland, #115006. By Kuno von

Wohlen ex Wanda von Brugg, by Rigo von der Krone, ex Mira von Augst, by Prinz Leo von Habsburg ex Flora von Habsburg. Rigo von der Krone by Hector von Schwaben ex Nellie von Eislingen. Kuno von Wohlen by Boewulf ex Hanny von Grafarth by Horaud von Grafarth ex Sigrum von Grafarth. Boewulf by Hector von Schwaben ex Cekla von der Krone. Owner: Adolph Vogt, Brooklyn. Breeder: Herman Troesch, Brugg, Switzerland. Whelped 8/20/1905. Gray, black saddle.

Giant Schnauzer (Registered as Schnauzer (Giant) until 1949)	March 1930	(46)	Bella v. Fuchspark Potzhaus, #721736. By Araber v. Alt-Worms ex Cissa v. Wertachof, by Bazi v. Wellerstein ex Russi. Bazi v. Wetterstein by Russl ex Russi. Araber v. Alt-Worms ex Cara II v. Kinzigtal, by Russ ex Lisbeth v. Kinzigtal. Owner: J. M. Hoyt. Breeder: K. Kaltenhaeuser, Germany. Whelped 2/17/1926. Black.
Great Dane	1887	(3)	Don Caesar, #6046. By Mentor ex Norma. Owner: Osceola Kennels, Osceola Mills, Wisconsin. Breeder: Otto Friedrich, Zahna, Prussia. Whelped 5/28/1886. Light fawn. Won 1st and spec. at Milwaukee, 1886; 1st at St. Paul, 1887.
Great Pyrenees	April 1933	(10)	Blanchette, #866751. By Haro du Givre ex Pastour du Givre, by Patou du Givre ex Gavarnie du Givre by Patou de Betpouey ex Aida du Givre. Patou du Givre by Patou du Givre ex Gavarnie du Givre. Haro du Givre by Satan II du Givre ex Beroye du Givre. Owner: Mr. and Mrs. Francis V. Crane. Breeder: Mrs. Andree Remier,

			France. Whelped 8/10/1930. White, brown markings.
Greyhound	1885	(8)	Baron Walkeen, #3241. By Farrier ex Countess Hatcliffe, by Brigadier ex Cerite. Farrier by Cavalier ex Carlton. Owner: Mr. L. C. F. Lotz, Chicago, Illinois. Breeder: Mr. Wilson Furness, England. Whelped 4/29/1877. Fawn and white.
Harrier	1885	(1)	Jolly, #3236. By Tyrant ex Tuneful, by Sontag ex Blameless. Tyrant by Safety ex Bertha. Owner: Mr. James Conlisk, Buffalo, New York. Breeder: Lord Fitzhardings, England. Whelped 10/1/1877. Black, white, and tan.
Ibizan Hound	1978	(568)	Asuncion, (B) #HC522350. Foundation Stock. By Hannibal ex Certera. Owner: Mr. W. O'Brien. Breeders: Col. and Mrs. C. A. Seoane. Whelped 8/3/1956. Red and white.
Irish Terrier	1885	(2)	Aileen, #3306. By Joe ex Norah (3309). Joe by Jimmy ex Gyp. Owner and breeder: Dr. J. S. Niven, London, Canada. No birth date given. Red.
Irish Wolfhound (Registered as Wolfhound (Irish) until 1953)	1897	(2)	Ailbe, #45994. By Fingall ex Zill, by Garryowen ex Roheen, by Brian ex Lufra of Ivanhoe. Garryowen by Scythian ex Spencer. Fingall by Dhuillart ex Cannac, by Blucher ex Lufra. Dhuillart by Hydra ex Sheelah. Owner: Roger Williams, Lexington, Kentucky. Breeder: Hon. E. Dillon, Charlbury, England. Whelped 7/30/1896. Gray.
Italian Greyhound	1886	(1)	Lilly, #4346. By Pet ex Blanche, by Dick ex Flora. Pet by Dick ex Flora. Owner and breeder: Mrs. E. P. Roberts, Alton, Illinois. Whelped 10/14/1879. Fawn and white. Won 1st at St. Louis, 1885.

Japanese Chin (Registered as Japanese Spaniel until 1977)	1888	(9)	Jap, #9216. Pedigree and breeder unknown. Owner: Fred Senn, New York City. Whelped 1886. Black and white.
Keeshond	October 1930	(8)	Bella v. Trennfeld, #751187. By Geron am Ziel ex Hilde am Ziel, by Fips Sauter ex Christel am Ziel, by Wolf II v.d. Folfsinsel ex Hexe v. Goslar. Fips Sauter by Wachter ex Greta v. Korberkopf. Geron am Ziel by Hans v. Solingen ex Christel am Ziel, by Wolf II v.d. Folfsinsel ex Hexe v. Goslar. Hans v. Solingen by Fritz ex Bella. Owner: Carl Hinderer. Breeder: Franz Schwab, Germany. Whelped 5/1/1926. Gray.
Kerry Blue Terrier	1922	(1)	Brian of Muchia, #349159. By Brian King of Munster ex Eileen Mavourneen, by Prince ex Eileen of Munster, by Joe ex Nell. Prince by Paddy ex Nora. Brian King of Munster by Dover ex Farranforeen, by Young Moucher ex Fanny. Dover by Jockey ex Jess. Owner: Eliz. Swords, 50 E. 67th St., New York City. Breeder: Mrs. J. Casey Hewitt, England. Whelped 5/28/1921. Blue gray.
Komondor	January 1938	(2)	Andrashazi Dorka, (B) #A199838. By Ketszeres Gyoztes Rozsadombi Pandur ex Pannonia Sari, by Pannoni Sobri II ex Pannonia Fuge, by Orokosgyoztes Pannonia Sobri ex Pannonia Diana; Pannoni Sobri II by Orokosgyoztes Pannonia Sobri ex Pannonia Diana. Ketszeres Gyoztes Rozsadombi Pandur by Derbygyoztes Itce Csakos ex Nadasdladanyi Buksi by Csori Bodri Aron ex Bakonyi Abel; Derbygyoztes Itce Csakos by Ifjabb Bodri Oregcserto ex Itce Berzek.

Owner: Tibor de Cholnoky, M.D. Breeder: Fellner Andras, Hungary. Whelped 10/25/1935. White.

Kuvasz	August 1931	(1)	Tamar v. Wuermtal, #791292. By Sultan v. Rosenhain ex Dumm v. Frauken, by Hadnagy v. Csikos Toth ex Diana (v. Ungarn), by Hadnagy ex Vitesz. Hadnagy v. Csikos Toth by Vitez Hortobagy ex Hattyn Hortobagy. Sultan v. Rosenhain by Jimmi ex Fuerge, by Vitez ex Hattyn. Jimmi by Dugo ex Rajna. Owner: Ignatz Schmidt. Breeder: Rudolf Fischer, Germany. Whelped 12/16/1925. White, black nose.
Lakeland Terrier	July 1934	(2)	Egton What A Lad of Howtown, #938424. By Egton Rock of Howtown ex Egton Sting of Cathra, by Bant ex Bet, by Gillet ex Dot. Bant by Tinker ex Floss. Egton Rock of Howtown by Crab of Wastwater ex Vic of Wastwater, by Grip ex Castle Queen. Crab of Wastwater by Bookwell Bristles ex Egton Lady of the Lake. Owner: Robert A. A. Johnston. Breeder: Mrs. G. Spence, England. Whelped 1/3/1933. Black and tan.
Lhasa Apso (Registered as Lhasa Terrier until 1944)	May 1935	(4)	Empress of Kokonor, #987979. By Chang Daw ex Ching Ming, by Taikoo of Kokonor ex Dinkie. Chang Daw by Taikoo of Kokonor ex Dinkie. Owner: B. Heathcote. Breeder: Miss M. Torrible, Canada. Whelped 8/28/1933. Cream.
Maltese	1888	(1)	Topsy, #12056. Pedigree and breeder unknown. Owner: Miss Ida Orme, New York City. Whelped 5/4/1885. White. Won 1st and spec. at Detroit, 1887; and in St. Paul, 1888.

Manchester Terrier (Toy) (Registered as Toy Manchester Terrier)	1886	(1)	Gypsy, #4485. By Jack ex Fanny. Owner: L. F. Whitman, Lake Shore Kennel, Chicago, Illinois. Breeder: Dr. Prittie, Detroit, Michigan. Whelped 3/1879. Black and tan. Won 2nd in Chicago, 1884; 2nd in New Orleans, 1885.
Manchester Terrier (Standard) (Registered separately until 1959)	1887	(1)	Lever, #7585. By Ch. Vortigern ex Fortune, by Reveller ex Lilly II, by Ch. Cupid ex Burton's Lilly. Reveller by Charlie ex Queen. Vortigern (E. 8633) by Viper (E. 7654) ex Gypsy, by Vanguard ex Music. Owner: C. P. Lawshe, Trenton, New Jersey. Breeder: Edward Lever, Philadelphia, Pennsylvania. Whelped 10/11/1886. Black and tan.
Mastiff	1885	(9)	Bayard, #3271. By The Monarch ex Gipsey. The Monarch by Marquis ex Empress. Owner: Mr. L. F. Delano, Boston, Massachusetts. Breeder: Mr. Wm. Wade, Pittsburgh, Pennsylvania. Whelped 10/10/1881. Fawn.
Mexican Hairless (Until 1959; no longer eligible for registration)	1887	(4)	Me Too, #6074. No pedigree or breeder listed. Owner: Mrs. Hubert T. Foote, New York City. Whelped 1882. Black. Won 1st and spec. New Haven; 1st New York; 1st Philadelphia; 1st New York, 1884. 1st and spec. New Haven; 1st Boston; 1st New York; 1st Philadelphia, 1885. 1st New Haven; 1st Boston; 1st and spec. Hartford; 1st New York, 1886.
Miniature Pinscher (Registered as Pinscher (Miniature) until 1972)	March 1925	(11)	Asta von Sandreuth, #454601. By Jean v. Falkenstein ex Lotte v. Sandreuth, by Prosper v. Niederbayern ex. Nelly, by Darling ex Malvine. Prosper v. Niederbayern by Pipifax v. Klein-Paris ex Prosperine v. Niederbayern. Jean v. Falken-

stein by Prosper v. Niederbay-
ern ex Liesl v. Nuernberg, by
Heinz v. Klein-Paris ex Nelly
Lilliput. (See above for Prosper
v. N.). Owner: Mrs. B. Seys-
chab. Breeder: J. Bauer, Germany.   Whelped   6/5/1924.
Black, red and brown.

Miniature Schnauzer (Registered as Schnauzer (Miniature) until 1972)	November 1926	(8)	Schnapp v. Dornbusch of Hitofa, #551063. By Hupp v. Dornbusch ex Litta v. Dornbusch, by Friedl v. Affentor ex Lenchen v. Dornbusch, by Rigo v. Dornbusch ex Hexe v. Dornbusch. Friedl v. Affentor by Rudi v. Lohr ex Mohra v.d. Werneburg. Hupp v. Dornbusch by Axel v. Dornbusch ex Betty v. Dornbusch, by Frick v. Dornbusch ex Maeus Chen v. Dornbusch. Axel v. Dornbusch by Rigo v. Dornbusch ex Hella v. Dornbusch. Owner: Frank Spiekerman. Breeder: Georg Riehl, Germany. Whelped 10/2/1924. Salt and pepper.
Newfoundland	1886	(2)	Fly, #4447. By Kiddy's Rover ex Morton's Hussey, by Barton's Nat ex Tuft's Gus. Rover by O'Grady's Juno ex Jollimore's Tillie. Owner: Acadia Kennels, J. A. Nickerson, Boston, Massachusetts. Breeder: Wm. Morton, Halifax, Nova Scotia. Whelped 1879. Black.
Norfolk Terrier(Registered as Norwich Terrier until 1979)	1979	(106)	Bar Sinister Little Ruffian, (B) #RA475550. Sire: Bethway's Sam I Am. Dam: Mt. Paul Vesper. Owner: Eileen Murphy. Breeders: John and Irene Mandeville. Whelped 2/12/1977. Red.
Norwegian Elkhound	1913	(3)	Koik, #170389. By Rap II ex Bibbi, by Bring ex Kjappa, by Prik ex Stussa. Bring by Storm ex Freia. Rap II by Rap ex Binna, by Bibi ex Storm. Rap by Storm ex Freia. Owner: Got-

			tlieb Lechner, Weiser, Idaho. Breeder: O. Hykket, Christiania, Norway. Whelped 3/1909. Gray.
Norwich Terrier	April 1936	(3)	Witherslack Sport, #A58858. By Witherslack George ex Witherslack Jane, by Kien ex Gyp, by Pepper ex Midge. Kien by Ky ex Pen. Witherslack George by Kien ex Pen, by Tommy ex Mustard. Kien by Ky ex Pen. Owner: G. Gordon Massey. Breeder: Lady Maureen Stanley, England. Whelped 2/24/1934. Red.
Old English Sheepdog	1888	(2)	Champion of Winkleigh, #9252. Pedigree and date of birth unknown. Owner: Edwin H. Morris, Exeter, England. Breeder: Mr. Isaacs, England. Brindle and white.
Otter Hound	1910	(2)	Hartland Statesman, #135334. By Hartland Spearman ex Alexandra of Hartland, by Dumfries Marauder ex Miranda of Annan, by Chaunter ex Darling. Dumfries Marauder by Smuggler ex Dowager. Hartland Spearman by Smiler ex Daisy of Dumfries, by Mawddwy Stanley ex Doubtless. Smiler by Sailor ex Safety. Owner and breeder: H. S. Wardner, New York City. Whelped 3/20/1907. Black, grizzle, and tan.
Papillon	1915	(8)	Joujou, #192537. By Gighi ex Mignonne. Owner and breeder: Mrs. De Forest Danielson, Medfield, Massachusetts. Whelped 4/14/1912. Sable. Reg. on wins.
Pekingese	1906	(6)	Rascal, #95459. by Chang ex Beauty, by Dick III ex Lady II, by Faust ex Lady. Dick III by Dick II ex Fanny. Chang by Fang ex Mocha, by Fu Hsi ex Ming. Fang by Hwang Ti ex Isi

An. Owner: Alfred J. S. Edwards, Glenolden, Pennsylvania. Breeder: Blanche Denton, Philadelphia, Pennsylvania. Whelped 6/10/1898. Black, tan, and white.

Pharaoh Hound	1983	(673)	Fqira, (B) #HD027750. Foundation Stock. Sire: Bahri. Dam: Mythra. Owner: Mrs. Ruth Taft Hobbs. Breeder: Mrs. J. W. Pownall-Gray. Whelped 3/8/1976. Chestnut, white markings.
Pointer	1878	(165)	Ace of Spades, #1187. By Button (1198) ex Topsey (1345), by Waddell's Phil ex Nelly. Button from Stewart's imported brace. Owner and breeder: J. J. Snellenberg, New Brighton, Pennsylvania. Whelped 6/1875.
Pointer (German Shorthaired)	March 1930	(1)	Greif v.d. Fliegerhalde, #723642. By Panther Furstenfeld ex Miss Schnaitberg, by Lux v. Wildbacher Waldeck ex Mathi Schnaitberg, by Roland Sand ex Bella Schnaitberg. Lux v. Wildbacher Waldeck by Panther v.d. Bode ex Olly v. Tannheim. Panther Furstenfeld by Panther v. Inn ex Rina Roggenstein, by Feldmann v. Furstenfeld ex Herta Roggenstein. Panther v. Inn by Treu v.d. Wessnitz ex Hella v. Ascholding. Owner: H. S. Rothschild. Breeder: Muller, Germany. Whelped 6/25/1928. Brown, spotted breast.
Pointer (German Wirehaired)	1959	(251)	Eiko vom Schultenhof (Germany), (D), #S963376. By Bodo v.d. Hammer Mark ex Blanka vom Schollenberg. Owner: W. D. Kyle, Jr. Breeder: Gustave Niederschult, Germany. Whelped 5/30/1950. Liver, white ticked.

Pomeranian	1888	(1)	Dick, #10776. By Texas ex Foulette. Owner: J. J. Jamison, San Francisco. Breeder: C. L. Meyer. Whelped 9/1885. White. Won 2nd at San Francisco, 1888.
Poodle	1887	(3)	Czar, #7597. By Boy (E. 15855) ex Queen, by Ch. Lyris ex Begum, by Puck ex Galatea. Imp. Boy by Boy ex Kiss. Owner and breeder: W. Lyman Biddle, Philadelphia, Pennsylvania. Whelped 6/14/1886. Black.
Portuguese Water Dog	1983	(721)	Renascenca do Al-Gharb, (B), #WF382950. By Lis Algarbiorum ex Enga Algarbiorum. Foundation Stock. Owner: Deyanne F. Miller. Breeder: Canil do Al-Gharb. Whelped 7/12/1968. Black, white markings.
Pug	1885	(3)	George, #3286. By Muggens ex Coquette. Owner: Mr. E. A. Pue, Philadelphia, Pennsylvania. Whelped 12/1878. Fawn and black. Won 2nd in New York, 1881; 1st in Pittsburgh, 1882; Champ in New York, 1882.
Puli	November 1936	(2)	Torokvesz Sarika, (B) #A107734. By Istenhegyi Almos Bago ex Promontori Morgo by Gazdag Allatkert ex Inal Allatkert by Banati Mufurc ex Pettendi Hamislany; Gazdag Allatkert by Anonymus ex Aniko Allatkert. Istenhegyi Almos Bago by Gazdag Allatkert ex Rakoshegyi Kis Kocos by Kassai Bator ex Hofeherke; Gazdag Allatkert by Anonymus ex Aniko Allatkert. Owner: Louis Kiss. Breeder: Cservenkai Karoly, Hungary. Whelped 10/2/1935. Black.
Retriever (Chesapeake Bay)	1878	(2)	Sunday, #1408. By Neptune ex Topsy, by Sandy ex Fan.

Neptune by Monday ex Judy. Owner: G. W. Kierstead, Laporte, Indiana. Breeder: O. D. Foulkes. Whelped 10/1875. Dark chestnut.

Retriever (Curly-Coated)	February 1924	(?)	Knysna Conjurer, #398399. By Bute Surprise ex Good Girl, by Penwortham Brown Boy ex Saucy Beauty, by Blackledges Nigger ex Caroline Bell. Penwortham Brown Boy by Penwortham Sportsman ex Penwortham Nana. Bute Surprise by Knysna Darkie ex Knysna Flora, by Knysna Sultan ex Dulock Fly. Knysna Darkie by Knysna Duke ex Knysna Princess. Owner: Charles H. Starr. Breeder: J. Browitt, Preston, England. Whelped 7/20/1922. Black.
Retriever (Flat-Coated)	1915	(?)	Sand Bridge Jester, #190223. By Jimmy of Riverside ex Toxca Banter, by High Legh Blarney ex Blossom of Riverside, by Rocket of Riverside ex Judy of Riverside. High Legh Blarney by Black Quilt ex High Legh Moment. Jimmy of Riverside by High Legh Blarney ex Duchess, by Wimpole Peter ex Pop of Riverside. Owner: J. C. O'Connor II, New York. Breeder: W. Simms, England. Whelped 8/18/1913. Black.
Retriever (Golden)	November 1925	(?)	Lomberdale Blondin, #490685. By Lomberdale Duke ex Brandy, by Noramby Balfour ex Ottershaw Bush, by Paxhill Brian ex Columbine. Noramby Balfour by Culham Brass ex Noramby Beauty. Lomberdale Duke by Astley Lad ex Glanduff Noblesse, by Bladen Boxer ex Bladen Beatrice. Astley Lad by Astley Storm ex Griff. Owner: Robert Appleton. Breeder: Capt. C.

Breed	Year	(No.)	Description
Retriever (Labrador)	1917	(?)	Waterhouse, England. Whelped 8/14/1922. Golden. Brocklehirst Floss, #223339. By Brocklehirst Bob ex Stewardess. by Munden Sovereign ex Susan, by Spratt ex Munden Solitary. Munden Sovereign by Sir Richard ex Munden Single. Brocklehirst Bob by Esk ex Flora, by Sam ex Bess. Esk by Warwick Collier ex Nell. Owner: Charles G. Meyer, New York City. Breeder: L. Rankine, Scotland. Whelped 1/2/1912. Black.
Rhodesian Ridgeback	1955	(142)	Tchaika of Redhouse (South Africa), (B), #H520551. By Faro ex Bergwag. Owner: Stephen Paine. Breeder: A., Uys. Whelped 9/10/1949. Wheaten.
Rottweiler	December 1931	(3)	Stina v. Felsenmeer, #805867. By Blucher v. Felsenmeer ex Alma (Gruner), by Mars v. Gaiberg ex Dina I v. Felsenmeer, by Ally v. Durnau ex Berna v. Felsenmeer. Mars v. Gaiberg by Bar v. Stolzenfels ex Alma v.d. Pfalz. Blucher v. Felsenmeer by Cito v.d. Breite ex Erna v. Karlstor-Molkenkur, by Cralo v.d. Festung ex Pitza v. Karlstor-Molkenkur. Cito v.d. Breite by Leo Silberzahn ex Gretel v.d. Steinlach. Owner: August Knecht. Breeder: Adolf Wagner, Germany. Whelped 3/8/1929. Black and brown.
Saint Bernard	1885	(6)	Chief, #3280. By Harold ex Judy, by Chamounix ex Alphe. Harold by Sultan III ex Dido II. Owner: Mr. A. V. de Goicouria, New York City. Breeder: Mr. J. P. Haines, Toms River, New Jersey. Whelped 5/12/1879. Orange, tawny, and white.

Saluki	March 1929	(1)	Jinniyat of Grevel, #674570. By Middain of Grevel ex Abu Kaff, by Ibn Hazael ex Abu Soufi, by Suafir Shemali ex Gaza Bint. Ibn Hazael by Hazael ex Bint Amman. Middain of Grevel by Ibn Hazael ex Abu Soufi. Owner: Mrs. S. Y. L'Hommedieu, Jr. Breeder: B. Berwick, England. Whelped 4/13/1927. Fawn.
Samoyed (Registered as Samoyede until 1948)	1906	(1)	Moustan of Argenteau, #102896. Pedigree, date of birth, and breeder unknown. Owner: Argenteau Kennels, Cold Spring Harbor, New York. White. Won 1st open in Danbury and Philadelphia, 1906.
Schipperke	1904	(1)	Snowball, #83461. By Majesto ex Cantsfield Kitty by El Dorado ex Helen of Troy, by Joppe ex Tad. El Dorado by Frity of Spa ex Miss Mephistopheles. Majesto by Fandango ex Cantsfield Peggy, by Prestwick Joe ex Walsoken Londa. Fandango by El Dorado ex Fleurette. Owner and breeder: A. Hunter, Philadelphia, Pennsylvania. Whelped 3/11/1904. Black.
Scottish Deerhound (Registered as Deerhound (Scottish) until 1972)	1886	(1)	Bonnie Robin, #4345. By Dunrobin ex Shellock, by Lord Grosvenor's Ossian ex Duke of Sutherland's Brenda, by Wallace ex Loyal. Dunrobin by Duke of Sutherland's Torrom, by Wallace ex Loyal, by Stag ex Kendeach, by Pirate ex Loyal. Stag by Torrom ex Loyal. Torrom by Glengarry ex Lioness. Owner: R. M. Boyd, Racine, Wisconsin. Breeder: G. S. Paige, Stanley, New Jersey. Whelped 5/9/1885. Brindle.

Scottish Terrier	1885	(2)	Prince Charlie, #3310. By Billy ex Lady. Owner: Mr. J. H. Naylor, Chicago, Illinois. Breeder: Mr. D. O'Shea, London, Canada. Whelped 4/1881.
Sealyham Terrier	1911	(2)	Harfats Pride, #151623. By Peer Gynt ex Nellie, by Trefgarn Crib ex Venom, by Tinker ex Nettle. Trefgarn Crib by Whiskey ex Sting. Peer Gynt by Dip II ex Tinny, by Diamond ex Smutt. Dip II by Dip ex Dinah. Owner: August Belmont, Jr., New York City. Breeders: Messrs. Lewis & Gwyther, England. Whelped 1/10/1909. White, badger pied.
Setter (English)	1878	(533)	Adonis, #1. By Leicester (148) ex Dart (335), by Llewellin's Prince ex Llewellin's Dora. Leicester by Llewellin's Dan, ex Llewellin's Lill II. Owner and breeder: George E. Delano, New Bedford, Massachusetts. Whelped 1875. Black, white and tan.
Setter (Gordon)	1878	(135)	Bank, #793. By Jerome's Shot ex White's Nell, by Stockton's Dash ex White's Fly. Owner: E.H. Nicoll. Breeder: J.H. White. Whelped 12/1875. Black and tan.
Setter (Irish)	1878	(259)	Admiral, #534. By Rufus (644) ex Belle (669), by King ex Jane. Rufus by Shot ex Linda. Owner: M. Ketchum, Westport, Connecticut. Breeders: Fisher & Bickarton. Whelped 8/1877. Deep red.
Shetland Sheepdog	1911	(3)	Lord Scott, #148760. By Carlo ex Daisy, by Hero ex Flossy, by Curley ex Janny. Hero by Roy ex Mootie. Carlo by Tootsie ex Old Daisy, by Wag ex Perrie. Tootsie by Princie ex Cora. Owner: E. H. McChesney, New York City. Breeder: A.

			Stephens, Shetland, Scotland. Whelped 2/11/1905. Sable.
Shih Tzu	1969	(2811)	Choo Lang of Telota (United Kingdom), (D), #TA573228. By Tensing of Shanreta ex Mai Mai of Talota. Owners: P. J. Federico and Wm. R. Guzzy. Breeder: Mrs. Olive Newson. Whelped 1/8/1968. White and golden.
Siberian Husky	December, 1930	(1)	Fairbanks Princess Chena, #758529. By Bingo II ex Alaska Princess, by Jack Frost ex Snowflake. Jack Frost by Scotty ex Vasta. Bingo II by Bingo ex Topsy. Owner: Mrs. Elsie K. Reeser. Breeder: Julien A. Hurley, Fairbanks, Alaska. Whelped 9/16/1927. White.
Silky Terrier	1959	(670)	Winsome Beau Ideal (Australia), (D) #T610051. By Winsome Beau Monde ex Winsome Gay Gold. Owner: Mrs. E. Page. Breeder: Mrs. D. Morris. Whelped 1/7/1945. Blue and tan.
Skye Terrier	1887	(1)	Romach, #6184. By Kingston Roy (E. 13643) ex Col. Legh's Zulu. Kingston Roy by Monarch (E. 6691) ex Venus (E. 7726), by Ben ex Topsey. Monarch by Tommy ex Queen Bess. Owner: Maizeland Kennels, Red Hook, New York. Breeder: Lt. Col. H. Cornwall, England. Whelped 7/1884. Blue.
Soft-Coated Wheaten Terrier	1973	(652)	Holmenocks Gramachree, CD (Ireland), (B), #RA44600. By Holmenocks Hartigan ex Griselda. Owner: Mrs. A. Cecelia O'Connor. Breeder: C. Graham Holmes. Whelped 3/23/1957. Wheaten.
Spaniel (American Water)	October 1940	(28)	Tidewater Teddy, (D), #A426838. By Redland's Sam Brown ex Quannah Queen by Billy Boy ex Exline Maggie by

			Buster Brown ex Queen's Lady Hollenbeck; Billy Boy by Mac ex Lady. Redland's Sam Brown by Redland's Rusty ex Marc's Lady Betty by Doc Brown ex Brownie Ferren; Redland's Rusty by Bud Brown ex Brown's Betty. Owner: Driscoll O. Scanlan. Breeder: Marc Woodmansee, Des Moines, Iowa. Whelped 8/1/1928. Brown.
Spaniel (Clumber)	1878	(5)	Bustler, #1353. By Bang ex Romp, by Thompson's dog ex Forman's Juno. Bang by Thompson's dog ex Forman's Juno. Owner: Benjamin Smith, Kentville, Nova Scotia. Breeder: George Piers. Whelped 4/1868. Orange and white.
Spaniel (Cocker)	1878	(22)	Capt, #1354. By Romeo ex Juliet; both imported by Bestor. Owner: M. P. McKoon, Franklin, New York. Breeder: S. J. Bestor. Whelped 6/1874. Liver and white.
Spaniel (English Cocker) (Separated from Spaniel (Cocker) in 1946)			
Spaniel (English Springer)	1910	(1)	Denne Lucy #142641. By Beechgrove Donaldson ex Beechgrove Clara, by Beechgrove Gorse ex Beechgrove Nelly, by Beechgrove Bert ex Beechgrove Lady. Beachgrove Gorse by Beechgrove Will ex Beechgrove Rubina. Beechgrove Donaldson by Beechgrove Donald ex Cottonham Nell, by Cottonham Roy ex Cottonham Bell. Beechgrove Donald by Don ex May. Owner: Hobart Ames, North Easton, Massachusetts. Breeder: F. Winton Smith, England. Whelped 1/30/1908. Liver and white.

Spaniel (Field)	1894	(?)	Coleshill Rufus, #33395. By Nebo ex Coleshill Lass, by Buckle ex Stately Lass, by Chelmford Caution ex Claisonne. Buckle by Sam ex Fern. Nebo by Bridford Bobbie ex Peeress, by Lord Bute ex Jewess. Bridford Bobbie by Easten's Bruce ex Bridford's Negress. Owner: R. P. Keasbey, Newark, New Jersey. Breeder: J. Smith, England. Whelped 7/21/1891. Liver.
Spaniel (Irish Water)	1878	(23)	Bob, #1352. By Sinbad (1371) ex Queen (1399), by Dash ex Cinder. Sinbad by Dyke ex Fan. Owner: Richard Tuttle, Chicago, Illinois. Breeder: J. H. Whitman. Whelped 11/1875. Liver. Won 2nd, St. Louis, 1877; 1st, St. Louis and Baltimore, 1878.
Spaniel (Sussex)	1878	(1)	Jack (alias Toby), #1363. By Read's Sailor ex Garlich's Bess. Owner: Capt. McMurdo, New Brunswick, Canada. Liver and white.
Spaniel (Welsh Springer)	1914	(6)	Faircroft Bob, #185938. By Faircroft Snip (185940) ex Faircroft Sue, by Buller of Llyan ex Longmynd May Gween, by Longmynd Morgan ex Colon Fach. Buller of Llyan by Buller of Bout ex Cora. Owner and breeder: Harry B. Hawes, Kirkwood, Missouri. Whelped 9/3/1914. Red and white.
Staffordshire Bull Terrier	1974	(371)	Tinkinswood Imperial (United Kingdom), (D), #RA161150. By Abbot of Rowenspur ex Tinkinswood Gypsy. Owner: Mrs. L. G. Rant. Breeder: J. Parsons. Whelped 8/3/1967. Fawn.
Standard Schnauzer (Registered as Schnauzer (Standard) until 1972)	1904	(2)	Norwood Victor, #77886. By Schnauzer ex Schnauzerl. Owner and breeder: Norwood

			Kennels, Philadelphia, Pennsylvania. Whelped 7/23/1901. Pepper and salt. Won 1st open at New York and Philadelphia, 1903.
Tibetan Spaniel	1983	(743)	Tritou Charlotte, (B), #NS789150. Foundation Stock. By Medrey's Win-A-Too ex Benagh Rue. Owner: Jeanne Holsapple. Breeder: Jenny Chalmers. Whelped 7/2/1978. Sable and white.
Tibetan Terrier	1973	(399)	Amandah Lamleh of Kalai, (B), #NS107000. By Kens-Pa Byis-Pa Lamleh of Kalai ex Yser-Bu-Mo Lamleh of Kalai. Owner: Mrs. Murray Klein. Breeder: Mrs. Henry S. Murphy. Whelped 12/20/1972. Brown and white.
Vizsla	1960	(325)	Rex Z. Arpadvar, (D), #SA63201. By Remi Z. Povazia ex Alma Olca. Owner: Marvin B. Marsh. Breeders: Tom Pratt and R. L. Davison. Whelped 7/26/1959. Golden rust.
Weimaraner	March 1943	(3)	Adda v. Schwarzen Kamp (B), #A646165. By Igor Uefingen ex Haida v. Zeubachtal by Armin v. Ahorntal ex Dora v. Zeubachtal by Pero v. Aurachstrand ex Asta v. Wesetal; Armin v. Ahorntal by Benno v. Puschendorf ex Blanka v. Zeubachtal. Igor Uefingen by Tell v.d. Kilver ex Adda v.d. Ileburg by Cosak Obermollrich ex Helga v. Feengrotten; Tell v.d. Kilver by Hellrud aus der Wulfsriede ex Luna aus der Wulfsriede. Owner: Howard Knight. Breeder: Herbert Vogel, Germany. Whelped 3/9/1934. Silver gray.
Welsh Corgi (Cardigan)	January 1935	(5)	Blodwen of Robinscroft, #965012. By Drudwyn ex Ha-

			wys, by Brenig Brilliant ex Yngharad, by Tit O'r Bryn ex Cassie. Brenig Brilliant by Bob Llwyd ex Cassie. Drudwyn by Toriad-y-Wawr ex Yngharad, by Tit O'r Bryn ex Cassie. Toriad-y-Wawr by Mimulus Musk ex Nell of Twyn. Owner: Mrs. Henry F. Price. Breeder: G. E. Owen, South Wales. Whelped 8/25/1932. Sable and white.
Welsh Corgi (Pembroke)	August 1934	(3)	Little Madam, #939536. By Bowhit Pepper ex Bowhit Bunny, by Bowhit Pimpo ex Bowhit Bisco, by Bowhit Pepper ex Bowhit Beda. Bowhit Pimpo by Bowhit Pepper ex Bowhit Betsy. Bowhit Pepper by Caleb ex Glandofan Fury. Caleb by Buller ex Phoebe. Owner: Mrs. Lewis Roesler. Breeder: Mrs. Sid Bowler, England. Whelped 12/16/1932. Red brown, white markings.
Welsh Terrier	1888	(2)	T'Other, #9171. Pedigree, date of birth and breeder unknown. Owner: Prescott Lawrence, Groton, Massachusetts. Black and tan grizzle.
West Highland White Terrier (Registered as Roseneath Terrier in 1908 only)	1908	(5)	Talloch, #116076. By Treach Bhan ex Kylach, by Conas ex Tedora, by Brogach ex Faslach. Conas by Badger ex Grougach. Treach Bhan by Boideach ex Robbin Bhan, by Frisk II ex Careagh. Boideach by Bodach ex Roddy. Owner: Mrs. Clinton E. Bell, Springfield, Massachusetts. Breeder: Mrs. Nana S. Hunter, Northamptonshire, England. Whelped 5/1/1907. White.
Whippet	1888	(1)	Jack Dempsey, #9804. By Eaves' Dear at a Gift ex Nell, by Chambers' Jack ex Maud S. Dear at a Gift by Let Me Go ex Turner's Lizzie. Owner: Chas.

O. Breed, Lynn, Massachusetts. Breeder: P. H. Hoffman, Philadelphia, Pennsylvania. Whelped 9/23/1885. White, brown and yellow markings. Won 2nd at Boston, 1888.

Wirehaired Pointing Griffon (Registered as Griffon (Wirehaired Pointing) until 1972)	1887	(1)	Zolette, #6773. By Guerre ex Tambour, by Chasseur ex Yankee, by Moustache I ex Auerida. Chasseur by Moustache II ex Clarette. Guerre by Moustache II ex Angot, by Moustache I ex Donna. Moustache II by Moustache I ex Zampa. Owner: C. C. Lamos, Chicago, Illinois. Breeder: Prince Solms, Braunsfels, Prussia. Whelped 1/6/1887. Brown.
Yorkshire Terrier	1885	(1)	Belle, #3307. No pedigree given. Owner: Mr. A. E. Godeffroy, Guymard, New York. Whelped 1877. Blue and tan.

Statistical Appendix

I REGISTRATIONS

Year	Breeds	Dogs	Litters	Year	Breeds	Dogs	Litters
1878- 1884-	8	1,416	-	1907	52	10,496	-
				1908	57	10,676	-
1885	26	1,896	-	1909	54	10,790	-
1886	26	2,085	-	1910	61	10,819	-
1887	38	2,202	-	1911	60	9,955	-
1888	49	4,457	-	1912	69	10,311	-
1889	39	4,217	-	1913	57	10,243	-
1890	37	2,866	-	1914	66	10,608	-
1891	36	4,308	-	1915	66	22,127	-
1892	37	4,469	-	1916	59	14,161	-
1893	38	4,028	-	1917	57	15,552	-
1894	37	3,667	-	1918	57	13,409	-
1895	36	3,473	-	1919	57	18,479	-
1896	37	3,512	-	1920	57	23,453	-
1897	42	3,738	-	1921	59	29,960	-
1898	49	3,649	-	1922	59	29,119	-
1899	46	4,351	-	1923	63	39,721	-
1900	43	4,881	-	1924	70	49,579	-
1901	43	5,445	-	1925	69	54,172	-
1902	45	6,319	-	1926	71	59,455	-
1903	46	6,595	-	1927	72	57,560	-
1904	51	7,396	-	1928	74	52,762	-
1905	49	8,276	-	1929	79	48,160	-
1906	53	9,730	-	1930	83	48,147	-

Year	Breeds	Dogs	Litters	Year	Breeds	Dogs	Litters
1931	83	46,724	-	1958	107	446,625	207,520
1932	81	47,112	29,200	1959	106	460,300	216,975
1933	85	51,497	44,309	1960	109	442,875	226,447
1934	93	60,196	50,891	1961	111	493,300	238,525
1935	96	72,390	52,520	1962	115	516,800	250,925
1936	100	84,475	57,225	1963	115	568,300	270,750
1937	103	84,156	54,925	1964	115	640,300	292,675
1938	102	82,797	56,925	1965	115	722,800	319,925
1939	100	79,989	53,425	1966	115	804,400	351,025
1940	105	83,345	53,950	1967	115	885,800	379,775
1941	99	87,968	55,300	1968	115	909,300	404,175
1942	99	89,383	53,250	1969	116	973,100	421,125
1943	100	78,200	46,025	1970	116	1,056,225	446,025
1944	98	77,400	47,275	1971	116	1,129,200	451,675
1945	97	147,707	73,089	1972	118	1,101,943	430,700
1946	100	206,978	92,662	1973	120	1,099,850	420,749
1947	100	235,720	110,092	1974	121	1,103,249	418,150
1948	105	227,647	115,384	1975	121	1,022,849	397,950
1949	106	241,811	119,493	1976	122	1,048,648	406,550
1950	104	251,812	113,557	1977	122	1,013,650	380,050
1951	104	264,415	123,788	1978	123	980,299	371,500
1952	105	294,240	139,550	1979	124	965,250	371,900
1953	105	326,234	142,551	1980	125	1,011,799	382,350
1954	102	346,525	152,475	1981	125	1,033,849	404,599
1955	104	359,900	159,684	1982	125	1,037,149	405,850
1956	104	430,900	188,482	1983	128	1,085,248	415,799
1957	106	436,600	192,262	1984	128	1,071,299	422,098

II EVENTS

Year	All-Breed Shows	Specialty Shows	Independent Obed. Tri.	Obed. Tr. With Shows	Tracking Tests	Field Trials
1884	11	0	-	-	-	-
1885	11	0	-	-	-	-
1886	18	1	-	-	-	-
1887	11	1	-	-	-	-

Year	All-Breed Shows	Specialty Shows	Independent Obed. Tri.	Obed. Tr. With Shows	Tracking Tests	Field Trials
1888	11	1	-	-	-	-
1889	14	0	-	-	-	-
1890	12	0	-	-	-	-
1891	25	1	-	-	-	-
1892	22	2	-	-	-	-
1893	20	0	-	-	-	-
1894	17	0	-	-	-	-
1895	12	0	-	-	-	-
1896	19	0	-	-	-	-
1897	23	0	-	-	-	-
1898	18	2	-	-	-	-
1899	22	5	-	-	-	-
1900	24	3	-	-	-	-
1901	22	0	-	-	-	-
1902	26	1	-	-	-	-
1903	32	4	-	-	-	-
1904	35	7	-	-	-	-
1905	55	6	-	-	-	-
1906	57	6	-	-	-	-
1907	72	8	-	-	-	-
1908	84	13	-	-	-	-
1909	91	12	-	-	-	-
1910	79	20	-	-	-	-
1911	71	29	-	-	-	-
1912	75	27	-	-	-	-
1913	70	28	-	-	-	-
1914	71	27	-	-	-	-
1915	77	27	-	-	-	-
1916	76	33	-	-	-	-
1917	72	37	-	-	-	-
1918	38	32	-	-	-	-
1919	52	33	-	-	-	-
1920	70	46	-	-	-	-
1921	73	48	-	-	-	-
1922	96	64	-	-	-	-
1923	128	78	-	-	-	18
1924	157	87	-	-	-	22
1925	169	103	-	-	-	22
1926	164	115	-	-	-	30
1927	183	109	-	-	-	30
1928	177	84	-	-	-	36
1929	166	93	-	-	-	36
1930	145	95	-	-	-	35
1931	125	93	-	-	-	39
1932	121	100	-	-	-	39

Year	All-Breed Shows	Specialty Shows	Independent Obed. Tri.	Obed. Tr. With Shows	Tracking Tests	Field Trials
1933	128	103	-	-	-	41
1934	166	110	-	-	-	53
1935	188	110	-	-	-	68
1936	181	121	-	-	-	82
1937	196	121	-	-	-	83
1938	212	124	4	-	-	98
1939	222	104	10	-	4	97
1940	223	112	11	-	9	111
1941	234	117	14	-	16	119
1942	164	60	13	-	13	103
1943	130	59	12	-	10	96
1944	196	100	16	-	15	115
1945	138	76	27	-	12	136
1946	254	178	26	-	21	168
1947	272	212	26	-	19	204
1948	305	214	37	-	12	231
1949	331	227	42	-	13	265
1950	361	273	59	-	15	309
1951	367	257	74	190	14	348
1952	382	269	87	206	15	386
1953	375	272	96	227	20	416
1954	384	304	110	241	21	473
1955	402	322	120	268	21	524
1956	411	317	128	282	20	592
1957	432	322	127	316	20	659
1958	440	337	136	331	22	699
1959	449	361	144	354	26	729
1960	459	392	143	382	26	737
1961	476	404	141	396	23	753
1962	480	421	142	406	31	752
1963	488	399	152	421	32	754
1964	496	421	154	428	34	773
1965	511	432	158	444	37	819
1966	520	456	159	454	41	833
1967	537	473	170	466	50	846
1968	545	512	176	489	48	851
1969	557	546	178	500	54	887
1970	569	599	190	511	56	902
1971	586	646	197	538	62	941
1972	606	690	196	569	62	974
1973	625	771	216	620	66	1,000
1974	656	838	215	679	73	993
1975	703	950	226	772	88	1,032
1976	732	1,050	230	844	92	1,069
1977	775	1,136	235	901	101	1,106

Year	All-Breed Shows	Specialty Shows	Independent Obed. Tri.	Obed. Tr. With Shows	Tracking Tests	Field Trials
1978	815	1,198	247	952	105	1,096
1979	823	1,238	264	940	110	1,113
1980	844	1,272	254	1,030	132	1,119
1981	877	1,302	263	1,087	161	1,138
1982	915	1,339	270	1,133	181	1,145
1983	961	1,360	276	1,165	173	1,134
1984	989	1,414	282	1,196	191	1,141

III DOGS IN COMPETITION

Year	Shows	Obedience Trials	Tracking Tests	Field Trials
1951	167,687	13,936	74	36,897
1952	171,412	16,358	90	39,391
1953	178,007	18,154	129	44,778
1954	190,461	22,224	115	50,805
1955	200,908	24,351	112	58,794
1956	208,764	24,611	107	66,383
1957	223,205	28,275	132	72,477
1958	225,756	30,316	164	76,655
1959	231,954	31,051	199	80,188
1960	246,200	31,874	177	81,301
1961	258,000	32,116	131	80,433
1962	270,168	33,360	195	82,467
1963	294,895	36,718	224	79,637
1964	322,299	38,661	226	82,436
1965	360,500	38,032	259	86,797
1966	398,752	41,292	311	88,844
1967	440,299	44,877	381	89,243
1968	490,471	50,500	352	94,597
1969	539,929	49,781	420	104,911
1970	597,174	56,524	452	104,111
1971	658,247	63,506	479	108,976
1972	705,117	66,490	537	112,755
1973	750,920	71,792	550	113,165
1974	789,612	75,890	627	113,240
1975	853,591	84,951	740	118,019
1976	894,934	86,989	805	122,965
1977	991,159	93,530	941	122,318

Year	Shows	Obedience Trials	Tracking Tests	Field Trials
1978	947,473	91,033	946	116,937
1979	938,898.	90,290	934	115,600
1980	949,053	91,547	1,053	111,694
1981	1,008,830	91,829	1,191	115,286
1982	1,050,863	100,846	1,236	113,853
1983	1,117,682	103,850	1,217	113,979
1984	1,133,084	103,501	1,310	114,204

IV FIELD TRIALS BY TYPE

Year	Basset Trials	Beagle Trials	Foxhounds Trials	Dachshund Trials	Pointing Breed Trials	Retriever Trials	Spaniel Trials
1923	-	17	1	-	1	-	-
1924	-	20	1	-	1	-	-
1925	-	22		-	-	-	-
1926	-	28	1	-	-	-	1
1927	-	26	1	-	-	-	4
1928	-	29	1	-	-	-	3
1929	-	30	1	-	-	-	3
1930	-	25	2	-	-	-	4
1931	-	31	2	-	1	1	5
1932	-	30	2	-	2	2	4
1933	-	30	2	-	3	2	4
1934	-	38	1	-	3	3	5
1935	-	44	1	2	7	4	12
1936	-	47	1	3	9	9	13
1937	1	48	1	3	5	10	15
1938	2	49	1	3	10	17	14
1939	1	50	1	3	7	17	17
1940	2	52	1	3	9	23	21
1941	1	63	1	1	6	23	25
1942	1	67	-	1	3	16	15
1943	1	70	-	1	2	13	9
1944	1	82	-	1	2	17	11
1945	2	92	-	1	6	22	12
1946	1	109	-	1	10	31	20
1947	2	135	-	-	15	35	16
1948	2	154	-	-	17	39	18
1949	2	170	-	-	22	49	21
1950	1	198	-	-	35	49	27

Year	Basset Hounds # of Trials	Basset Hounds # of Starters	Beagles # of Trials	Beagles # of Starters	Dachshunds # of Trials	Dachshunds # of Starters	Pointing Breeds # of Trials	Pointing Breeds # of Starters	Retrievers # of Trials	Retrievers # of Starters	Spaniels # of Trials	Spaniels # of Starters
1951	2	38	220	29,813	1	18	42	1,759	54	3,974	29	1,295
1952	2	41	243	31,588	1	13	51	2,204	59	4,106	30	1,439
1953	2	51	259	36,109	1	22	61	2,700	61	4,518	32	1,378
1954	2	83	286	39,510	1	17	82	4,183	71	5,565	31	1,447
1955	3	116	313	45,612	1	26	104	5,933	73	5,447	30	1,528
1956	3	154	342	50,024	1	25	125	6,706	88	7,588	33	1,886
1957	4	267	372	53,858	1	33	148	7,736	100	8,742	34	1,841
1958	6	507	380	56,249	1	30	170	8,731	106	9,404	36	1,734
1959	7	583	406	57,996	2	33	173	9,673	108	10,236	33	1,667
1960	11	759	399	57,322	1	16	181	10,681	111	10,727	34	1,796
1961	11	771	397	54,778	1	26	195	11,950	115	11,130	34	1,778
1962	12	867	400	56,308	1	27	186	11,741	119	11,754	34	1,770
1963	13	832	401	53,576	1	26	184	12,615	123	12,153	32	1,830
1964	12	787	403	54,619	1	31	196	13,550	126	11,727	35	1,720
1965	15	978	411	56,861	1	30	225	15,182	135	12,226	32	1,520
1966	15	1,029	407	57,193	1	25	236	15,740	140	13,265	34	1,592
1967	15	1,186	411	55,859	2	53	244	17,307	139	13,235	35	1,603
1968	15	1,151	412	57,394	2	53	255	19,392	134	15,019	33	1,588
1969	17	1,113	408	60,485	2	51	282	24,522	138	16,865	40	1,875
1970	19	1,212	395	59,665	2	54	310	24,241	139	17,351	37	1,588
1971	19	1,216	405	61,197	3	87	329	26,155	144	18,735	41	1,586
1972	22	1,353	413	60,244	3	85	355	29,184	144	20,241	37	1,648
1973	24	1,600	402	57,651	3	65	380	29,589	152	22,497	39	1,763
1974	24	1,811	386	55,890	3	58	386	30,603	156	23,177	38	1,701

Year	Basset Hounds		Beagles		Dachshunds		Pointing Breeds		Retrievers		Spaniels	
	# of Trials	# of Starters	# of Trials	# of Starters	# of Trials	# of Starters	# of Trials	# of Starters	# of Trials	# of Starters	# of Trials	# of Starters
1975	30	2,017	394	56,611	3	75	407	32,164	165	25,430	33	1,668
1976	29	1,735	390	56,993	3	73	428	34,429	173	27,546	46	2,189
1977	31	1,599	397	53,881	3	117	445	35,567	184	29,115	46	2,039
1978	31	1,541	382	50,266	3	68	446	34,058	190	28,929	44	2,075
1979	31	1,478	387	49,152	5	124	453	34,463	192	28,298	45	2,085
1980	32	1,349	391	47,735	7	133	454	32,783	191	27,585	44	2,109
1981	35	1,544	391	50,082	8	195	464	33,071	192	27,939	48	2,455
1982	37	1,464	393	49,345	9	175	462	33,230	195	27,219	49	2,420
1983	38	1,561	402	49,106	10	206	435	32,029	201	28,639	48	2,438
1984	37	1,532	406	48,981	14	346	434	32,064	203	28,869	47	2,412

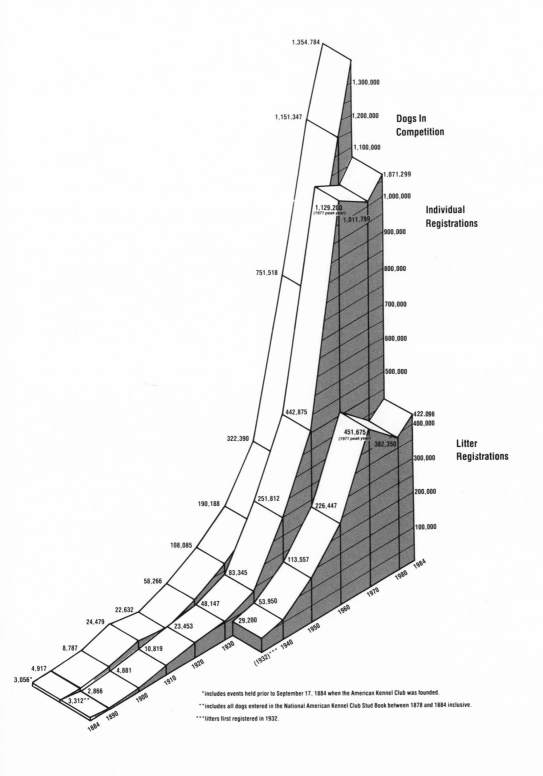

1,354,784

1,300,000

1,151,347

1,200,000

**Dogs In
Competition**

1,100,000

1,071,299

1,000,000

**Individual
Registrations**

1,129,200
(1971 peak year)

1,011,799

900,000

751,518

800,000

700,000

600,000

500,000

442,875

422,098

400,000

322,390

451,675
(1971 peak year)

**Litter
Registrations**

382,350

300,000

190,188

251,812

226,447

200,000

108,085

113,557

100,000

83,345

58,266

48,147

53,950

1984

22,632

23,453

29,200

1980

24,479

1970

10,819

1930

1960

8,787

(1932)***

1950

4,881

1940

4,917

1920

3,056*

4,881

1910

2,866

1900

3,312**

1890

1884

*includes events held prior to September 17, 1884 when the American Kennel Club was founded.

**includes all dogs entered in the National American Kennel Club Stud Book between 1878 and 1884 inclusive.

***litters first registered in 1932.

Epilogue

The *Source Book* covers the high points and historical facts that are significant landmarks in American Kennel Club's century of growth. I am certain that many of the changes recorded herein for the reader relating to the early days of the American Kennel Club were accompanied by debate, argument, and resistance. Dog fanciers and dog breeders of eras past probably were just as divided on the subject of breed standards, dog show and field trial rules and procedures as we are today!

The important point is that the American Kennel Club was responsive to the need for change. Had we not been, our growth would have slowed and stopped.

The American Kennel Club's record of positive change throughout the last century is a marvelous heritage. Cherish it, and look forward to greater growth and achievements in our second century.

Charles A. T. O'Neill

Index

Note: page numbers in italics refer to illustrations and/or captions.

D

E

F

M

O

P

S

Y